Birthplace

Birthplace

Report of the Confidential Enquiry into Facilities Available at the Place of Birth conducted by The National Birthday Trust

Geoffrey Chamberlain, MD, FRCS, FRCOG,
Obstetrician

Philippa Gunn, SRN, SCM,
Midwife

A Wiley Medical Publication

JOHN WILEY & SONS
Chichester · New York · Toronto · Brisbane · Singapore

Copyright © 1987 by John Wiley & Sons Ltd.

British Library Cataloguing in Publication Data:

Birthplace: report of the confidential
    enquiry into facilities available at place of
    birth conducted by the National Birthday
    Trust.
    1. Maternal health services — Great
    Britain
    I. Chamberlain, Geoffrey, *1930–* II. Gunn,
    Philippa III. National Birthday Trust
    362.1'982'00941   RG964.G7

    ISBN 0 471 91477 0

Typeset by Inforum Ltd, Portsmouth
Printed and bound in Great Britain

Contents

Foreword

DAME JOSEPHINE BARNES, DBE, MA, DM, FRCP, FRCS, FRCOG
President, National Birthday Trust Fund

The National Birthday Trust Fund for the Extension of Maternity Services was founded in 1928, one year before the Royal College of Obstetricians and Gynaecologists. For almost sixty years it has existed as a charity devoted to the improvement of the lot of mothers and their babies.

The moment of birth is the most important, and the most dangerous, moment in all our lives. The care that mothers receive and the place where the birth takes place is therefore of vital importance. During this century the trend has been away from home birth to hospital. This is a controversial matter and it is important that wherever a birth occurs there should be facilities and skilled staff available. In a few cases things can still go wrong, when the life of the mother and baby may be at risk or there is a further risk that the baby may suffer life-long handicap.

The National Birthday Trust has sponsored and undertaken much valuable research, in particular to show where facilities for maternity care were deficient. As a result much has been done to achieve the Fund's original purpose. The present confidential survey is unique as an independent assessment of facilities and services available at the place of birth. It is a worthy successor to the previous surveys which have looked at the social aspects of childbearing, perinatal mortality and childbirth.

The fact that this report has appeared so soon after the study is in itself a tribute to all those who have worked so hard on it. It should be looked on as a blueprint for future parents and their children in the continuing search for happier and safer childbirth.

London 1986

Preface

This report concerns a survey performed by the National Birthday Trust into the facilities available in the birthplace; it is the direct successor to the series of studies performed by the Trust in 1946, 1958 and 1970, as a part of its work in the interests of the maternity services. The report examines the contemporary scene in the United Kingdom; it has the great advantage of being impartial and being produced independently and not by a self-interested body of employers, professionals or consumers. There is a great need for such national data to be collected and reported without bias.

To make this study possible, the Trust worked in amicable cooperation with regulatory bodies and colleges of the professions and to them we are indebted. We are happy to thank the DHSS for providing a generous grant which combined with Trust funds made the survey possible. We are appreciative of and acknowledge the work done by the Advisory Committee and Working Party to the survey who have spent many hours getting the planning right. Our greatest thanks, however, go to the midwives in service who took time to complete the questionnaire and answered our questions so patiently and precisely. The United Kingdom is unique in the world in having this body of trained professionals looking after mothers and their babies — we must not waste this midwifery resource in the next few years nor lose it for any administrative convenience of reorganization.

The report has been written by the Working Party who have spent a lot of time drafting and revising chapters. The editors thank them for their individual and collective work. We are grateful to Dr Timothy Peacock and Mr Elliot Philipp both of whom read through the work and made many helpful suggestions; however, the errors which may be present are not theirs but the editors. The figures, which greatly help elucidation of the material, were done by Mr Duncan Larkin, Medical Artist at St George's Hospital Medical School. We are happy to thank Patricia Sharp of John Wiley for her willing assistance given in publication.

CEFPOB Survey
National Birthday Trust
57 Lower Belgrave Street
London, SW1W OLR

GEOFFREY CHAMBERLAIN
Director

PHILIPPA GUNN
Administrative Officer

List of Bodies Represented on the Steering Committee

Association of Anaesthetists
British Medical Association
British Paediatric Association
Department of Health & Social Security
Department of Health & Social Services, Northern Ireland
Faculty of Anaesthesia, Royal College of Surgeons
Faculty of Community Medicine, Royal College of Physicians
Institute of Obstetrics & Gynaecology
Obstetric Anaesthetists' Association
Office of Population Censuses & Surveys
National Birthday Trust Fund
Royal College of General Practitioners
Royal College of Obstetricians & Gynaecologists
Royal College of Midwives
Scottish Home and Health Department
Welsh Office

Working Party

Miss Ruth Ashton SRN SCM MTD (to January 1984)
Dr Martin Bland MSc PhD
Professor Geoffrey Chamberlain MD FRCS FRCOG (Chairman)
Miss Josephine Golden SRN SCM MTD (to February 1985)
Miss Philippa Gunn SRN SCM
Dr Adrian Grant DM MRCOG
Dr Peter Lambert MB BCh DPH FFCM (to February 1983)
Dr Barbara Morgan MB ChB FFARCS
Dr Michael Murphy MB BCh MAO (from March 1983)
Dr Naren Patel MB ChB MRCOG
Dr Brian Speidel MD FRCP
Miss Betty R.Sweet SRN SCM MTD (from April 1985)

CHAPTER 1

The Background and Mounting of the Survey

GEOFFREY CHAMBERLAIN
PHILIPPA GUNN

The National Birthday Trust has been associated with surveys of the maternity services of the United Kingdom previously in 1946, 1958 and 1970. The first of these studies, by Professor J.W.B. Douglas, was conducted in conjunction with the Population Investigation Committee and examined 14 000 births occurring in March 1946; the results were published in *Maternity in Great Britain* (1948). Information was analysed about the effects of childbearing on the economics of the household, the survey being performed just before the introduction of the National Health Service. Some medical aspects were not assayed but relief of pain was analysed and the methods of delivery were detailed.

In 1958, the National Birthday Trust, in conjunction with the Royal College of Obstetricians and Gynaecologists, performed the Perinatal Mortality Survey, organized by Professor Neville Butler and Professor Dennis Bonham: 17 000 births during one week in England, Wales and Scotland were fully surveyed in a detailed questionnaire completed by midwives. In addition, the perinatal deaths for three months were examined in an extensive pathological study of the causes of perinatal death. That survey was reported in two volumes:, *Perinatal Mortality* (1963) and *Perinatal Morbidity* (1969). The results of the Perinatal Mortality Survey were far reaching; policies for the reduction of perinatal death at local, national and international level have been formulated since, based upon the data and conclusions of this survey. Much research has been, and is still being, generated from the data. The concept of pregnancies at higher risk for socio-economic reasons, from increased age and from greater parity was quantified. The effects of cigarette smoking were shown here for the first time in a large survey.

In 1970, the British Births Survey was performed by Roma and Geoffrey

Chamberlain. This study, under the joint auspices of the National Birthday Trust and the Royal College of Obstetricians and Gynaecologists, investigated the quality of life of the mother and the care of the mother in pregnancy, labour and the first week after delivery. It purposely concentrated on the living, dealing more with morbidity because the previous 1958 study had examined perinatal mortality: 17 000 births were surveyed; results and analyses were presented in *British Births 1970*, Volume 1 (1975) and Volume 2 (1978).

From the 1946, 1958 and 1970 studies, three cohorts of children were generated whose antenatal and intrapartum details had been well documented; these results are available for further analysis and are being followed up by groups associated with the University of Bristol and the International Centre for Child Studies. Valuable information is still being extracted and published about developmental and educational standards in relation to childbirth. The coordination of these studies is under the care of Professor Neville Butler and this work will go on for many years.

THE PRESENT ENQUIRY

In 1980 the National Birthday Trust was considering performing another national survey into obstetrical matters along the lines of the previous ones carried out at twelve-year intervals. However, by 1980 many other groups of doctors and social scientists all over the world were active in this field. In addition, there was then a possibility that the statutory collection of material and child care information was about to be expanded by the Office of Population, Censuses and Surveys, so that much of what had been collected by National Birthday Trust surveys in previous years would become available from officially collected data sources in the OPCS publications. Further, the Birthday Trust was advised that cohorts of children collected in the manner used previously were not necessarily the best way of generating such studies; the group of children so produced may be biased in some seasonal way and so could influence the follow-up of education and developmental factors. In consequence, it was decided not to hold another cohort survey of the same nature.

However, the reputation of the Trust in data collecting was such that it was pressed by obstetricians and midwives to conduct another confidential enquiry. It was considered that an entirely different type of study should be mounted to learn about what was available to all the women in the United Kingdom at the place where they had their babies. We decided to examine the facilities which were actually present at all the places where women give birth. Such a survey would not be based upon individual women but on the places where they deliver; it would aim to learn about the facilities available in hospitals, in general practitioner units and in the homes where women have babies.

It was considered essential to ask questions about staffing by midwives and nurses, obstetricians, anaesthetists and paediatricians of all seniorities. The services available such as blood transfusion and dedicated operating theatres were to be considered and the equipment that was actually available at the place of birth was to be assessed.

Much is known about the expected plans and organization of staff and equipment levels as laid down by the health authorities; we wanted to know who and what were really there. A proforma would be constructed to be asked at certain sample times about staffing and the availability of specified samples of equipment at all places where women had babies in 1984.

All professionals who deliver babies have their own ideas about what is essential for a safe delivery; the Working Party to the Confidential Enquiry considered in detail certain samples of equipment and services that would epitomize aspects of labour care. Such a sampling technique may be considered as a management biopsy. If the sites are well chosen, biopsies give information about the state of the rest of the tissues in an organ; similarly, if the samples of equipment and services are well chosen, they will reflect the availability of the whole service.

In all surveys, the National Birthday Trust has relied upon midwives to collect information. This has always yielded a very high response rate and a high validity of data when checked against outside sources.

PLANNING THE ENQUIRY

The National Birthday Trust considered these ideas carefully at general and medical committees and then convened a meeting in 1980 of all the bodies that had helped with previous Trust surveys (listed on page xi). Helpful discussions took place and many ideas were generated.

The Trust was then asked to form a small Working Party (see page xiii) to identify the subjects about which information could be collected in a questionnaire format. The Working Party was also to plan the proforma for such a questionnaire and to examine ways of funding the project.

All this was done over the next two years and at a second meeting of the Steering Committee in January 1983, the recommendations of the Working Party were considered. In general, the Committee agreed with all the suggestions but a few points required referral back to parent bodies. The Director of the Enquiry and other members of the Working Party met with various groups and secured agreement by discussion. The Trust is grateful to all the representatives of the bodies listed who gave their time and helped to prepare this survey.

The enquiry was run from the National Birthday Trust headquarters in London. It was funded by the Trust and a generous grant from the Department of Health and Social Security; the Trust is grateful to the Department for its substantial help.

The tactical planning of the survey was in the hands of the Working Party and the Survey Administrator, Miss Philippa Gunn, who worked with us from April 1984. Details of this phase of the enquiry are described later in the chapter.

TIMING OF THE ENQUIRY

The aim was to find out what was really happening in all places where women deliver in a manner compatible with the proper collection of information. The two aspects of the fullness of data collection and the practicality of getting the information were not always reconcilable but the Working Party considered if one asked midwives to fill in data at set points in a 24-hour period for several days, this would give a representative series of samples. Different days of the week were chosen over several months of the year to allow for seasonal staffing variations. It was eventually decided to use the first day of the months of August, September, October and November 1984 to give a variety of working conditions.

August 1 was a Wednesday. At many hospitals this is the date when the house officers and registrar posts change their staff. Thus there was a reshuffling of medical staffing but the midwifery staff would be constant. It is also in the holiday period. September 1 was a Saturday and so would reflect weekend conditions. October 1 was a Monday and November 1 was a Thursday, two weekdays away from the holiday time.

It was hoped that by selecting these four days a variety of conditions of working practice could be examined. To have sampled more days would have taxed the midwives who were filling in the forms; additionally, more forms would have to have been transferred between the hospital and the collecting centre with an increased resultant loss. Two questionnaires were derived. The first was for use in hospitals and general practitioner units while the second was for community deliveries; the equipment and personnel would obviously be very different from that at the hospital unit. Details of these questionnaires are reproduced in Figures 1.1 and 1.3 to 1.12.

THE HOSPITAL QUESTIONNAIRE

Background of the units

It was decided to ask about the unit to give background information about its size and workload (Figure 1.1). The number of deliveries in the previous year was requested.

Please complete at 9 a.m.

Over the next 24 hours we would like you to record the details of equipment, women and staff present at specified times.

At the end of 24 hours we would like you to record the events and procedures that have occurred. We suggest that you ensure that the following details are recorded in the delivery book over the next 24 hours.

1 Time of delivery
2 Type of delivery (including elective or emergency Caesarean Section).
3 Time that General Anaesthetic started.

4 Neonatal endotracheal intubation.
5 Transfer of baby to SCBU.
6 Other major procedures.
7 Time epidural inserted.

TO BE COMPLETED BY THE MIDWIFE IN CHARGE OF THE DELIVERY AREA

For Office Use:

Please tick one only

1-13

NHS Consultant Unit	☐
Combined GP and Consultant Unit	☐
Combined Consultant Unit and Private Unit	☐
General Practitioner Unit	☐
Private Unit in NHS Hospital	☐
Armed Services	☐
Private Hospital	☐
Other — please specify	☐

☐ 14

. . . .

THE PLACE OF BIRTH UNDER REVIEW

Please complete the following details for the year of 1983

Perinatal Mortality Rate per 1,000 total births . . . . :   15-17

Number of deliveries   18-21

Number of Caesarean Sections   22-24

Number of babies born at this address with a birth weight of less than 2.5Kg   25-27

To obtain some measure of the geography of your unit please complete the following questions:

How many delivery rooms are there at the place of birth under review? i.e. rooms planned for deliveries to take place; do not include admission and first stage rooms.   28-29

Are these in a central delivery area?   Yes/No   ☐ 30

If NO, are these in wards that have antenatal and/or postnatal beds?   Yes/No   ☐ 31

Figure 1.1

6 BIRTHPLACE

TABLE 1.1   Distribution of 1983 load by size of unit

	Small (1–500)	Medium (501–2000)	Large (2001–4000)	Very large (4000+)
Units	217	149	129	26
Units (%)	41	29	25	5
Deliveries (to nearest 1000)	35 000	197 000	350 000	120 000
Delivery (%)	5	28	50	17

It was hoped by August 1984 that the data of 1983 would be completed and known to the senior midwife. This proved to be so in 95 per cent of the centres (Figure 1.2 and Table 1.1).

Of all units reporting deliveries in 1983, 41 per cent performed less than 500 a year. Hence, while they constituted almost a half of units, only 5 per cent of births in the country took place in them. At the other end of the scale, 30 per cent of units reported delivery over 2000 a year and they performed two-thirds of the workload. In between, the medium units (500–2000 deliveries a year) took 29 per cent of the work. The number of Caesarean sections and of babies born with a birthweight of less than 2500 g was requested as another measure of the workload, for both of these factors would use up extra facilities.

It was realized by the Working Party that many hospitals had patterns of labour wards laid down by traditional building of the previous decades if not the last century. Thus all births might not be in the same locus. Midwives were asked if there was a central delivery area with all the labour facilities of staff and equipment gathered in one place or whether the delivery rooms were scattered around the hospital.

In addition, we asked about the number of delivery rooms. The need for these would obviously differ between a unit having a first stage room where women were admitted and only transferred to a labour room for delivery itself, and those units where women were admitted straight to a labour room where they stayed for the whole of the labour. It was the room where delivery took place which concerned this survey.

Staff present

We collected information about the staff actually present and available for the delivery area at 11 am (Figures 1.3 and 1.4). The midwifery staff questions related only to those who were actually in the labour area while those about the medical staff, particularly those in more senior positions, included information about those on call for the labour ward but on duty elsewhere (Table 1.2); unless a problem requiring their attention was actually occurring in the labour ward at the sample time, there was no reason for them to be there.

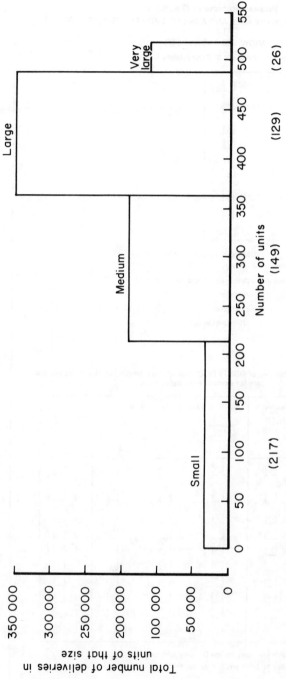

Figure 1.2 Proportion of deliveries by units of differing size (see text)

Please complete at 11 a.m.

STAFF PRESENT IN THE DELIVERY AREA AND AVAILABLE FOR THE DELIVERY AREA AT 11 a.m.

MIDWIVES AND NURSES

Please record the number and grade of those present at 11 a.m.

The survey has tried to cover all groups of midwives and nurses but if there are some that have been excluded please enter these under the heading of 'OTHER'

Please check that the various grades of midwives and nurses are actually in the delivery areas If they are away for a meal break or escorting a patient they should not be counted

*THEATRE TRAINED NURSING STAFF
Are those with a minimum of one year experience in theatre work employed for theatre area and not included in any other grade on the list

- NURSING OFFICER (Senior Midwife Grade)
- MIDWIFERY SISTER
- COMMUNITY MIDWIFE
- STAFF MIDWIFE (Not Agency or Bank)
- AGENCY MIDWIFE
- BANK MIDWIFE
- STUDENT MIDWIFE
- *THEATRE TRAINED NURSING STAFF
- STUDENT NURSE
- OTHER NURSING OR MIDWIFERY (please specify). . . . .

32-51

WOMEN IN THE DELIVERY AREA AT 11 a.m.

How many women are in the delivery area in labour? 52-53

How many women are in the delivery area and not in labour?

Antenatal 54

Postnatal 55

Other please specify

. . . . 56

. . . . 57

Please record the number of OBSTETRICIANS who are on duty at 11 a.m. to provide care for women in the delivery area

NHS EQUIVALENT STATUS OF DOCTORS	PRESENT in the DELIVERY AREA	AVAILABLE FOR THE DELIVERY AREA			How many of these were short term locums of 2 weeks or less
		Not present in the Delivery area BUT on duty in the same Hospital premises	Not in the hospital premises BUT on call outside the hospital for the delivery area within 20 minutes	greater than 20 minutes	
1 CONSULTANT	⊔	⊔	⊔	⊔	⊔
2 SENIOR REGISTRAR	⊔	⊔	⊔	⊔	⊔
3 ASSOCIATE SPECIALIST	⊔	⊔	⊔	⊔	⊔
4 REGISTRAR post M	⊔	⊔	⊔	⊔	⊔
5 REGISTRAR pre M	⊔	⊔	⊔	⊔	⊔
6 CLINICAL ASSISTANT	⊔	⊔	⊔	⊔	⊔
7 GENERAL PRACTITIONER	⊔	⊔	⊔	⊔	⊔
8 SHO	⊔	⊔	⊔	⊔	⊔
9 OTHERS	⊔	⊔	⊔	⊔	⊔
10 MEDICAL STUDENT	⊔	⊔	⊔	⊔	⊔

If a doctor is in a DOCTOR'S ROOM which is attached to the delivery area please count this as being in the delivery area

If in doubt please check the availability pre MRCP and post MRCP registrar status

58-111

Are there any OBSTETRICIANS on duty for the Delivery area *only*?

(i.e. with no other responsibilities for other areas of the maternity unit, accident and emergency department etc.)

Yes/No 112

If YES, what is their status — as listed above?. 113

Figure 1.3

Please complete at 11 a.m. continued

Please record the number of PAEDIATRICIANS who are on duty at 11 a.m. to provide care for women in the delivery area

NHS EQUIVALENT STATUS OF DOCTORS	PRESENT in the DELIVERY AREA	AVAILABLE FOR THE DELIVERY AREA			How many of these were short term locums of 2 weeks or less
		Not present in the Delivery area BUT on duty in the same Hospital premises	Not in the hospital premises BUT on call outside the hospital for the delivery area within 20 minutes	greater than 20 minutes	
1 CONSULTANT	⊔				⊔
2 SENIOR REGISTRAR	⊔	⊔	⊔	⊔	⊔
3 ASSOCIATE SPECIALIST	⊔	⊔	⊔	⊔	⊔
4 REGISTRAR post MRCP	⊔	⊔	⊔	⊔	⊔
5 REGISTRAR pre MRCP	⊔	⊔	⊔	⊔	⊔
6 CLINICAL ASSISTANT	⊔	⊔	⊔	⊔	⊔
7 GENERAL PRACTITIONER	⊔	⊔	⊔	⊔	⊔
8 SHO	⊔	⊔	⊔	⊔	⊔
9 OTHERS	⊔	⊔	⊔	⊔	⊔
10 MEDICAL STUDENT	⊔	⊔	⊔	⊔	⊔

If a doctor is in a DOCTOR'S ROOM which is attached to the delivery area please count this as being in the delivery area

If in doubt please check the availability pre MRCP and post MRCP registrar status

Are there any PAEDIATRICIANS on duty for the Delivery area *only?*

(i.e. with no other responsibilities for other areas of the maternity unit, accident and emergency department etc.)

Yes/No

If YES, what is their status — as listed above? . . . .

Please record the number of ANAESTHETISTS who are on duty at 11 a.m. to provide care for women in the delivery area

NHS EQUIVALENT STATUS OF DOCTORS	PRESENT in the DELIVERY AREA	AVAILABLE FOR THE DELIVERY AREA			How many of these were short term locums of 2 weeks or less
		Not present in the Delivery area BUT on duty in the same Hospital premises	Not in the hospital premises BUT on call outside the hospital for the delivery area within 20 minutes	greater than 20 minutes	
1 CONSULTANT	⊔	⊔	⊔	⊔	⊔
2 SENIOR REGISTRAR	⊔	⊔	⊔	⊔	⊔
3 ASSOCIATE SPECIALIST	⊔	⊔	⊔	⊔	⊔
4 REGISTRAR post FFA	⊔	⊔	⊔	⊔	⊔
5 REGISTRAR pre FFA	⊔	⊔	⊔	⊔	⊔
6 CLINICAL ASSISTANT	⊔	⊔	⊔	⊔	⊔
7 GENERAL PRACTITIONER	⊔	⊔	⊔	⊔	⊔
8 SHO	⊔	⊔	⊔	⊔	⊔
9 OTHERS	⊔	⊔	⊔	⊔	⊔
10 MEDICAL STUDENT	⊔	⊔	⊔	⊔	⊔

If a doctor is in a DOCTOR'S ROOM which is attached to the delivery area please count this as being in the delivery area

If in doubt please check the availability pre FFA and post FFA registrar status

Are there any ANAESTHETISTS on duty for the Delivery area *only?*

(i.e. with no other responsibilities for other areas of the maternity unit, accident and emergency department etc.)

Yes/No

If YES, what is their status — as listed above? . . . .

Figure 1.4

TABLE 1.2   Sampling times for staff and equipment on each of the survey days

	11 am	3 pm	7 pm	11 pm
Staff midwifery	X	X	X	X
Obstetrical	X			X
Paediatric	X			X
Anaesthetic	X			X
Services		X		
Equipment		X		
Women in labour	X	X	X	X

We asked about the numbers and grades of midwives and nurses present in the labour area at 11 am. We enquired about obstetricians, paediatricians and anaesthetists on duty for the delivery area at the same time even though they were not actually in it, for many doctors do not stay in the labour ward if there is no need. The questionnaire differentiated between those doctors who were present in the delivery area, those in the hospital and those on call for deliveries, dividing them into those who were within 20 minutes of the unit and those more than 20 minutes away. We asked about long-term locums (more than two weeks) to gauge some measure of the proportion of medical staff who were not on permanent appointments.

In this survey we divided up the medical and midwifery staff to assess the seniority and experience of the people who were dealing with women in labour. The doctors were analysed by their grade and also were subdivided by their geographical closeness to the hospital or the labour ward. The midwifery staff were a little easier to categorize by seniority alone for they were usually allocated to the labour area. In some cases when they were nursing mixed labour and ward areas, they would go into the delivery area as required, spending the rest of their time in the ward with antenatal and postnatal women.

We considered several ways of dividing the doctors by their experience but in the end used the National Health Service grades as the best understood and most acceptable categorization. We are well aware that a senior house officer (SHO) can be everything from a first day tiro to a fairly experienced doctor in his third SHO post, who, having spent eighteen months in obstetrics, makes a good assessment of a difficult emergency situation and knows exactly how to call the right people on duty. The grades were those that were well understood by the midwives filling in the forms. Further, we determined the most senior doctor in the hospital who was on sole call for the delivery area.

In our questionnaire, we asked for details about the following:

1. *Consultant*   A specialist trained to take responsibility inside his own speciality for the total care of patients. He may hold a whole or part-time

appointment in the National Health Service and has undergone a rigorous training. He or she is a member of The Royal College of Obstetricians and Gynaecologists, The Royal College of Physicians, or a Fellow of the Faculty of Anaesthetists of the Royal College of Surgeons depending on the speciality. Consultants have been appointed by the health authority to be in clinical charge of all the women or babies attending the unit. In the United Kingdom most consultants in obstetrics, paediatrics or anaesthesia have undergone over ten years' postgraduate training between qualification and their appointment and so are experienced doctors. It must be realized conversely that not all members or fellows of the appropriate colleges are consultants, for these higher degrees are gained in the course of the training; many are registrars or senior registrars. In 1984, there were 764 consultant obstetricians, 573 consultant paediatricians and 1878 consultant anaesthetists in England and Wales to give some idea of the relative staffing. However, very few would be devoting their whole time to the care of childbirth. Obstetricians usually perform gynaecology as well; paediatricians spend much of their time looking after older children as well as the newborn; anaesthetists are occupied mostly in helping in general surgical departments.

2. *Senior registrar* This is a senior training grade from which the consultants are chosen. He too will be a fellow or member of the appropriate college or faculty and will have been at least seven years in postgraduate training before reaching this grade. Generally speaking he is well trained and capable of carrying out most of the duties performed by a consultant. He will probably be on call for emergencies in a group of units and not necessarily resident in any one of them. In 1984 there were 134 senior registrars in obstetrics, 134 in paediatrics and 399 in anaesthesia in England and Wales.

3. *Registrar* He or she is a member of an even more junior training grade to which doctors of some two to four years' experience in their obstetrical training are appointed. Some of them may have achieved a higher degree of fellowship or membership of the appropriate college but many have not. In consequence, in this survey we added one split-level by dividing registrars into pre- or post- their higher diploma for this would make some difference to their experience. We had expected some problems with the completion of this and advised midwives to consult the respective doctors but in the pilot studies these answers came in well and so we proceeded to the main study. In fact, no one reported difficulties in this area and it was greatly to the credit of the midwives filling in the forms that they were able to obtain this information tactfully and apparently with little trauma.

In 1984, there were 495 registrars in obstetrics, 227 in paediatrics and 835 in anaesthesia in England and Wales. In fact, in the analysis we grouped the pre- and post-registration registrars together, for most units used them for duties by their grade and not by their experience.

4. *Senior house officers* These make up most of the posts in obstetrics, paediatrics and anaesthetics; they are held by junior doctors who care for women in labour in the hospitals. They are all post-registration, meaning that the doctor has done at least a year of general medicine and surgery before coming forward to this level; in some cases they will have done one or two years in further training before achieving this post. Not all doctors at senior house officer level are going to specialize in the subject they are working in for some may wish to enter general practice having some experience of one of the specialities behind them. Others may wish for experience in one of the three disciplines under review in this survey in order to help their career in another discipline. For example, somebody wishing to do obstetrics as a career may do a SHO post in paediatrics to learn about the problems of that discipline. In 1984, there were 1272 SHOs in obstetrics, 975 in paediatrics and 901 in anaesthesia in England and Wales. The data given in all these grades are full time equivalents but their relative numbers show the proportion of working doctors at each level and speciality.

5. *Associate specialist* This is a senior non-career grade in obstetrics, paediatrics or anaesthesia; there are few of them in the United Kingdom. They are usually people who have gone a long way along the training ladder, being post-diploma workers in their own speciality. However, they do not wish to go for consultant grades and have been appointed at the career level of associate specialist.

6. *Clinical assistants* They are usually general practitioners who wish to do one or two sessions in hospital work. Their experience will be that of a senior house officer although occasionally that of a registrar in the speciality. They usually do sessional work in the hospital and few of them actually look after labouring women.

We categorized the nursing grades and their role in the delivery area as follows:

1. *Nursing officer (senior midwife grade)* This is generally the highest grade of midwife maintaining clinical skills and working at the place of birth. Her role is predominantly administrative but what she does in the delivery area will vary widely according to the size of the unit and the demand. In the small unit, she may be both the most senior midwife and nurse available or even the sole midwife in the hospital. With increasing size of unit, the senior midwife's responsibilities become more focused on the delivery area. In a medium or large unit, her responsibility during her shift may be confined to two or more clinical areas within the maternity department, while in the very large units, she may take responsibility for the delivery area only.

The questionnaire was completed by the midwife in charge of the delivery area. Nursing officers fulfilling this role, while also being responsible for other clinical areas, may have planned their visits to the delivery area to coincide with the sample times. For this reason, there may be some over-reporting of the most senior midwife present.

2. *Midwifery sister*   She will be generally the most senior midwife present in the delivery area. In smaller hospitals she could also be the only midwife on duty. In the other clinical areas of the maternity unit, there is frequently only one sister on duty each shift and her role is largely to administrate but in the labour ward, a higher proportion of sisters are present and they also do clinical work. In the absence of a senior midwife covering the maternity unit or hospital, the midwifery sister will often act up.

3. *Community midwife*   She is an experienced midwife whose skills are mainly clinical. She may be present in the delivery area as a part of a shift or by the virtue of being called in for a *domino delivery*. Her availability in the *domino scheme* will vary according to the type of unit. S. Robinson (1979)[1] showed that 31 out of 53 districts provided a domino scheme and of these 22 districts stated they took place in a GP unit. In the same study, it was revealed that 785 (76.1 per cent) of the community midwives questioned did not do any *domino deliveries*.

4. *Staff midwife*   She carries out mainly clinical care in the delivery area. Her duties include care of women in normal labour, assisting at interventions and in the operating theatre. She may also be responsible for the teaching and supervision of student midwives, nurses or medical students. The staff midwife may act up for the sister in the latter's absence.

5. *Agency and bank midwives*   They generally meet the demand for midwifery cover when staffing shortages and sickness occur. It is not unknown for some midwives to work on a regular basis in one unit and at the same time through an agency or bank in another so that the midwife can meet her financial commitments. The nursing agency provides midwives for any hospital on a commercial basis while the nursing and midwifery banks exist within individual hospitals and pay employees according to the NHS scales.

6. *Student midwives*   They appear in this enquiry for they are required to gain sufficient experience in the conduct of the normal deliveries and to attend abnormal deliveries during their period of training. In the initial training, student midwives spend a minimum of six weeks in the management of normal labour and in their final period of 32–34 weeks they must spend another six weeks during which time their role is extended to the management of abnormal labour. Further experience in the delivery area may occur during the 15–21 weeks of community experience and the student midwife may also be called to witness a delivery or accompany midwifery tutors. During her training the student midwife must conduct 40 normal deliveries and attend a further 40 women in whom the labour or delivery may be complicated, e.g. acceleration of labour or forceps delivery.

With the exception of the special care baby unit, the Central Midwives Board states 'Any clinical area which will be involved in midwifery training should have 24 hours' direct supervision by a midwife to provide instruction of student midwives'.

7. *Theatre trained nursing staff* An assessment was made of those with a minimum of one year's experience and be employed specifically for theatre work; they should hold the Joint Board of Clinical Studies Diploma in Theatre Work, which is a one-year course, or have the equivalent experience. In this survey they were only recorded if they had not been included in a grade of midwife or student midwife. This skilled group of nurses, although unable to take responsibility for women in labour, run the delivery operating theatre which otherwise places a demand on the midwives' time.
8. *Student nurses* They are at present in the delivery area as part of the community or family module in their three-year training for state registration. Generally eight weeks will be spent in this phase and their role in the delivery area is therefore supernumerary. They are not qualified to conduct deliveries.
9. *Other nursing or midwifery staff* This group included a large number of nursing auxiliaries. Very few state enrolled or state registered nurses were recorded in this group. Within the delivery area, there is a large proportion of duties that they would be unable to carry out and their role would therefore be general nursing and domestic.

Minor variations may occur in the work performed but these are small compared with the major variations and skills described at each level.

We asked about the numbers of *medical students* for we were interested to know about training. All universities require that students have some practical experience in delivery of babies. Sometimes quotas are laid down (the supervised delivery of ten normal women is a common one) while in other cases, a minimum attendance time in the labour ward is recommended. Every potential doctor needs to know what is involved in the process of childbirth so that he can help his patients later in his career.

Students will now be found not just in the teaching hospitals but in the labour wards of district general hospitals in the country. We realized that four days throughout the year are not necessarily a large sample but as with the collection of all the data, these days were spread throughout the week and at various times in the academic year and so we report on the information we gathered there.

We gained information by seniority about the availability of obstetricians, paediatricians and anaesthetists. Perhaps one of the more important sections of this part of the questionnaire was where we asked about those who were on duty for the delivery area only with no other responsibilities for any other areas of the hospital: that is they were not on call for the antenatal or postnatal wards of the maternity unit, gynaecology, accident and emergency department or other part of the hospital. If there were such persons we wanted to know their seniority. In some cases people gave us the rankings of several doctors who apparently were only on call for the labour ward duties in that hospital at the

Please complete at 3 p.m.

STAFF PRESENT IN THE DELIVERY AREA AND AVAILABLE FOR THE DELIVERY AREA AT
3 p.m.

MIDWIVES AND NURSES

Please record the number and grade of those present at 3 p.m.

The survey has tried to cover all groups of midwives and nurses but if there are some that have been excluded please enter these under the heading of 'OTHER'

Please check that the various grades of midwives and nurses are actually in the delivery areas. If they are away for a meal break or escorting a patient they should not be counted.

*THEATRE TRAINED NURSING STAFF. Are those with a minimum of one year experence in theatre work employed for theatre area and not included in any other grade on the list

NURSING OFFICER (Senior Midwife Grade)	⎿⏄⏄⎿
MIDWIFERY SISTER	⎿⏄⏄⎿
COMMUNITY MIDWIFE	⎿⏄⏄⎿
STAFF MIDWIFE (Not Agency or Bank)	⎿⏄⏄⎿
AGENCY MIDWIFE	⎿⏄⏄⎿
BANK MIDWIFE	⎿⏄⏄⎿
STUDENT MIDWIFE	⎿⏄⏄⎿
*THEATRE TRAINED NURSING STAFF	⎿⏄⏄⎿
STUDENT NURSE	⎿⏄⏄⎿
OTHER NURSING OR MIDWIFERY	⎿⏄⏄⎿
(please specify)	

....

....

1-13

14-33

WOMEN IN THE DELIVERY AREA AT 3 p.m.

How many women are in the delivery area in labour?   ⎿⏄⎿   34-35

How many women are in the delivery area and not in labour?

Antenatal   ⎿⎿   36

Postnatal   ⎿⎿   37

Other please specify

.........................⎿⎿   38

.........................⎿⎿   39

SERVICES AVAILABLE TO THE DELIVERY AREA

Please tick the appropriate box

SERVICES	AVAILABLE			NOT AVAILABLE
	In the Delivery area	On the same premises	Elsewhere	
Blood storage area with Rhesus Negative blood					40
Operating Theatre on the same premises and exclusively for obstetrical use.					41
Operating Theatre on the same premises shared with other disciplines					42
Recovery for mothers					43

	AVAILABLE		NOT AVAILABLE
	On demand	When possible	
Epidural service				44

Figure 1.5

Please complete at 7 p.m.

STAFF PRESENT IN THE DELIVERY AREA AND AVAILABLE FOR THE DELIVERY AREA AT 7 p.m.

MIDWIVES AND NURSES

Please record the number and grade of those present at 7 p.m.

1-13

The survey has tried to cover all groups of midwives and nurses but if there are some that have been excluded please enter these under the heading of 'OTHER'

Please check that the various grades of midwives and nurses are actually in the delivery areas. If they are away for a meal break or escorting a patient they should not be counted.

*THEATRE TRAINED NURSING STAFF
Are those with a minimum of one year experience in theatre work employed for theatre area and not included in any other grade on the list.

NURSING OFFICER (Senior Midwife Grade)	☐☐☐
MIDWIFERY SISTER	☐☐☐
COMMUNITY MIDWIFE	☐☐☐
STAFF MIDWIFE (Not Agency or Bank)	☐☐☐
AGENCY MIDWIFE	☐☐☐
BANK MIDWIFE	☐☐☐
STUDENT MIDWIFE	☐☐☐
*THEATRE TRAINED NURSING STAFF	☐☐☐
STUDENT NURSE	☐☐☐
OTHER NURSING OR MIDWIFERY	☐☐☐

(please specify)

....

....

14-33

WOMEN IN THE DELIVERY AREA AT 7 p.m.

How many women are in the delivery area in labour?   ☐☐   34-35

How many women are in the delivery area and not in labour?

       Antenatal   ☐   36

       Postnatal   ☐   37

       Other please specify

.... ☐   38

.... ☐   39

Figure 1.6

Please complete at 11 p.m.

STAFF PRESENT IN THE DELIVERY AREA AND AVAILABLE FOR THE DELIVERY AREA AT 11 p.m.

MIDWIVES AND NURSES

Please record the number and grade of those present at 11 p.m.

For Office Use:

The survey has tried to cover all groups of midwives and nurses but if there are some that have been excluded please enter these under the heading of 'OTHER'

Please check that the various grades of midwives and nurses are actually in the delivery areas. If they are away for a meal break or escorting a patient they should not be counted

NURSING OFFICER (Senior Midwife Grade)
MIDWIFERY SISTER
COMMUNITY MIDWIFE
STAFF MIDWIFE (Not Agency or Bank)
AGENCY MIDWIFE
BANK MIDWIFE
STUDENT MIDWIFE

*THEATRE TRAINED NURSING STAFF
Are those with a minimum of one year experience in theatre work employed for theatre area and not included in any other grade on the list

*THEATRE TRAINED NURSING STAFF
STUDENT NURSE
OTHER NURSING OR MIDWIFERY
(please specify)

40-59

WOMEN IN THE DELIVERY AREA AT 11 p.m.

How many women are in the delivery area in labour?   60-61

How many women are in the delivery area and not in labour?

Antenatal   62

Postnatal   63

Other please specify   64

Please record the number of OBSTETRICIANS who are on duty at 11 p.m. to provide care for women in the delivery area

NHS EQUIVALENT STATUS OF DOCTORS	PRESENT in the DELIVERY AREA	AVAILABLE FOR THE DELIVERY AREA			How many of these were short term locums of 2 weeks or less
		Not present in the Delivery area BUT on duty in the same Hospital premises	Not in the hospital premises BUT on call outside the hospital for the delivery area within 20 minutes	greater than 20 minutes	
1 CONSULTANT					
2 SENIOR REGISTRAR					
3 ASSOCIATE SPECIALIST					
4 REGISTRAR post MRCOG					
5 REGISTRAR pre MRCOG					
6 CLINICAL ASSISTANT					
7 GENERAL PRACTITIONER					
8 SHO					
9 OTHERS					
10 MEDICAL STUDENT					

If a doctor is in a DOCTOR'S ROOM which is attached to the delivery area please count this as being in the delivery area

If in doubt please check the availability pre MRCOG and post MRCOG registrar status

65-118

Are there any OBSTETRICIANS on duty for the Delivery area *only?*

(i.e. with no other responsibilities for other areas of the maternity unit, accident and emergency department etc.)

Yes/No   119

If YES, what is their status -- as listed above?   120

Figure 1.7

Please complete at 11 p.m. continued

Please record the number of PAEDIATRICIANS who are on duty at 11 p.m. to provide care for women in the delivery area

For Office Use:

1-13

If a doctor is in a DOCTOR'S ROOM which is attached to the delivery area please count this as being in the delivery area.

If in doubt please check the availability pre-MRCP and post-MRCP registrar status.

NHS EQUIVALENT STATUS OF DOCTORS	PRESENT in the DELIVERY AREA	AVAILABLE FOR THE DELIVERY AREA			How many of these were short term locums of 2 weeks or less
		Not present in the Delivery area BUT on duty in the same Hospital premises	Not in the hospital premises BUT on call outside the hospital for the delivery area		
			within 20 minutes	greater than 20 minutes	
1 CONSULTANT	⊔	⊔	⊔	⊔	⊔
2 SENIOR REGISTRAR	⊔	⊔	⊔	⊔	⊔
3 ASSOCIATE SPECIALIST	⊔	⊔	⊔	⊔	⊔
4 REGISTRAR post-MRCP	⊔	⊔	⊔	⊔	⊔
5 REGISTRAR pre-MRCP	⊔	⊔	⊔	⊔	⊔
6 CLINICAL ASSISTANT	⊔	⊔	⊔	⊔	⊔
7 GENERAL PRACTITIONER	⊔	⊔	⊔	⊔	⊔
8 SHO	⊔	⊔	⊔	⊔	⊔
9 OTHERS *(please specify)*	⊔	⊔	⊔	⊔	⊔
10 MEDICAL STUDENT	⊔	⊔	⊔	⊔	⊔

14-63

Are there any PAEDIATRICIANS on duty for the Delivery area *only?*

(i.e. with no other responsibilities for other areas of the maternity unit, accident and emergency department etc.)

Yes/No

☐ 64

☐ 65

If YES, what is their status — as listed above? . . . .

Please record the number of ANAESTHETISTS who are on duty at 11 p.m. to provide care for women in the delivery area

If a doctor is in a DOCTOR'S ROOM which is attached to the delivery area please count this as being in the delivery area.

If in doubt please check the availability pre-FFA and post-FFA registrar status.

NHS EQUIVALENT STATUS OF DOCTORS	PRESENT in the DELIVERY AREA	AVAILABLE FOR THE DELIVERY AREA			How many of these were short term locums of 2 weeks or less
		Not present in the Delivery area BUT on duty in the same Hospital premises	Not in the hospital premises BUT on call outside the hospital for the delivery area		
			within 20 minutes	greater than 20 minutes	
1 CONSULTANT	⊔	⊔	⊔	⊔	⊔
2 SENIOR REGISTRAR	⊔	⊔	⊔	⊔	⊔
3 ASSOCIATE SPECIALIST	⊔	⊔	⊔	⊔	⊔
4 REGISTRAR post-FFA	⊔	⊔	⊔	⊔	⊔
5 REGISTRAR pre-FFA	⊔	⊔	⊔	⊔	⊔
6 CLINICAL ASSISTANT	⊔	⊔	⊔	⊔	⊔
7 GENERAL PRACTITIONER	⊔	⊔	⊔	⊔	⊔
8 SHO	⊔	⊔	⊔	⊔	⊔
9 OTHERS *(please specify)*	⊔	⊔	⊔	⊔	⊔
10 MEDICAL STUDENT	⊔	⊔	⊔	⊔	⊔

66-115

Are there any ANAESTHETISTS on duty for the Delivery area *only?*

(i.e. with no other responsibilities for other areas of the maternity unit, accident and emergency department etc.)

Yes/No

116

If YES, what is their status — as listed above? . . . .

117

Figure 1.8

time. We made a ranking judgement by taking the most senior grade and considered him or her to be the senior doctor on duty for the delivery area.

Having enquired about staff at 11 am, we performed similar sampling for the midwives at 3 pm, 7 pm and 11 pm on that day (Figures 1.5, 1.6, 1.7 and 1.8), trying to avoid the commonest changeover times. Doctors on the labour ward usually work longer duty rotas lasting often 12 hours or, more usually, 24 hours. Hence we collected data on them once more only, at 11 pm, to assess medical staffing in the night time.

As well as the professional staff, we asked questions about the clerical staff available in the delivery area during the 24 hours under review. We assessed this category as an important para-medical group who assist the smooth running of a labour ward.

We were not performing this survey to assess individual units but groups of places of delivery. Hence any one department might have been temporarily understaffed (or, very rarely, overstaffed) for a specific reason. For example the effects of August and September, traditionally holiday months, or a temporary closure of some part of the labour suite to allow repainting. We asked compilers to let us know about any such unusual aspect of their hospital life but the replies were few. Five units reported redecorating, four renovation and one replumbing. On 1 August, nineteen units commented on the presence of a new SHO and eight units had actually planned a diminished elective workload on that day because of the expected medical staff changeover.

Services

The Working Party considered it important to examine the services available in the delivery area during the 24 hours (Figure 1.5). The results could be expressed on each of the days surveyed but the agreement between these days was great so that they are given only once for each group of units.

The actual services assessed are only samples of what we thought was important but those selected are ones that the Working Party felt would represent the availability of other services. Blood storage areas in the delivery suite, on the same premises or elsewhere were asked for. Those units which had no blood available were also examined.

The Working Party examined the availability of an operating theatre for emergency operative obstetrics not just geographically close but that it was dedicated to obstetrics. Thus it would not be blocked by general surgery when there was a need for an urgent Caesarean section. Similarly, the availability of recovery rooms for mothers was examined and the provision of an epidural service on demand or when possible was checked. The theoretical provision of both obstetrical and paediatric flying squads was examined. The Working Party considered assessing some measure of the degree of preparedness of such squads and how frequently this service was used. At the pilot survey stage, however, difficulties were experienced; so this area was omitted from the final questionnaire for questionnaire surveys must be pragmatic and embrace the art of the practical. The availability and staffing of special care baby units were also examined and the information analysed in the paediatric section of the report (Chapter 7).

Equipment

The items of equipment assessed were obviously samples (Figure 1.9) selected as examples to obtain a picture of what was actually available at the place of birth. The list could have been much longer but the Working Party considered that it had to be kept to about fifteen items and chose those in the questionnaire after testing a variety of others at the pre-pilot and pilot stages. It is of interest to note that a year later, the Maternity Services Liaison Committee published a list of equipment which it considered should be available in every delivery suite. It matched the samples which the National Birthday Trust had chosen previously to survey in all but two items.

Among the obvious obstetrical items, the delivery bed was considered an important example; a continuous fetal heart rate monitor was going to be present in any sizeable unit and a fetal pH meter is considered by many to be an item which should be paired with the fetal heart rate monitor. We asked about both real-time ultrasound and birth chairs; these might be thought to represent items at the extremes of the equipment spectrum and which, for different reasons, we expected would be present in fewer units. Oxygen for the mother might be expected to be available in all units while an infusion pump might only be used when intravenous infusions were used frequently for the induction or augmentation of labour.

Samples of paediatric equipment included the presence of a neonatal laryngoscope, a bag and mask for newborn resuscitation and a resuscitation table. These would be of high priority in most units while an overhead radiant heater, though important, is a more recent addition to standard equipment and its presence might depend on the finances available.

In the anaesthetic field, an anaesthetic machine, which allows an anaesthetist to give a general anaesthetic immediately, was considered one of the essentials while an ECG monitor and a ventilator are considered desirable anywhere general anaesthesia is given. A cardiac arrest trolley was also enquired about as a measure of the capacity of that unit to cope with emergencies promptly.

Work done

In order to assess the workload we asked about the deliveries occurring at the various phases of the day with some details about vaginal deliveries, breech

Please complete at 3 p.m. continued

Definition A special care baby unit gives care in a special nursery or transitional ward providing observation and treatment falling short of intensive care but exceeding normal care. Care includes monitoring of ECG, respiration, TcPO₂, use of supplemental oxygen IV fluids, tube feeding, care of babies requiring constant nursing supervision and medical advice.

Definition An intensive care baby unit gives care in a special or intensive care nursery which provides continuous skilled supervision by nursing staff and 24 hour resident medical cover. Care includes long term mechanical ventilation, CPAP, care of babies of 1.5 Kg or 30 weeks gestation and parenteral nutrition.

SPECIAL CARE BABY UNIT

Is there a special care baby unit available at the place of birth?	Yes/No	45
If Yes, how many cots are there?		46-47
How many of these cots are available for intensive care?		48-49
How many of these cots are fully staffed and equipped for intensive care?		50-51

DO YOU PROVIDE

An obstetrical flying squad – emergency team?	Yes/No	52
A paediatric flying squad – emergency team?	Yes/No	53

PARAMEDICAL PERSONNEL

Are any of the following hospital personnel available for the delivery area at any time in 24 hours under review?

Hospital porter	Yes/No	54
Ward Clerk	Yes/No	55

56-59

60-63

64-67

EQUIPMENT AVAILABLE IN THE DELIVERY AREA

Please indicate from this wide range of possible items of equipment the number in the delivery area and the number functioning.

AN OBSTETRIC DELIVERY BED is one most of us use: it can be divided to allow operative procedures and has the capacity for rapid head up and head down tilting.

OXYGEN may be from a central piped supply or from portable cylinders but should not include mixtures with nitrous oxide (Entonox).

A MONITOR is to provide an ECG trace if the anaesthetist requires.

AN ANAESTHETIC MACHINE is one that allows the Anaesthetist to give a general anaesthetic immediately. If unsure we suggest you ask the anaesthetist.

EQUIPMENT	Number in delivery area	Number in working order	If equipment being mended — How long has it been away — Where did it go?	
Real time Ultrasound				68-69
Continuous Fetal Heart Monitor				70-73
Fetal pH Monitor				74-75
*Obstetric Delivery Bed				76-79
Birth Chair				80-81
Infusion Pump				82-85
Oxygen for the mother				86-89
Neonatal Laryngoscope				90-93
Neonatal Resusitation Table				94-97
Neonatal Overhead Radiant Heater				98-101
Bag and mask for resusitation of newborn				102-105
*Anaesthetic Machine				106-107
ECG Monitor (Adult)				108-109
Anaesthetic Ventilator				110-111
Cardiac Arrest Trolley				112-113

Figure 1.9

PLEASE COMPLETE AT 9 A.M. THE NEXT MORNING

HOW MANY OF THE FOLLOWING PROCEDURES OCCURRED IN THE LAST 24 HOURS?

1-13

EVENTS	09.00 TO 12.59 HOURS	13.00 TO 16.59 HOURS	17.00 TO 20.59 HOURS	21.00 TO 00.59 HOURS	01.00 TO 08.59 HOURS	TOTAL 24 HOURS
SINGLETONS ONLY Normal deliveries	☐	☐	☐	☐	☐	☐☐
Vaginal Breech Deliveries	☐	☐	☐	☐	☐	☐☐
Vaginal Operative Cephalic						
Forceps & Vacuum Extractions	☐	☐	☐	☐	☐	☐☐
*Elective Caesarean Section	☐	☐	☐	☐	☐	☐☐
*Emergency Caesarean Section	☐	☐	☐	☐	☐	☐
TWIN DELIVERIES	☐	☐	☐	☐	☐	☐☐
TOTAL DELIVERIES	☐☐	☐☐	☐☐	☐☐	☐☐	☐☐
General Anaesthetic started	☐	☐	☐	☐	☐	☐☐
Epidural inserted	☐	☐	☐	☐	☐	☐☐
Babies intubated	☐	☐	☐	☐	☐	☐☐
Babies sent to a special care baby unit	☐	☐	☐	☐	☐	☐☐
OTHER major procedures: (Please specify):	☐	☐	☐	☐	☐	☐☐

Only enter one event in each column

*If C S went from 12.30 to 13.30 enter it at the time the baby was born, say 12.52

*Enter under delivery time of second twin

Please consult with the paediatrician or Special Care Baby unit to record accurate timing of these events.

14-74

75-109

Are there any features which made this 24 hours unusual, e.g., excessive staff sickness, repainting of rooms, rooms closed due to staff shortage, transfer-in of women in labour from another unit or home?

110

We plan to present the results of the survey in the autumn of 1985.

Thank you very much for your help in completing this form.

You might like to compare your own unit's data with the national figures. We suggest you Xerox the forms before returning to the National Birthday Trust and compare them with the regional and national figures published in the report.

Figure 1.10

TABLE 1.3   Deliveries performed (and % of total) on August 1984 survey day by size of unit

Size of unit	Small 500	Medium 501– 2000	Large 2001– 4000	Very large 4000+	Not grouped
Normal deliveries	86 (90.5)	448 (77.3)	779 (78.4)	214 (67.5)	
Operative vaginal	8 (8.4)	52 (8.9)	108 (10.3)	54 (17.0)	5
Caesarean section					
Elective	0 (–)	33 (5.6)	58 (5.6)	17 (5.3)	3
Emergency	1 (1.0)	35 (6.0)	76 (7.3)	25 (7.8)	3
Breech	0	4	13	4	1
Twin	0	7	7	3	0
Total deliveries (2054)	95	579	1041	317	22

presentations, elective and emergency Caesarean sections (Figure 1.10 and Table 1.3).

Table 1.4 outlines and Figure 1.11 illustrates the comparative data about method of delivery in the last three National Birthday Trust surveys. While the editors accept that the method of data collection and the number of days of the enquiry differed between the three surveys, the trends shown are obvious. Normal deliveries have reduced by over 10 per cent while operative vaginal

TABLE 1.4   Methods of delivery in 1958, 1970 and 1984

Method of delivery	1958 (7 days) No.	%	1970 (7 days) No.	%	1984 (4 days) No.	%
Normal	14 991	88.2	14 178	83.9	6 198	76.1
Forceps and vacuum extraction[a]	799	4.6	1 361	8.0	890	10.9
Breech	385	2.3	454	2.8	131	1.5
Caesarean section	457	2.7	765	4.6	923	11.3
Destructive operation[b]	11	0.1	1	–	–	–
No trained person[b]	350	2.1	124	0.7	–	–
TOTAL	16 993	100.0	16 883	100.0	8 142	99.8

[a] No vacuum extraction in 1958.
[b] No data for 1984.

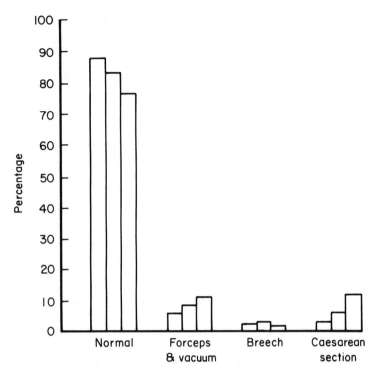

Figure 1.11   Comparison of the methods of delivery in the 1958, 1970 and 1984 surveys

delivery has more than doubled and the Caesarean section rate increased by greater than four-fold.

As might be expected the proportion of operative vaginal delivery increased with size of hospital while the normal deliveries reduced. However, both elective and emergency Caesarean section rates were about the same in all the units delivering more than 500 a year; in the small units only one emergency Caesarean section took place on the survey day, a rate below one in a hundred, implying a reasonable section of women for delivery.

To assess the paediatric load, we asked similarly about babies intubated and babies sent to the special care baby unit and for the anaesthetic load, the number of general anaesthetics and epidural analgesics started at that time. These allowed us to analyse data about staff, services and facilities against load and so obtain some valuation of the work done against the facilities available.

THE COMMUNITY QUESTIONNAIRE

The information to be collected from the community was very different from that involved with the institutional deliveries. The questionnaire was distri- buted to the heads of the Community Midwifery Services for each district or

NOTES OF GUIDANCE

This questionnaire should be under the supervision of the Head of Community Midwifery Services for the District (or Health Board in Scotland and Northern Ireland). We would be grateful if she would fill in the details below and ask the individual midwives who attend domiciliary deliveries to fill in the five tables. We have allowed enough space for three deliveries to occur outside the hospital in 24 hours; it would be unusual to get more than that number of home deliveries in the time but if in your district this has happened, would you please Xerox the form and fill in the other appropriate pages. This will be a most unusual event.

When the form has been completed at the end of 24 hours would you please return it to the National Birthday Trust Fund at 57 Lower Belgrave Street, London SW1W 0YY as soon as possible. Using the Business Reply label attached.

It may be that no domiciliary deliveries occurred in your district or Health Board in the 24 hours under review. We would still welcome your filling in the front page indicating that there was no deliveries so that we can have a complete report of the day's activities throughout the country.

We would stress that all this information is fully confidential. Neither your name or your district will appear in any analysis. We will block out personal details from the front page when we fill in the survey number immediately the proforma arrives at the National Birthday Trust. From then on, the form has a number only.

TO BE COMPLETED BY THE HEAD OF COMMUNITY MIDWIFERY
SERVICES OR HER DEPUTY

For Office Use:

Please complete this section even if there have been no deliveries in the community during the 24 hours under review. To give us some measure of your workload, please complete the number of deliveries in your District outside the hospital during 1983.

1-8

Total number of deliveries outside the hospital for 1983:   9-11

Of the above, how many were:

Booked for a home delivery: 12-14

Booked elsewhere but a home delivery: 15-16

Unbooked but delivered at home: 17-18

Booked elsewhere but delivered in transit: 19-20

Figure 1.12

health board in the United Kingdom. They were asked to fill in some details about the previous year to give a background picture of the District Community Services' activities, for example the number of deliveries that occurred outside hospital and some breakdown of the population of those booked for home delivery (Figure 1.12).

The questionnaire then devoted a single page to the domiciliary delivery under review (Figure 1.13). To cover the unlikely eventuality of a district having more than one delivery in the day of the survey, there were three such pages bound in each questionnaire sent to each district. In fact on one survey day, against the odds, one district did have two home deliveries but no district had to use the third page.

The head of the District Community Services was responsible for the distribution of the forms and for their collection; the midwife in charge of the delivery filled in the page. We asked about the booking arrangements of the mother and whether that delivery was booked to take place at home. The personnel present (by grade) were obviously different from those expected at a hospital delivery. We enquired if the midwife or general practitioner who attended the delivery had actually been booked for that delivery.

Transfer of the mother and/or baby in the first 24 hours after delivery and the reasons for this were assessed as were details about where they had gone.

We chose samples of equipment that might be expected at a domiciliary delivery but, as discussed previously, the Working Party realized these were only samples. To examine communications we asked about range of equipment from a telephone, through Aircall bleeps, to two-way radios. To assess fetal monitoring equipment in labour, we enquired if a Doppler fetal heart rate machine was present. To examine the care of the mother we asked both about the capacity for intravenous therapy and the presence of oxygen for the mother. Neonatal cover was assessed with questions about neonatal laryngoscopes and oxygen for the baby. We enquired about the medical personnel present during the labour, their booking arrangements and the availability of obstetrical and paediatric flying squads.

In the United Kingdom there are approximately 21 domiciliary deliveries a day, both booked and unbooked. Thus in the four survey days one might have expected 84 deliveries and we received forms for 86. We have no other way of checking the completeness of our domiciliary records but they are probably in the right zone.

MOUNTING THE SURVEY

After the Survey Working Party had agreed a semi-final version of the form, eight hospitals were approached to complete the institutional questionnaire as a pre-pilot assessment. Of these, one was a private sector unit, the Wellington Hospital, and the remaining seven were from widespread NHS regions within

DELIVERY 1 — TO BE COMPLETED BY THE MIDWIFE WHO ATTENDED THE DELIVERY

Would the individual midwives attending the home deliveries in the 24-hour period under review, please enter the details of equipment and services available. We would like to emphasise that this is a national survey of facilities at the place of birth and not an assessment of individual arrangements. The list of personnel and services may not describe well your own arrangements. The list of equipment may not include items felt important to you and no criticism is intended of any individual who does not have these items. This survey can only ask about samples of the facilities available at the place of birth and we would ask you to be as accurate as possible in completing the form.

BOOKING ARRANGEMENTS FOR THE MOTHER		For Office Use:
Please tick one		
WAS THE MOTHER		
Booked for a home delivery:	☐	
Booked elsewhere but a home delivery:	☐	
Unbooked but delivered at home:	☐	☐ 21
Booked elsewhere but delivered in transit:	☐	

PERSONNEL PRESENT AT THE DELIVERY:

How many of these professionals were present at the delivery:

Nursing Officer (Senior Midwife Grade)	☐	22
Community Midwife	☐	23
Hospital Based Midwife	☐	24
Student Midwife	☐	25
General Practitioner	☐	26
Other (please specify)	☐	27

Was the Midwife or General Practitioner who attended the delivery booked for that delivery?

Midwife: YES/NO/NOT APPLICABLE — ☐ 28

General Practitioner: YES/NO/NOT APPLICABLE — ☐ 29

TRANSFER

Was the mother transferred in the first 24 hours after the birth? YES/NO — ☐ 30

If YES, to where: — ☐ 31

Was the baby transferred in the first 24 hours after the birth? YES/NO — ☐ 32

If YES, to where: — ☐ 33

EQUIPMENT

From this range of possible equipment please indicate the items on the premises of delivery:

	Please tick:	For Office Use:
Telephone (working in the premises)	☐	☐ 34
Two way Radio control	☐	
Bleep	☐	☐ 35
Ultrasound/Doppler fetal heart rate machine	☐	☐ 36
Neonatal laryngoscope	☐	☐ 37
Oxygen for baby	☐	☐ 38
I.V. giving set	☐	☐ 39
I. V. fluids	☐	☐ 40
Oxygen for mother	☐	☐ 41

MEDICAL PERSONNEL:

Was a General Practitioner booked for labour care? YES/NO — ☐ 42

If NO, what medical cover was there? — ☐ 43

Did a General Practitioner attend during labour? YES/NO — ☐ 44

Was an Obstetric emergency team (flying squad) available? YES/NO — ☐ 45

Was a Paediatric emergency team (flying squad) available? YES/NO — ☐ 46

Do you wish to make any further comment about this delivery?: — ☐ 47

— ☐ 48

Figure 1.13

the United Kingdom. These were the Aberdeen Maternity Hospital; Ninewells Hospital, Dundee; Queen Charlotte's Hospital, London; St George's Hospital, London; St Mary's Hospital, London; Norfolk & Norwich Hospital; and Southmead Hospital, Bristol. The hospital questionnaires were completed by the nursing officer or sister in charge of the labour ward. At the same time, Norfolk and Norwich District completed some of the community questionnaires.

The return of these questionnaires, together with valuable comments from the midwives who completed them, enabled the Working Party to reconsider certain aspects of the questionnaire. The general comments did not suggest that the forms took too long to complete (a mean of seventeen minutes) or that they made unreasonable demands on the midwife in charge of the labour ward at any of the sample times. Following the pre-pilot study, the main alterations were to provide clearer definitions about the facilities and equipment being examined and to exclude certain ill-understood questions.

These modifications enabled a full pilot study to be performed in April 1984. The midwifery managers of two health authorities, the Paddington and North Kensington District and the Norfolk and Norwich District, were approached and asked to complete both community and institutional forms for all deliveries in 24 hours within their district; details of community deliveries were completed by the community midwifery sister under the supervision of the director of midwifery services. The first district was in an inner city area and the second was a rural one including both a district general hospital and isolated GP units. Following the return of the questionnaires of the pilot study, the Working Party was able to plan for 1 August 1984 as the first day of the survey. We are grateful to the midwifery supervisors and all staff who helped refine the questionnaires by testing them at the formative stages.

At the beginning of 1984 an approach had been made to senior medical and midwifery staff through the Departments of Health in England and Wales, the Scottish Home and Health Office and the Department of Health and Social Services in Northern Ireland asking for their cooperation by participating in the enquiry. At the same time publicity was given to the survey both by articles published in the medical and midwifery journals and by members of the Working Party attending professional meetings to discuss the survey. The Survey Director attended meetings in Northern Ireland at the Department of Health and Social Services, the Scottish Home and Health Department and the Welsh Office. In England, the Director and the Survey Coordinator addressed a meeting of heads of midwifery services at the Royal College of Midwives. Posters were made and used for publicity at medical conferences and courses. A display was mounted at the Royal College of Midwives' Annual General Meeting in Cardiff in July 1984.

From May 1984, the nursing and midwifery managers within the United Kingdom were approached to ask for their cooperation in the survey. In view of the varying nursing and midwifery management structures in the different countries, the methods of approach differed in England, Wales, Scotland and Northern Ireland.

In England, approaches were made to regional nursing officers, the district nursing officers and arrangements were made to distribute the questionnaires through the directors of midwifery services. In the vast majority of districts this presented no problems. However, in a few districts the midwifery and community services were fully integrated and some questionnaires were sent to the directors of community services for completion in isolated GP units and community deliveries. Two further districts were managed on a geographical basis and this necessitated questionnaires being sent to more than one director of nursing services.

In Scotland, the Department of Home and Health was in the middle of a reorganization of its area health boards at the time of our survey and we were asked to forward the questionnaires to the chief area nursing officers for distribution within their health boards. During the course of the survey, two health boards asked for the questionnaires to be sent to the midwife managers.

In Northern Ireland the chief area nursing officers were approached and the questionnaires were either sent to them or the midwifery managers within that health board.

A list of hospitals undertaking deliveries was obtained and checked against places of delivery held at both the National Perinatal Epidemiology Unit in Oxford and at the Office of Population and Census Surveys. The list of hospitals and separate places of delivery within each district or unit of management was forwarded to the head of midwifery services for each district for confirmation. A few units had closed since the hospital list had been drawn up and some hospitals had opened (or re-opened). The head of midwifery services was also asked to inform us if she had any independent midwives anticipating undertaking a delivery during the survey period so that we could forward additional community questionnaires for them.

The names and addresses of hospitals in the private sector providing obstetric care were obtained with the cooperation of the Private Patients Plan; their administrative officers and head nurses were approached.

Six hospitals under the aegis of the Ministry of Defence provided maternity services which were also included in the study. Their cooperation was gained through the directors of the medical services of the Army and Royal Air Force and the medical officers in charge of the respective maternity services. The Royal Navy has no obstetrical service nor were there any delivery services functioning within the prison service.

Movement of the questionnaires

The questionnaires, together with spare copies, were forwarded to the respective heads of services two or three weeks prior to each survey day; they were asked to return them as soon as possible after the first of each month. During July 1984 there was a postal strike at the sorting office serving the area of the National Birthday Trust while a similar strike affected the Manchester area during August. However, with willing volunteers posting material away from the Trust's headquarters, these did not create any major problems for the running of the survey. Heads of service were asked to check the number of forms on arrival and confirm this to the National Birthday Trust by returning a prepaid printed postcard.

The questionnaires were returned by the heads of services and the first set was received at the Birthday Trust's headquarters on 3 August, two days after the survey day. It came from Kidderminster Health District. Some 95 per cent of the questionnaires were returned by the 25th of each month. Missing questionnaires were pursued by post and telephone through the heads of services by the Survey Administrator. The final response rate over the four survey days was 99.1 per cent. The main delay in returning the questionnaires occurred in those districts with a number of hospitals providing maternity services where it took a little longer to collect the questionnaires together.

Handling the data

On arrival at the National Birthday Trust, a unique number was allocated to each place of birth. Then the cover of the questionnaires, which provided details of the hospital and place of birth, was removed so that the information in the body of the questionnaire was completely anonymous and could not be traced to the unit. From this point, all analyses were performed on these anonymous data sheets. Much of the information collected was pre-coded and the remainder was coded by the survey staff at the National Birthday Trust office as the forms came in from 3 August. This work was done by Philippa Gunn and Sarah Clive Powell.

The first batch of forms was sent for punching in September 1984; the last batch of questionnaires was returned from punching in March 1985. This included the last returns of the November survey day and those which had been held back from the other days of the enquiry because of queries.

Data analysis

The editing of the data started in December 1984 and was completed by September 1985; it was carried out in the Computer Department at St George's Hospital Medical School with the help of the data processing manager, Miss Valerie Dickinson. The work was done by the Survey Administrator, Miss Gunn, who was greatly helped by the staff of that department.

The data from the hospital deliveries were filed at the University of London Computer Centre and analyses with the Statistical Analysis System (SAS) package. A total of 820 units were used in the analysis of data over the period of twelve months. The correcting of data on the tape was carried out with five small files which were joined together for the final analysis. Some data were required for one month only (August), further analysis was carried out joining the results for all four months in each particular unit and for this the data were divided into four separate months. The data files were stored in the form of SAS Data Libraries. Analyses of the profiles of units within groups, size and types were performed by merging the results of each unit for four months (or less with the few cases where four questionnaires had not been returned) and these provided within-unit results. The remaining results were obtained from the entire file and these assessed variations between the unit.

The community questionnaires were edited and analysed on a microcomputer in the Department of Clinical Epidemiology and Social Medicine at St George's Hospital Medical School.

The editing and analyses were under the aegis of the survey statistician, Dr Martin Bland, Senior Lecturer at St George's Hospital Medical School, to whom we are grateful for the assistance given by him and many members of staff in his department.

CONCLUSIONS

This survey belongs to the midwives for without them we could not have performed it. They filled in the forms at the hospitals and to them the ultimate thanks must be given for they have once again assisted the National Birthday Trust in performing a survey which we hope to be of use to all who provide health care for pregnant women. The information shown in the pages of this report may not always please factions in medicine or midwifery but it has at least the merit of having been collected impartially and analysed without bias to allow those who wish to further the obstetrical services to do so with a firm data base.

REFERENCE

1. Robinson, S. (1979). *The Role and Responsibility of the Midwife*. Chelsea College, London, (1979).

CHAPTER 2

The Place and Day of Birth

GEOFFREY CHAMBERLAIN

THE BIRTHPLACE

The vast majority of births occurred in obstetric units, mostly in hospitals. The size of hospitals examined in the survey varied widely from one where only one baby had been delivered in the previous year to six units where over 5000 women a year were delivered (Table 2.1).

For geographical reasons in the periphery of the United Kingdom there may have to be a number of units delivering very few babies a year; over 40 per cent of all the units reporting in August, however, had delivered less than 500 babies in the previous year, a minute population of the total obstetrical workload spread widely in small units not all of which were in the periphery of the country. Some are still to be found in large towns near to larger hospitals.

We divided the hospitals reporting to the survey into roughly equal functional groups and have designated these with names which we use throughout the report.

Small units

These were units that reported between 1 and 500 deliveries a year in the previous year, 1983. Many of these were GP units. Their facilities and problems are highlighted in the sub-analysis performed in Chapter 9. Although there are 217 of these (41 per cent of all units) they covered only 35 000 deliveries, 5 per cent of the total.

Medium units

These were the hospitals performing between 501 and 2000 deliveries a year; there were 149 and they accounted for 28 per cent of all deliveries. They could

TABLE 2.1   A representation of the spread of the deliveries in United Kingdom in 1983 throughout 531 units

In up to 10% of these units there were less than	60 deliveries in 1983
20%	125
30%	232
40%	410
50%	1023
60%	1554
70%	1989
80%	2495
90%	3190
In the largest unit there were	5476 deliveries in 1983

have been split further on either side of the 1000 deliveries a year point but there was a uniformity of data throughout the group, and so we maintained the whole cluster as one.

Large units

These units performed between 2001 and 4000 deliveries a year and into this group came most of the district general hospitals. The 129 units had delivered 50 per cent of the population in the previous year, so that this group which contained only a quarter of the units provided care for half the deliveries.

Very large units

This term was applied to the 26 units delivering more than 4000 babies a year. These, although few in number (less than 5 per cent of hospitals) had a large workload and were responsible for 17 per cent of all deliveries in the country.

The division of the units into these groups was to aid analysis. Individual district midwifery managers know exactly the size of their own units in this confidential enquiry and can therefore place them in context with the other units reporting in the survey.

TABLE 2.2   Distribution of units and deliveries in United Kingdom

	Small (1–500)	Medium (501–2000)	Large (2001–4000)	Very large (4001+)
Units	217	149	129	26
Deliveries in 1983 (to nearest 1000)	35 000	197 000	350 000	120 000
Total deliveries (%)	5	28	50	17

Note: Not grouped in this table are the private and service hospitals — see text.

TABLE 2.3   Number of units open and return of forms by month

	Aug (Wed)	Sept (Sat)	Oct (Mon)	Nov (Thurs)
Units returning forms	531	523	521	523
Units open but forms not returned	1	8	6	5
Units closed	6	7	11	10

Units open on the survey days

Table 2.3 details the units open on each survey day and those we know that were temporarily closed. The response rate by unit each day was 99.8, 98.5, 98.9 and 99.0 per cent with an overall rate of 99.1 per cent. Enthusiasm seems to have been sustained for the four months, as the Working Party had predicted. Many letters and comments were received which confirmed this (but also letting us know that a longer study would not have been so welcome).

Of the 538 units open on one or other of the survey days, there were 57 units (10.5 per cent) which reported having neither a woman in labour at any of the survey times nor any deliveries in the four 24-hour periods under review. As could be expected, these units were in the group of small hospitals.

If no one was in labour, there was no need for attending doctors, and in some cases midwives, to be there and so in these small hospitals no return was obtained. Under-reporting of midwifery and medical staff in these cases cannot then be excluded but in most of the small units the total availability of GP obstetricians, paediatricians and anaesthetists on call for the delivery area was recorded thus giving results for cover of these hospitals per thousand women in labour.

THE REGIONS

The regions used in the survey are those of the National Health Service for England. Fourteen geographical areas are managed by regional health authorities and we followed the boundaries laid down by these. Wales has only one region while Scotland and Northern Ireland have several health boards each but on population sizes, we considered these two kingdoms as equivalent to one region each. The special units included the private units, those in the Armed Services and a unit each in Guernsey, Jersey and the Isle of Man.

The National Birthday Trust decided not to release the result of any analyses at a district health authority level. This is a confidential enquiry and we received returns from district midwifery managers on this understanding. To publish data at the district level in our opinion would have been a breach of this confidence for in many districts there is only one large unit providing obstetric

TABLE 2.4   Number of units by region, August 1984

	Total	Type of unit		
	no. of units	Con. and + GP	GP	Other
Northern	28	21	7	0
Yorkshire	31	21	10	0
Trent	35	19	16	0
East Anglia	16	10	6	0
North-West Thames	22	18	2	2
North-East Thames	30	23	7	0
South-East Thames	27	23	4	0
South-West Thames	17	16	1	0
Wessex	31	12	19	0
Oxford	22	10	12	0
South-Western	37	13	23	1
West Midlands	41	23	18	0
Mersey	10	10	0	0
Northern	30	21	9	0
Wales	37	21	16	0
Scotland	72	34	38	0
Special health authority	2	2	0	0
Northern Ireland	27	16	11	0
Others				
Private hospitals	7			
Service hospitals	6			
Channel Islands and				
Isle of Man	3			

care. Were we to publish district data, this could quickly be extrapolated into the information about performance and facilities at a recognized unit. The outline profiles of maternity performance indicators in the Appendix of this volume will enable the district midwifery managers who hold this information to set their units against national data of units of the same size or region in confidence.

The type and size of delivery unit showed a wide variation when examined by region. Some of this reflects geographical needs; for example the largest number of units was found in Scotland and this can be accounted for by the large number of small GP units providing services in isolated parts of the region (Table 2.4).

The region with the largest percentage of units delivering less than 500 a year was the South-Western region where over two-thirds of units fell into this

TABLE 2.5   Hospitals and delivery areas (August 1984)

Central delivery services	495
Separate GP delivery area	32
Separate private unit delivery area	2
Divided consultant delivery areas with separate staffing and equipment	2
TOTAL NUMBER OF DELIVERY AREAS	**531**

group. Scotland, Wales, Wessex and Oxford also had half their units delivering less than 500 babies in the previous year. In Mersey there were no units delivering less than 1000 a year. In Wales and South-West Thames there were no units delivering over 3000 babies in the previous year.

THE TYPE OF HOSPITAL UNITS

Hospitals reported providing 531 maternity delivery areas on 1 August 1984. In 495 of these (93 per cent), there was one central delivery area with a uniform equipment and policy for staffing (Table 2.5).

Thirty-two hospitals had a separate GP delivery area on the same site and two had a separate delivery area for private patients. A further two units provided separate consultant delivery areas, each with separate equipment and staffing.

TABLE 2.6   Numbers of delivery units of each type (August 1984)

NHS consultant unit	195
Combined NHS consultant and GP unit	114
Combined NHS consultant and private unit	7
Separate GP unit	199
Private unit in NHS hospital	2
Armed Services hospital	6
Private hospital	6
Other	2
TOTAL	531

Table 2.6 shows that 195 hospitals were purely NHS consultant units while another 114 shared facilities with GP obstetricians. Some 37 per cent (199) were separate GP units. Obviously for the data presentation such a detailed breakdown would provide too many small categories and so they were grouped as follows:

NHS consultant unit   ⎫
Consultant and GP unit   ⎬ Consultant units
Consultant and private unit   ⎭

GP unit isolated from consultant unit   } Separate GP units

Service hospital   ⎫
Private hospital   ⎬ Other units
Private unit in hospital   ⎬ Other
Units in Channel Isles and Isle of Man ⎭ Other

1. *Consultant units*   The majority of units fell into this group. The consultant unit was on the same site as the GP services or the private facilities so that consultant facilities were available in all delivery areas. In some cases there may still have been separate wards but generally there were central delivery services.
2. *Separate GP units*   This grouping included both isolated GP units and those covered by general practitioners in a hospital but kept separate from the consultant unit with a delivery area separate from the consultant unit. This had implications in the levels of staffing and provision of equipment.
3. *Other units*   These few units have been grouped together although they did not always produce similar findings. In general, the staffing and facilities were peculiar to that unit and its type of work. Private hospitals worked differently from those in the Armed Services but the type of deliveries and the absence of student midwives and medical students were common to all.

The delivery area

The delivery area or labour ward is well known to most who work in obstetrics and hardly needs definition. However, in some cases there was a blurring of boundaries. We intended to examine those places where women normally would be expected to deliver; these should be equipped and staffed to cope with deliveries and any complications that might arise at those deliveries. In the United Kingdom most women have antenatal care and know they should go to hospital early in labour. We do not have the problems of other countries where women turn up in the second stage of labour and need delivery in emergency rooms close to the casualty department. While some deliveries do take place in casualty deartments, we were not assessing such emergencies in this survey.

Further variation between delivery areas was anticipated in the type and siting of the labour rooms. Although hospitals generally provide a central delivery area, some units existed in which each ward consisted of antenatal and postnatal beds with a labour room for these women. There also existed units where rooms were provided for successive antenatal care, labour care and postnatal stay so that the woman stayed in the one room for all her time in hospital; these are described as all-purpose rooms. Many of the integrated and all-purpose delivery areas were in the smaller units. This classification in the analysis of data and in particular in the aspect of midwifery staffing was considered important and analysis between these two types of wards is used in Chapter 4.

Another problem was the number of delivery areas in any given hospital. We tried to cope with this by the instructions that we gave to the senior midwives who filled in the forms. We suggested that forms be used for different places of birth along the following guidelines:

1. Where all deliveries take place within one geographical area, please complete one form (regardless of GP, Consultant or private cases).
2. Where there are separate delivery areas within one institution, proviued they are staffed and equipped as one, please use only one form, e.g. a unit where deliveries do not occur within one central delivery area but may be integrated into a series of combined antenatal and postnatal wards.
3. Where separate delivery areas with separate arrangements for staffing and equipment exist within one institution, please count these as separate places of birth and use more than one form, e.g. separate GP or private units.

Do not forget to add into your delivery areas the following possibilities: birth rooms and isolation labour wards for infectious cases.

We considered that the examples we quoted of special birth rooms and isolation delivery wards were important for those are places where women might be expected to deliver and so should be included in any survey of facilities.

The denominators

To understand the relative importance of the numbers relating to equipment or staff collected in a survey of this nature, the data must be set against their background. Ratios of numbers to some measure of work done are essential for this allows us to compare like with like. In this report we have tried to show ratios with denominators which indicate the size of the unit or its workload.

Unfortunately there is no one denominator which does this in all circumstances and so three denominators have been used at various points in the presentation of the data: (1) the number of places at which women deliver; (2) the number of women in labour at the four survey times (1984); (3) the number of deliveries in that unit in 1983.

1. The number of units has been used to show the variation of facilities in any geographical areas.

2. The number of women in labour during each survey day is a measure of workload; this can be related to changing facilities including medical and midwifery staffing levels. There was a good correlation between the number of women in labour in any unit and deliveries reported in the previous year.

   The number of women in labour (excluding the numbers of other non-labouring women, for example antenatal and post-delivery patients) in the delivery area and the type of delivery carried out vary according to the size of unit. There were relatively more postnatal and antenatal women recorded in the smaller units. A finer determinant is found by looking at the proportion of different types of deliveries recorded over the 24-hour periods. Obviously larger units undertook more vaginal instrumental and operative deliveries and carried out more epidural anaesthetics.

3. The data on the previous year's deliveries were reported and completed well. In a small number of cases, the delivery unit did not function or even exist in 1983 and so data were not available in these cases (0.4 per cent of units reporting in August 1984 were not open in 1983). This denominator was used as a measure of the workload which could be anticipated in the unit and against which the fixed facilities could have been planned such as labour rooms, equipment and special care baby units.

CHANGES IN THE PLACE OF BIRTH IN THE FOUR MONTHS

During the course of the survey, 538 units were open on one or more survey days. Seven units closed after the first month and three units opened during the following three months. Two units changed site; one, a moderate sized and separate maternity unit, moved from an isolated site on to the site of a district general hospital and the other was an isolated GP unit which closed but continued deliveries in a GP ward of an existing maternity unit. Three GP units within consultant maternity units were reportedly closed during the survey time due to the lack of staff. One very large unit and one small unit open throughout the survey were identified to the National Birthday Trust office after the first two months and completed part of the first two forms in retrospect.

THE SURVEY DAYS

The first day of the month for four months in autumn 1984 was selected. The first survey day was Wednesday August 1, a midweek day during a peak holiday season. The highest number of questionnaires was returned on this day (531) and 2058 deliveries took place in institutions (Table 2.7).

   In England, August 1 was one of the two days in the year when there was a complete change of junior medical staff in many hospitals. In this survey we found that this affected both elective deliveries and medical cover. Eight units

TABLE 2.7 Number of deliveries reported by month

	August (Wednesday)	September (Saturday)	October (Monday)	November (Thursday)
No. of institutional deliveries	2058	1853	2234	2017
No. of home deliveries	26	16	25	19

reported a reduction in booking elective deliveries and planned procedures nineteen units reported that special arrangements for that day were made because of temporary changes in medical cover. It may be administratively convenient to have a massive change of all junior staff on the same day but it can produce poorer cover for the whole team of relatively experienced juniors to be replaced by new doctors of less experience. Many hospitals have given up this archaism by changing SHO and registrar posts in a planned fashion at different months through the year.

The least active day by the number of deliveries was the second survey day on September 1. This was a Saturday, still within the holiday season and falling a week after the English and Welsh Late Summer Bank Holiday. Eight smaller units open on that day failed to return questionnaires to the survey and this was the highest rate of missing forms in the four months; three units had sent off the forms and these had been lost in the post and five units had forgotten to complete them. A further three larger units had completed part of the information in retrospect. There were fewer deliveries both in hospital and in the community and the lowest rate of operative deliveries was reported on this day. This fits with national data which confirm that fewer deliveries take place at the weekend.

The third survey day was Monday October 1, and although it was not considered to be within the major holiday season, it is the day on which approximately half the Scottish hospitals traditionally take their Late Statutory Holiday to coincide with the school half-term. There were fewer units open on 1 October, eleven of the total of 538 being closed although some only temporarily. On the first day of the week there was the highest number of hospital deliveries recorded in the four days.

The final day of the survey was Thursday 1 November—All Saints' Day. Although the number of units which was open had been falling over the first three months, three dormant units opened on this last day of the survey.

A number of midwives commented that each of the four days had been exceptionally quiet. This is in line with the well-known horticultural comment that you should have seen the garden last week. The Director of Nursing Services from one district, commenting on home deliveries, wrote after the last survey day that there had been a home delivery on the 31st and another on the

TABLE 2.8   Type of delivery by day and month

	Aug (Wed)		Sept (Sat)		Oct (Mon)		Nov (Thurs)	
	No.	%	No.	%	No.	%	No.	%
Normal deliveries	1540	74.8	1436	77.5	1665	74.5	1495	74.6
Forceps and vacuum extractions	227	10.8	220	11.9	235	10.5	212	10.7
Vaginal breech deliveries	23	1.0	24	1.2	42	1.8	43	2.1
Twin deliveries	17	0.8	18	0.9	34	1.5	27	1.3
Caesarean section Elective	111	5.4	23	1.2	91	4.0	110	5.5
Caesarean section Emergency	140	6.8	132	8.1	167	7.4	130	6.5
TOTAL	2058		1853		2234		2017	

2nd but none on the day surveyed. One midwife telephoned at the end of November to report that she had not received her questionnaries for 1 December. We thought this reflected the keenness of midwives who did the real work for this survey.

CHANGES BETWEEN THE FOUR DAYS

The highest number of deliveries recorded over the four days was on the Monday and the number of deliveries in 24 hours then fell to the lowest on the Saturday. Although numbers were fewer, it was also noted that a higher number of home deliveries occurred at the beginning of the week and fewest on Saturday.

The type of delivery also varied between weekdays and weekend (Table 2.8). The vaginal delivery rate and forceps delivery rate showed little variation between the four days; both were highest on the Saturday but the differences were not major. Although small in number, breech and twin deliveries were highest on the Monday and Thursday. As might be expected, the number of elective Caesarean sections was greatly reduced on the Saturday and was only a quarter of the weekday rate; the emergency Caesarean section rate continued and was indeed highest on the Saturday, 8.1 per cent compared with 6.8, 7.4 and 6.5 per cent on other survey days.

The other procedures and events recorded during the 24 hours related respectively to anaesthetic and to paediatric loads (Table 2.9). The variation noted already between weekday and weekend was also demonstrated in the

TABLE 2.9   Number of procedures and percentage of total deliveries in 24 hours

	August (Wednesday)		September (Saturday)		October (Monday)		November (Thursday)	
	No.	%	No.	%	No.	%	No.	%
General anaesthetic started	232	11.2	161	8.7	222	9.9	275	16.0
Epidural inserted	341	16.6	251	13.5	326	14.5	317	16.0
Babies intubated	81	3.9	74	4.0	87	3.8	73	3.6
Admission to SCBU	203	9.8	186	10.0	123	5.5	178	9.0
TOTAL DELIVERIES	2058		1853		2234		2017	

number of general anaesthetics started and epidurals inserted and these data corresponded well with the reduction in elective Caesarean rate over the weekend.

The paediatric procedures recorded were intubation of the baby and admission to special care baby units and both were a little higher on Saturday than weekdays. The rate of babies intubated was raised (insignificantly) on the Saturday (4.0 per cent compared with 3.9, 3.8 and 3.6 per cent on the other days) although the rate of admission of babies to the special care baby units was significantly lowest on the Monday, 5.5 per cent compared with 10.0, 9.8 and 9.0 per cent on the other three days.

CHANGES WITHIN THE DAY

The variation of deliveries and other labour-intensive procedures over the 24 hours was also analysed. The workload was recorded in five blocks during the 24 hours. The first from 9 am to 1 pm was the morning period, 1 pm to 5 pm reflected the afternoon activity. From 5 pm to 9 pm was the early evening while 9 pm to 1 am was the late evening activity. From 1 am to 9 am was the night period.

The distribution of deliveries over the 24-hour period (Figure 2.1) showed a larger proportion of deliveries occurring during the two daytime periods and fewest occurring during the night. There was also a higher rate of operative deliveries occurring during the day than at night regardless of the day of the week.

A further assessment of workload in the delivery area, that of the number of women in labour, shows a similar trend over 24 hours. Irrespective of the month or day of the week the largest number of women in labour is recorded at 11 am and this figure falls over the twelve-hour period so that by 11 pm there

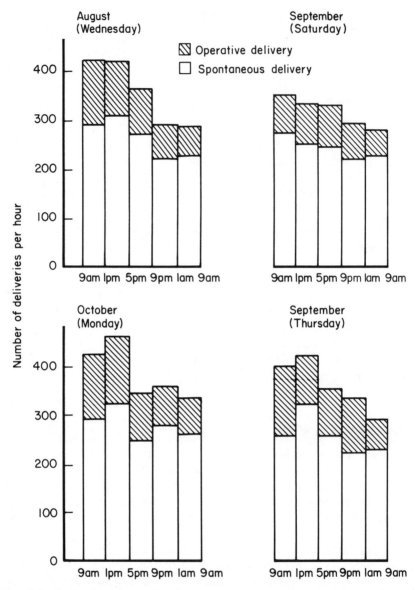

Figure 2.1   Deliveries on each day of the survey. The numbers are divided between the time intervals in which data were collected for the 24 hours

are on average one-third fewer women in labour in the delivery area (Table 2.10).

A number of other procedures occurring in the deliver area were also recorded over the same five periods of time in 24 hours (Figure 2.2). The

TABLE 2.10   Number of women in labour by time of day

	August (Wednesday)	September (Saturday)	October (Monday)	November (Thursday)
11 am	810	737	875	828
3 pm	722	648	783	723
7 pm	622	569	644	618
11 pm	539	549	631	584

number of general anaesthetics started and of epidurals inserted reflected the anaesthetic load. These were highest during the morning period for both procedures in all four survey days. The number of general anaesthetics started dropped over the 24-hour period to less than half by the night period which was a reflection of the numbers of women in labour. On Saturday, there were the fewest general anaesthetics but the diminution of epidurals inserted was not

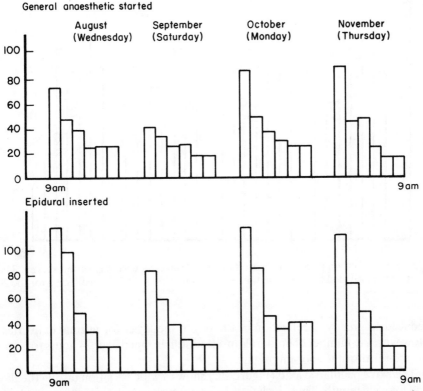

Figure 2.2   Certain anaesthetic procedures performed on each day of the survey. The numbers are divided between the time intervals in which data were collected for the 24 hours.

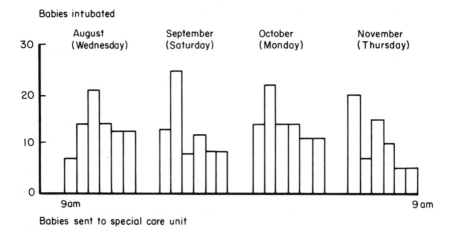

Babies sent to special care unit

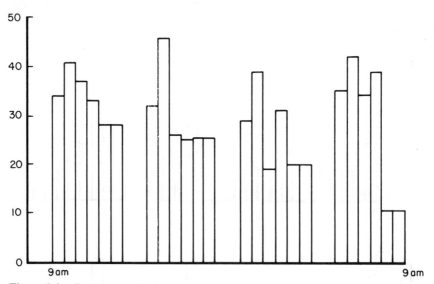

Figure 2.3   Certain paediatric procedures performed on each day of the survey. The numbers are divided between the time intervals in which data were collected for the 24 hours

reduced so greatly, a reflection of the use of the latter for normal deliveries. However, the number of epidurals inserted still dropped over 24 hours to a rate of one-third of the morning figure.

The extra paediatric load (Figure 2.3) shows a wide variation during the day and for each month. There is slightly less activity during the night hours and this compares with the number of deliveries for the 24-hour period. However, the

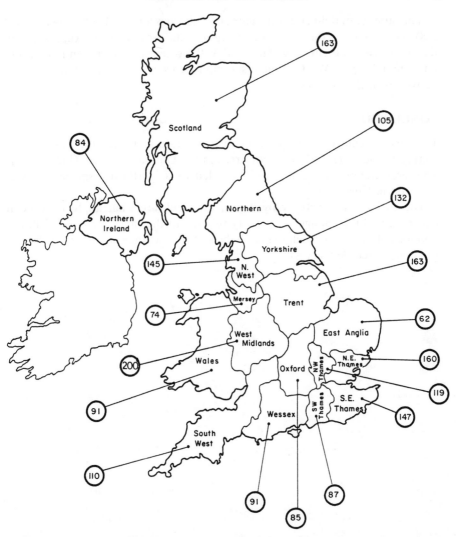

Figure 2.4   The numbers of deliveries in each region for the first survey day (August)

August and September data differ from those of October and November. Comparisons of data in Figure 2.3 show that in the latter two months, admissions to special care baby units and intubations reflect roughly the numbers of babies born. However, in August and September, admissions and intubations were more common in the afternoon and early evening although the highest delivery numbers were in the morning.

The number of deliveries on each survey day has already been shown (Table 2.8). These were further analysed by regions; the results for the August survey day are shown in Figure 2.4. They follow the general pattern seen in monthly and annual data—West Midlands region deals with the most number of deliveries in the country.

CONCLUSIONS

The survey achieved a 99 per cent response rate and gives the first precise picture of the workload in labour areas in the United Kingdom (Figure 2.4). The large number of minute units has led us to perform a special analysis reported in Chapter 9.

The variations of activity by day of the week are what might have been expected and the changes of activity relating to the time of day confirm the opinions of those who seek to match the staffing facilities of labour wards with the anticipated delivery load.

CHAPTER 3

Equipment and Services

ADRIAN GRANT

INTRODUCTION

Despite calls for 'minimum requirements for essential equipment in common use in obstetric and neonatal practice' by the Social Services Committee[1] there is no consensus as to what provision of equipment or services in a delivery area is either essential or the minimum requirement. Several recommendations have been made based on the opinions both of those working in the health services and of others; the most recent was the Report of the Maternity Services Advisory Committee[2]. Such advice was based on only limited information about what was available at the places where British women had babies. This survey provides this information on a national scale.

Information about fifteen specific pieces of equipment was sought at 3 pm on all four days of the survey. The format of the relevant question is shown in Table 3.1.

The definitions of most types of equipment were considered to be unambiguous but supplementary description was provided in the questionnaire for four: an obstetric delivery bed, oxygen for the mother, an ECG monitor (adult) and an anaesthetic machine. To save time during questionnaire completion, respondents were not required to fill in every box on the questionnaire, the assumption being made that empty boxes indicated non-availability. To test this assumption in respect of equipment, delivery areas were identified for which no entries at all had been made. This applied to only three units— one very large, one large and one small—and these have been excluded from the analyses of equipment.

Information about various services was also sought at 3 pm on all four days of the survey. Epidural services, special neonatal care facilities and provision of obstetric and paediatric flying squads are discussed in the sections on anaesthesia, paediatrics and obstetrics. This chapter will cover blood storage areas

TABLE 3.1   Equipment available in the delivery area
Respondents were asked to indicate from this wide range of possible items of equipment
the number in the delivery area

Real-time ultrasound
Continuous fetal heart monitor
Fetal pH monitor
Obstetric delivery bed
Birth chair
Infusion pump
Oxygen for the mother
Neonatal laryngoscope
Neonatal resuscitation table
Neonatal overhead radiant heater
Bag and mask for resuscitation of newborn
Anaesthetic machine
ECG monitor (adult)
Anaesthetic ventilator
Cardiac arrest trolley

---

with rhesus negative blood, operating theatre facilities and recovery areas for mothers. The format of the questions about these is shown in Table 3.2. The availability of ward clerks will also be described.

Nine special hospitals—that is Armed Forces, special authority and private hospitals—have been included in the results for the total survey but not in the sub-analyses based on caseload size, type of unit and geographical region.

Analyses based on annual caseload sizes of 1–500, 501–2000, 2001–4000 and more than 4000 births have been used to compare provision in groups of units with differing caseloads. A contrast has also been made between GP units and units with consultant cover. The third type of sub-analysis has assessed geographical variation by comparing equipment in the English health authority regions, Wales, Scotland and Northern Ireland.

METHOD OF ANALYSIS

The responses varied so little between the four days surveyed that provision will be described as for a single day only—the first day in August. For convenience, the equipment surveyed has been divided into three broad groups: firstly, equipment which is primarily obstetric or midwifery (real-time ultrasound, continuous fetal heart monitor, fetal blood pH meter, infusion pump, obstetric delivery bed and birth chair); secondly, equipment which is primarily paediatric (neonatal resuscitation table, neonatal radiant heater, neonatal laryngoscope and bag and mask); and thirdly, equipment which is primarily anaesthetic (oxygen for the mother, anaesthetic machine, anaesthetic ventilator, ECG monitor and cardiac arrest trolley). It should be recognized,

TABLE 3.2   Services available to the delivery area
Respondents were asked to indicate which of the following services were available

Services	Available			Not available
	In the delivery area	On the same premises	Elsewhere	
Blood storage area with rhesus negative blood				
Operating theatre on the same premises and exclusively for obstetrical use				
Operating theatre on the same premises shared with other disciplines				
Recovery for mothers				

though, that more than one discipline may actually use a particular type of equipment.

The Working Party considered surveying a much longer list of equipment. This list was subsequently shortened at the pre-pilot and pilot phase and the fifteen items chosen included some equipment which was considered essential and some non-essential. The aim was to provide a profile of how British labour rooms were equipped in 1984 and to contrast provision in places of delivery with different patterns of work.

Two approaches have been used to describe the provision of the equipment. The first is based on absolute availability; that is, whether a unit did have at least one piece of equipment of that type. These analyses are presented both as proportions of units which have the equipment, and as proportions of deliveries in 1983 which occurred in units with at least one piece of the equipment. In some situations, particularly where units of markedly varying size are being compared, absolute availability presented as a proportion of units may give a somewhat distorted picture of provision: small units tend not to have equipment but they are responsible for relatively few women in labour. Analyses based on the number of deliveries with access to the equipment adjust for this. Some kinds of equipment, for example the obstetric delivery bed and neonatal laryngoscope, were reported in nearly every unit. For these, the numbers of items in the units have also been described.

A more pertinent statistic about the types of equipment which were reported in nearly every delivery area is their provision relative to the caseload of the unit. The second approach which has been used for describing the provision of equipment is therefore based on relative provision, defined in terms of the number of deliveries in 1983 per piece of equipment. This has been described in two ways. The first method is by simple frequency histograms with the number of annual deliveries per piece of equipment (at intervals of 100 annual deliveries per piece of equipment) on the horizontal axis and with the number of delivery areas on the vertical axis. The second method has used the same data converted into cumulative frequency graphs showing the 10th, 25th, 50th, 75th and 90th percentiles. These cumulative frequency graphs have a standard format. The lines show the interdecile range, that is the range between the 10th and 90th percentiles; the boxes show the interquartile range; and the median value is indicated with a vertical clear line near the middle. Tables of the figures from which these graphs were derived are included in an appendix. Although it is not possible to say from a survey such as this what is the correct amount of equipment that a unit of a particular size should have, it is possible to describe the usual provision. The graphs give a visual impression of this in terms of the provision which is most common and the extent of variation between units. The latter was found to be highly dependent on caseload size and for this reason separate percentile graphs have been presented throughout the chapter for the four standard caseload-size groupings.

In addition to describing variations in provision for units of similar sizes these cumulative frequency graphs can also be used for assessing the provision of specific individual units in comparison with others of the same size. Units with fewer (or more) pieces of equipment than would be expected from the appropriate 90th (or 10th) percentile value may be arbitrarily considered to be relatively under- (or over-) provided.

The provision of the services has also been described in terms of absolute availability, that is whether or not a place of delivery had access to a particular service. Again, this has been presented both in terms of availability to the units and in terms of availability to women who are delivered in the units.

Regional variation in the provision of equipment and services has been presented in terms of annual deliveries per item for equipment which is available in nearly all units, and in terms of absolute availability (see above) for equipment for which no item was reported in the delivery area in an important proportion of units. The latter approach was also used to describe geographical variations in the provision of services.

OBSTETRIC EQUIPMENT

Real-time ultrasound

Small portable ultrasound machines have appeared only recently on the delivery wards. As well as the availability of portable equipment with good

TABLE 3.3   Real-time ultrasound
Units (%) and 1983 deliveries (%) with real-time ultrasound machine in delivery area

	Delivery areas (%)	Deliveries (%)
All institutional delivery areas ($n = 528$)	18	23
Unit size		
Small 1–500 ($n = 217$)	12	12
Medium 501–2000 ($n = 148$)	19	20
Large 2001–4000 ($n = 129$)	20	21
Very large 4001+ ($n = 25$)	31	36
General practitioner units ($n = 197$)	10	9
Consultant-covered units ($n = 315$)	23	24

resolution, this change had to await the clinical obstetric staff with requisite skills. In the last five years, obstetric registrars and senior registrars have been gaining experience with ultrasound and can carry their knowledge into the labour ward for emergency scans, particularly when the main ultrasound department is closed.

Real-time ultrasound may be useful in an emergency, for example to identify the position of the placenta, to check the fetal presentation, to exclude the possibility of an undiagnosed multiple pregnancy or to confirm or refute a diagnosis of fetal death. Many modern machines are mobile, however, and in interpreting the survey ultrasound figures it is important to bear in mind that some units without a machine in the delivery area at the sampling time may have had real-time ultrasound facilities easily available elsewhere in the hospital; the survey did not provide information about this.

Ninety-five units (18 per cent) were reported to have a real-time ultrasound machine in the delivery area; these units were responsible for 23 per cent of all deliveries. Table 3.3 shows the proportion of delivery areas with real-time ultrasound and the proportion of women with access to a machine in the delivery area, in the four standard groups of units based on caseload size.

About one-third of the very large units had a real-time ultrasound machine in the delivery area and this covered 36 per cent of all their deliveries. Ten per cent of GP units reported that they had an ultrasound machine in the delivery area compared with 23 per cent of consultant-covered units.

Regional variation in the provision of real-time ultrasound in the delivery area is shown in Table 3.4. Some regions such as Oxford and Northern Ireland appear to be relatively well equipped whereas others such as the West Midlands, North-Western and North-West Thames regions, appear to be relatively underprovided.

TABLE 3.4   Real-time ultrasound
Regional variation in the presence of at least one real-time ultrasound machine in
delivery areas (%) and for women who labour in the delivery areas with rank position in
parentheses

	Number of delivery areas in region	Delivery areas with ultrasound (%)	Deliveries in units with ultrasound (%)
Northern	28	18	15 (12=)
Yorkshire	31	10	12 (14)
Trent	35	17	21 (7=)
East Anglia	16	6	19 (10)
North-West Thames	22	14	9 (16)
North-East Thames	29	24	34 (4=)
South-East Thames	27	19	17 (11)
South-West Thames	17	18	21 (7=)
Wessex	31	13	34 (4=)
Oxford	22	32	70 (1)
South-Western	37	14	27 (6)
West Midlands	41	2	5 (17)
Mersey	10	20	21 (7=)
North-Western	30	7	11 (15)
Wales	37	11	15 (12=)
Scotland	70	26	36 (3)
Northern Ireland	27	48	48 (2)

Continuous fetal heart monitor

A total of 1725 fetal heart monitors (FHMs) were reported in the survey.
Sixty-five per cent of all institutions had at least one FHM; these units tended to
be the larger ones and delivered 96 per cent of all women (Table 3.5).

Virtually all units with an annual caseload of more than 500 deliveries had at
least one FHM compared with only 18 per cent of the smaller units. This was
reflected in the fact that only 19 per cent of women who labour in GP units had
access to a FHM compared with 99 per cent of women in units with consultant
cover.

The relative provision of FHM in units which have one or more is shown in
Figure 3.1. It shows the frequency distribution of units based on the annual
number of deliveries per monitor; the commonest provision is one monitor for
between 300 and 400 deliveries annually. The top line of Figure 3.2 describes
the same data in terms of percentiles. From it, it can be seen that about
one-quarter of units had a monitor for fewer than 300 and one-quarter one
monitor for more than 500 deliveries each year.

To an important extent, this variation reflects differences in unit caseloads.
Units with fewer than 500 deliveries per year which have a machine appear to

TABLE 3.5   Fetal heart monitors
Presence of at least one continuous fetal heart monitor in delivery areas (%) and for
women who labour in the delivery area (% 1983 deliveries)

	Delivery areas (%)	Deliveries (%)
All institutional delivery areas ($n = 528$)	65	96
Unit size		
Small 1–500 ($n = 217$)	18	28
Medium 501–2000 ($n = 148$)	95	98
Large 2001–4000 ($n = 129$)	100	100
Very large 4001+ ($n = 25$)	100	100
General practitioner units ($n = 197$)	12	19
Consultant-covered units ($n = 315$)	96	99

be well provided (second line of Figure 3.2). It is important, however, to
remember that this figure refers to the 18 per cent which actually had a monitor
and that these few units almost invariably had only one machine.

Provision in the other three groups is relatively similar. The medians are
between 350 and 430 annual deliveries per machine. The greatest variation is in
the 2001–4000 group and the cumulative frequency distribution of this group is
skewed on the right suggesting that some units are relatively underprovided, as
many as 10 per cent having more than 750 annual deliveries per monitor.

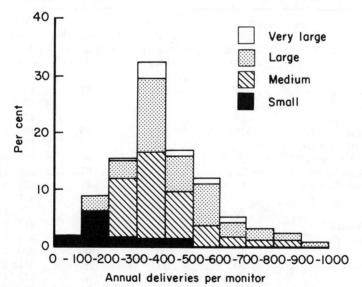

Figure 3.1   Fetal heart rate monitor: frequency distribution of annual deliveries per
monitor by the percentage of units with monitors

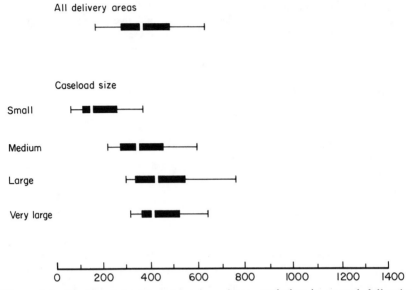

Figure 3.2   Profile of fetal heart rate monitors—variation in annual deliveries per monitor (see page 54)

TABLE 3.6   Continuous fetal heart monitor
Regional variation in availability of at least one continuous fetal heart monitor in delivery areas and to women who labour in the delivery areas (with rank position in parentheses)

	Number of delivery areas in region	Delivery areas (%) with fetal monitors	Deliveries (%) with access to monitor	Average annual deliveries per monitor
Northern	28	79	97	433 (10)
Yorkshire	31	71	95	379 (5)
Trent	35	54	95	423 (9)
East Anglia	16	63	96	300 (1)
North-West Thames	22	91	100	354 (3)
North-East Thames	29	86	93	440 (11)
South-East Thames	27	81	97	385 (6)
South-West Thames	17	87	99	403 (8)
Wessex	31	45	91	464 (15)
Oxford	22	45	93	476 (16)
South-Western	37	38	91	512 (17)
West Midlands	41	63	92	460 (14)
Mersey	10	100	100	400 (7)
North-Western	30	77	97	441 (13)
Wales	37	62	98	327 (2)
Scotland	70	47	95	371 (4)
Northern Ireland	27	63	93	438 (12)

TABLE 3.7   Fetal pH meter
Availability of fetal pH monitor in delivery areas (%) and to women who labour in the
delivery areas (% 1983 deliveries)

	Delivery areas (%)	Deliveries (%)
All institutional delivery areas ($n = 528$)	15	31
Unit size		
Small 1–500 ($n = 217$)	1	2
Medium 501–2000 ($n = 148$)	15	17
Large 2001–4000 ($n = 129$)	31	32
Very large 4001+ ($n = 25$)	60	60
General practitioner units ($n = 315$)	1	1
Consultant-covered units ($n = 197$)	24	33

Geographical variation in the absolute availability of continuous fetal heart monitors is described in Table 3.6. The wide range in the proportion of delivery areas with at least one monitor largely reflects differences between the regions in their numbers of units with small caseloads (South-Western, Wessex, Oxford, Trent and Scotland are the five regions with the highest proportion of GP units). In most regions, the proportion of women delivering in units with continuous fetal heart monitors is close to 100 per cent. For this reason availability has also been expressed as the annual number of deliveries per monitor in each region. Overall the average annual number of deliveries per machine was just over 400. The figures for most regions are near this, the range being from a low of 300 in East Anglia to a high of 512 in the South-Western region.

Fetal blood pH meter

The use of intrapartum fetal acid–base assessment in conjunction with continuous electronic fetal heart rate monitoring is still controversial and this was reflected in the findings of the survey.

Fifteen per cent of units reported that there was a fetal pH meter in the delivery area and between them these units were responsible for 31 per cent of all deliveries. These proportions rose progressively with increasing annual caseload size (Table 3.7) but even among the largest units only 60 per cent had a pH meter in the delivery area. Virtually no general practitioner units had a pH meter.

There were also striking differences between the regions in this respect (Table 3.8). For example, a fetal pH meter was available for only 5 per cent of women who delivered in the North-East Thames region compared with 50 per cent in the North-West Thames region.

TABLE 3.8   Fetal pH meter
Regional variation in availability of at least one fetal pH meter in delivery areas and for
women who labour in the delivery areas (with rank position in parentheses)

	Number of delivery areas in region	Delivery areas (%) with pH meter	Deliveries (%) with access to pH meter
Northern	28	21	34 (7)
Yorkshire	31	13	28 (10=)
Trent	35	14	40 (5)
East Anglia	16	6	19 (13=)
North-West Thames	22	36	50 (2)
North-East Thames	29	3	5 (17)
South-East Thames	27	22	29 (9)
South-West Thames	17	24	28 (10=)
Wessex	31	13	31 (8)
Oxford	22	14	49 (3)
South-Western	37	11	42 (4)
West Midlands	41	12	19 (13=)
Mersey	10	30	38 (6)
North-Western	30	37	59 (1)
Wales	37	8	19 (13=)
Scotland	70	9	24 (12)
Northern Ireland	27	7	12 (16)

It should be recognized that the actual use of pH meters and FH monitors is
not the same. One FH monitor can be in exclusive, continuous use for one
woman during her labour while a fetal pH machine can cover many women for
it is used only intermittently. Thus one pH machine per unit (with perhaps a
second as back-up) is all that is required. Furthermore, some delivery areas
may use a pH machine in a nearby neonatal unit and this might not have been
recorded in this survey of labour ward facilities. Nevertheless, some experts
would consider FH monitoring without fetal pH assessment facilities to be
suboptimal. Only 60 per cent of the largest units and 30 per cent of units
delivering between 2000 and 3000 women a year has such a machine. Hence,
for some 70 per cent of women there was apparently no facility of pH measure-
ment in the labour ward in contrast with only 4 per cent of women who had no
access to a FH monitor.

Infusion pump

A total of 1741 infusion pumps were identified in the survey. Only 66 per cent
of units had one or more but these units delivered 93 per cent of all women.
This reflected the fact that 97 per cent of units with an annual caseload of more
than 500 deliveries had at least one pump compared with 26 per cent of the units
with fewer than 500 deliveries per year (Table 3.9). This was also evident in the

TABLE 3.9   Infusion pump
Availability of at least one infusion pump in delivery areas (%) and for women who
labour in the delivery areas (% 1983 deliveries)

	Delivery areas (%)	Deliveries (%)
All institutional delivery areas (n = 528)	66[a]	93[a]
Unit size		
Small 1–500 (n = 217)	26	35
Medium 501–2000 (n = 148)	95	96
Large 2001–4000 (n = 129)	98	98
Very large 4001+ (n = 25)	88[a]	89[a]
General practitioner units (n = 197)	20	24
Consultant-covered units (n = 315)	94[a]	97[a]

[a] One very large unit did not make an entry and two others reported that they had no infusion
pump.

figures for general practitioner and consultant-covered units (bottom of Table
3.9).

The relative provision of infusion pumps in units which have one or more is
shown in Table 3.9 and their frequency distribution in Figure 3.3. Although the
median value is close to that of the fetal heart monitor the variation in provision
is wider (10th percentile 149 and 90th percentile 680).

Figure 3.4 shows graphically the cumulative frequency distributions of
the annual deliveries per pump by caseload size. Even after taking caseload size
into account a wide variation in provision is still evident. As is the case for other
types of equipment it was the small units with pumps which appeared relatively
well provided. Again, this must be interpreted with caution because only 26 per

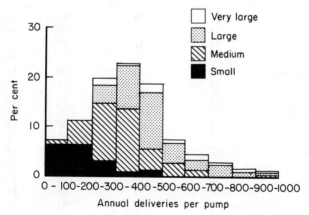

Figure 3.3   Infusion pump: frequency distribution of annual deliveries per pump (see
caption to Figure 3.1)

BIRTHPLACE

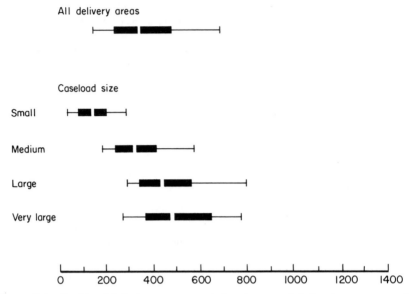

All delivery areas

Caseload size

Small

Medium

Large

Very large

0   200   400   600   800   1000   1200   1400

Figure 3.4 Profile of infusion pumps variation in annual deliveries per pump (see caption to Figure 3.2)

TABLE 3.10 Infusion pump
Regional variation in availability of at least one infusion pump in delivery areas and to women in labour in the delivery areas (with rank position in parentheses)

	Number of delivery areas in region	Delivery areas (%) with pump	Deliveries (%) with access to pump	Average annual deliveries per pump
Northern	28	79	98	382 (5)
Yorkshire	31	74	97	310 (2)
Trent	35	51	87	423 (11)
East Anglia	16	56	77	408 (7)
North-West Thames	22	95	100	332 (3=)
North-East Thames	29	76	93	473 (14)
South-East Thames	27	85	98	420 (10)
South-West Thames	17	88	99	419 (9)
Wessex	31	58	90	451 (15)
Oxford	22	41	85	549 (17)
South-Western	37	49	92	435 (12)
West Midlands	41	98	90	500 (16)
Mersey	10	100	100	416 (8)
North-Western	30	77	86	437 (13)
Wales	37	59	97	397 (6)
Scotland	70	44	96	332 (3=)
Northern Ireland	27	81	96	243 (1)

TABLE 3.11   Obstetric delivery bed
Frequency distribution of number of obstetric delivery beds in delivery areas

	No. of obstetric delivery beds						
	0	1	2	3–5	6–10	11–20	21+
All institutional delivery areas (n = 528)	20	96	130	139	109	32	2
Unit size							
Small 1–500 (n = 217)	20	92	89	15	1	0	0
Medium 501–2000 (n = 148)	0	2	34	80	30	2	0
Large 2001–4000 (n = 129)	0	0	3	41	69	16	0
Very large 4001+ (n = 25)	0	0	0	2	8	13	2

cent of these units had an infusion pump at all and the majority of those that did, had only one. Using this figure it is possible to compare the provision of infusion pumps in a particular unit of known caseload size with similar units elsewhere. For example, a unit which delivers 1500 babies each year would be expected to have about five pumps; it is relatively underprovided if it only has two (=95th percentile).

As was the case for the fetal heart monitors, the wide regional range in the proportion of delivery areas with an infusion pump reflected the numbers of small units in the regions (Table 3.10). The proportion of a region's deliveries in units with a pump were generally near 90 per cent. The average annual deliveries per pump ranged from 243 in Northern Ireland to 549 in the Oxford region.

Obstetric delivery bed

A total of 2182 obstetric delivery beds (ODBs) were reported in the survey.

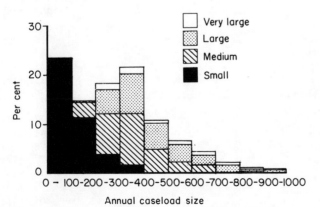

Figure 3.5   Obstetric delivery bed—frequency distribution of annual deliveries per bed (see caption to Figure 3.1)

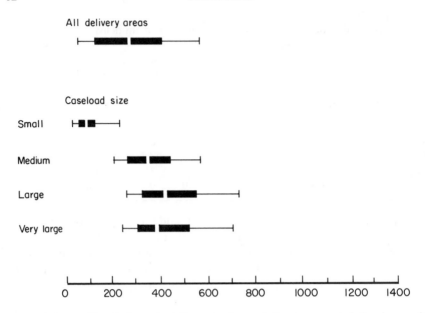

Figure 3.6   Profile of obstetric delivery beds—variation in annual deliveries per bed
(see caption to Figure 3.2)

TABLE 3.12   Obstetric delivery bed
Regional variation in average number of annual deliveries per obstetric delivery bed
(rank position in parentheses)

Region	Average annual deliveries per bed
Northern	337 (12)
Yorkshire	302 (6)
Trent	309 (7)
East Anglia	318 (9)
North-West Thames	287 (4)
North-East Thames	338 (13)
South-East Thames	323 (10)
South-West Thames	334 (11)
Wessex	251 (1)
Oxford	277 (3)
South-Western	341 (14)
West Midlands	398 (15)
Mersey	427 (17)
North-Western	418 (16)
Wales	295 (5)
Scotland	261 (2)
Northern Ireland	312 (8)

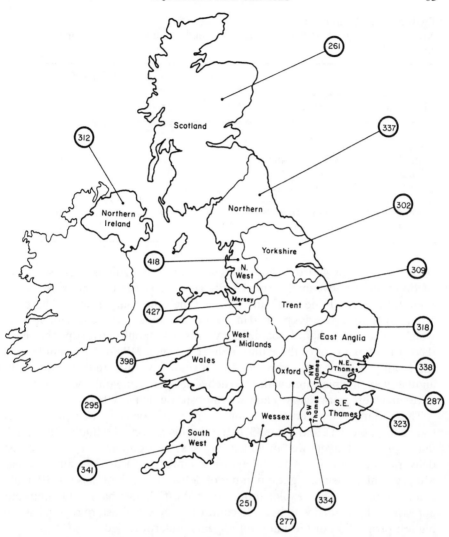

Figure 3.7   Average number of deliveries per obstetric delivery bed (by regions)

Some 96 per cent of all delivery areas had at least one and these units delivered 99 per cent of all babies; the few units which did not have an ODB all delivered fewer than 365 babies per year. Although most units have at least one ODB the variation between units of similar size is striking. The actual numbers of beds in the units is described in Table 3.11. The frequency distribution of annual deliveries per bed also shows this variation (Figures 3.5 and 3.6). The distribution is in fact bimodal with a peak between 100 and 200 and a second peak

TABLE 3.13   Birth chair
Availability of birth chair in delivery areas (%) and to women who labour in the delivery
areas (% 1983 deliveries)

	Delivery area (%)	Deliveries (%)
All institutional delivery areas (n = 528)	18	28
Unit size		
Small 1–500 (n = 217)	9	14
Medium 501–2000 (n = 148)	16	16
Large 2001–4000 (n = 129)	31	34
Very large 4001+ (n = 25)	36	36
General practitioner units (n = 197)	9	14
Consultant-covered units (n = 315)	23	29

between 300 and 400 deliveries per bed per year. This is a consequence of differences between the small units (less than 501 deliveries per year) seen in the second line on Figure 3.6, and the other, larger units. There are strikingly fewer deliveries per bed in the smallest units. The median for all units which deliver more than 500 babies per year is 364 (or one delivery per bed each day). Eighty per cent of these units deliver between 219 (10th percentile) and 632 (90th percentile) babies per bed each year. To illustrate this variation in another way, a typical unit with 1500 deliveries per year would be expected to have anywhere between two and seven obstetric delivery beds.

The variation between the regions in obstetric delivery bed provision is shown in Table 3.12 and Figure 3.7. In part this reflects the finding that small units appear relatively well provided. Wessex, for example, which has fewest deliveries per bed, has a relatively large number (19) of GP units whereas Mersey, which has the highest number of deliveries per bed, has no GP units. But this is not the whole explanation. North-West Thames has few GP units but appears well provided with beds. In contrast the South-Western region has the highest proportion of GP units yet appears underprovided.

Birth chair

Ninety-nine birth chairs were reported in the survey, six units having more than one. The 18 per cent of units which had a birth chair delivered 28 per cent of mothers but the difference in provision in the four caseload groups was less marked than for other equipment (Table 3.13). Even among the largest units only a minority had a birth chair. The difference between consultant units and GP units (23 per cent compared with 9 per cent) reflected these findings.

There was very marked regional variation in birth chair provision. Over 50

TABLE 3.14   Birth chair
Regional variation in availability of at least one birth chair in delivery areas and to
women who labour in the delivery areas (with rank position in parentheses)

	Number of delivery areas in region	Delivery areas with birth chair (%)	Deliveries with access to birth chair (%)	
Northern	28	14	16	(13)
Yorkshire	31	39	56	(1)
Trent	35	17	25	(9)
East Anglia	16	19	47	(3=)
North-West Thames	22	9	9	(15=)
North-East Thames	29	17	21	(11)
South-East Thames	27	15	22	(10)
South-West Thames	17	29	32	(6)
Wessex	31	13	9	(15=)
Oxford	22	5	2	(17)
South-Western	37	16	27	(8)
West Midlands	41	12	20	(12)
Mersey	10	50	53	(2)
North-Western	30	40	47	(3=)
Wales	37	8	13	(14)
Scotland	70	14	43	(5)
Northern Ireland	27	11	30	(7)

per cent of women delivering babies in the Yorkshire and Mersey regions did so
in hospitals with a birth chair in the delivery area (Table 3.14). The equivalent
figure was 9 per cent for North-West Thames and Wessex and only 2 per cent
for the Oxford region.

The use of a birth chair is a regeneration of a very old idea probably going
back to Egyptian times in 3000 BC. Birth chairs have been requested as part of
the resurgence of interest in greater self-determination for women in labour.
Some consider they feel more in control in the sitting position, others feel it to
be more physiological. Randomized controlled trials are currently investig-
ating the advantages and disadvantages of birth chairs as opposed to delivery
beds.

PAEDIATRIC EQUIPMENT

Neonatal resuscitation table

As many as 98 per cent of all delivery areas had at least one neonatal
resuscitation table and these units delivered 99.9 per cent of all women. The
survey identified 1419 resuscitation tables with a wide range in the numbers in

TABLE 3.15   Neonatal resuscitation table
Frequency distribution of number of tables in delivery areas

	No of tables					
	0	1	2	3–5	6–10	11–20
All institutional delivery areas ($n = 528$)	13	204	104	152	48	7
Unit size						
Small 1–500 ($n = 217$)	13	174	26	4	0	0
Medium 501–2000 ($n = 148$)	0	20	54	67	7	0
Large 2001–4000 ($n = 129$)	0	5	21	70	30	3
Very large 4001+ ($n = 25$)	0	0	2	9	10	4

individual units; 38 per cent of delivery areas had only one and 1 per cent (7) had more than ten (Table 3.15). In the 2001–4000 annual deliveries grouping five units were reported to have only one whereas one had as many as fifteen.

There is no apparent usual provision of neonatal resuscitation tables in terms of annual deliveries per table (Figure 3.8). To some extent, as for other equipment, this reflects a marked difference between the small units and larger units, there being little overlap between them in their relative provisions (Figure 3.9). But even within the broad caseload groupings there is extraordinary variation. For example, there is a four-fold difference between the 10th and 90th percentiles for units which deliver more than 2000 women annually; one implication of this is that one in four of the larger units has more than 1000 deliveries each year per resuscitation table. These data suggest that in some units resuscitation tables are moved from delivery room to delivery room when needed, whereas other units have a table in each delivery room.

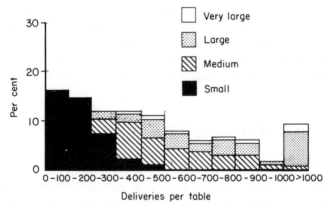

Figure 3.8   Neonatal resuscitation table — frequency distribution of annual deliveries per table (see caption to Figure 3.1)

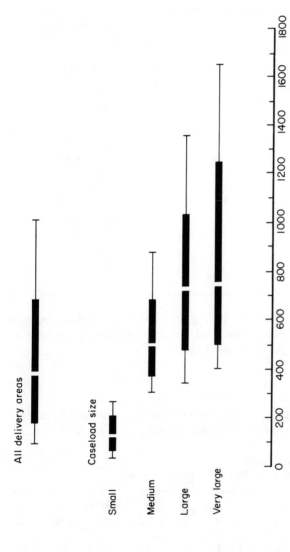

Figure 3.9 Profile of neonatal resuscitation tables—variation in annual deliveries per table (see caption to Figure 3.2)

TABLE 3.16   Neonatal resuscitation table
Regional variation in average number of annual deliveries per neonatal resuscitation table (with rank position in parentheses)

Region	Average annual deliveries per table
Northern	631 (14)
Yorkshire	562 (12)
Trent	522 (10)
East Anglia	400 (3)
North-West Thames	431 (6)
North-East Thames	529 (11)
South-East Thames	494 (9)
South-West Thames	484 (8)
Wessex	427 (5)
Oxford	635 (16)
South-Western	409 (4)
West Midlands	634 (15)
Mersey	588 (13)
North-Western	641 (17)
Wales	397 (2)
Scotland	456 (7)
Northern Ireland	297 (1)

This variation was also evident in the regional comparison, there being a more than two-fold difference between the lowest and highest number of deliveries per resuscitation table (Table 3.16).

Neonatal radiant heaters

As would be expected, the availability of neonatal radiant heaters closely parallels that of neonatal resuscitation tables: 92 per cent of all delivery areas

TABLE 3.17   Neonatal radiant heater
Frequency distribution of number of heaters in delivery areas

	No. of heaters					
	0	1	2	3–5	6–10	11–20
All institutional delivery areas ($n = 528$)	45	162	107	140	64	10
Unit size						
Small 1–500 ($n = 217$)	38	136	34	9	0	0
Medium 501–2000 ($n = 148$)	3	19	53	57	16	0
Large 2001–4000 ($n = 129$)	2	3	16	65	41	2
Very large 4001+ ($n = 25$)	0	0	3	7	7	8

TABLE 3.18   Neonatal radiant heater
Regional variation in average number of annual deliveries per neonatal radiant heater
(rank position in parentheses)

Region	Average annual deliveries per heater
Northern	545 (13)
Yorkshire	506 (12)
Trent	417 (6)
East Anglia	409 (4=)
North-West Thames	408 (3)
North-East Thames	502 (10)
South-East Thames	433 (7)
South-West Thames	562 (15)
Wessex	445 (8)
Oxford	635 (17)
South-Western	409 (4=)
West Midlands	617 (16)
Mersey	503 (11)
North-Western	551 (14)
Wales	363 (2)
Scotland	446 (9)
Northern Ireland	329 (1)

had at least one and these delivered 98 per cent of women. A total of 1496 heaters was reported to the survey; 30 per cent of units had only one and 2 per cent (10) had more than ten. Like the resuscitation table, the widest variation in the numbers per unit is in the 2001–4000 group (Table 3.17).

There is no obvious typical provision in terms of annual deliveries per heater (Figure 3.10). There is as much as a four-fold difference between the upper and lower quartiles and a fifteen-fold difference between the deciles. As for other equipment, the small units which have heaters appear relatively well provided. When units with larger caseloads than 500 deliveries per year are considered separately the commonest (modal) provision is between 400 and 500 annual deliveries but even for these larger units there is a remarkably wide variation in provision. In the 2001–4000 annual deliveries group 10 per cent of units had fewer than 335 deliveries per heater each year (10th percentile) and 10 per cent had more than 1290 (90th percentile)—again, a near four-fold difference. In the very large units this variation was even greater, nearer six-fold.

Variation between the regions is shown in Table 3.18. The rank order is very similar to that for the neonatal resuscitation table.

The modern proprietary neonatal resuscitation table comes complete with a heater, so the similarity in the provision of resuscitation tables and heaters is not surprising; in 6 per cent of units, however, a resuscitation table was present without a heater. These tables were probably earlier commercial or 'home-

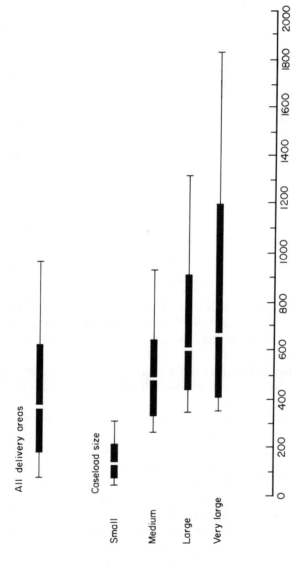

Figure 3.10   Profile of neonatal radiant heaters—variation in annual deliveries per heater (see caption to Figure 3.2)

TABLE 3.19   Neonatal laryngoscope
Frequency distribution of number of laryngoscopes in delivery areas

	\multicolumn{7}{c}{No. of laryngoscopes}
	0	1	2	3–5	6–10	11–20	21+
All institutional delivery areas (n = 528)	5	126	111	135	110	39	2
Unit size							
Small 1–500 (n = 217)	4	121	77	14	1	0	0
Medium 501–2000 (n = 148)	1	2	24	80	38	3	0
Large 2001–4000 (n = 129)	0	0	7	38	61	23	0
Very large 4001+ (n = 25)	0	0	0	3	9	11	2

made' models. These are perfectly adequate for resuscitation if they have the facility to group around them the essential needs for this emergency—oxygen, suction, bag and mask, working neonatal laryngoscope with endotracheal tubes, and essential drugs. However, it is now recognized that during the minutes needed for effective resuscitation and establishment of respiration, the baby can cool rapidly in the British labour ward. After being at 38°C in the uterus for months, the newborn is exposed to a 20–25°C environment and needs protection from this sudden potential cooling.

Neonatal laryngoscope

All except five units were reported to have a neonatal laryngoscope and four of these five had small caseloads (Table 3.19).

Most units (76 per cent) had more than one laryngoscope, the largest number reported being 29 in a unit with over 5000 deliveries per year. Like the radiant heater, there was a bimodal frequency distribution of numbers of annual deliveries per laryngoscope which again reflected the relatively small numbers of deliveries per instrument in the smallest units which had a laryngoscope (Figure 3.11). The commonest (modal) provision in the larger units (more than 500 annual deliveries) was 200–300 deliveries per laryngoscope.

The cumulative frequencies of annual deliveries per laryngoscope for the four standard caseload size groupings are shown in Figure 3.12. The width of the cumulative frequency distribution, especially the extension of the right-hand tail beyond 600 annual deliveries, suggests that some of the larger units have significantly fewer laryngoscopes than is the usual.

Most of the regions averaged about 300 deliveries per laryngoscope, ranging from a low in the South-Western region, the region with the most GP units, to a high in Mersey, the region with no GP units (Table 3.20).

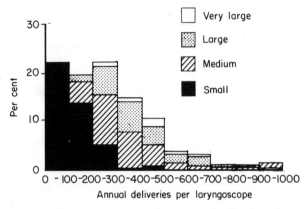

Figure 3.11   Neonatal laryngoscope — frequency distribution of annual deliveries per laryngoscope (see caption to Figure 3.1)

Bag and mask

Like other paediatric equipment, most units had a bag and mask for neonatal resuscitation but there was no normal provision after taking into account a unit's caseload.

Of the total number of units, 97 per cent were reported to have at least one bag and mask for neonatal resuscitation and these units were responsible for 98 per cent of all deliveries. Whereas one-third of units reportedly had only one

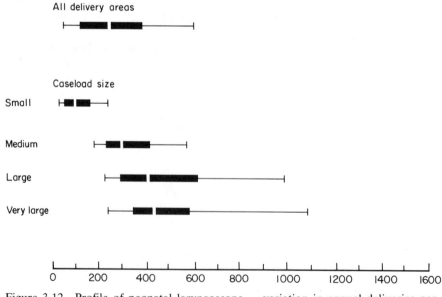

Figure 3.12   Profile of neonatal laryngoscope — variation in annual deliveries per laryngoscope (see caption to Figure 3.2)

TABLE 3.20   Neonatal laryngoscope
Regional variation in average number of annual deliveries per neonatal laryngoscope
(with rank position in parentheses)

Region	Average annual deliveries per laryngoscope	
Northern	394	(15)
Yorkshire	310	(9)
Trent	342	(13)
East Anglia	267	(5)
North-West Thames	296	(8)
North-East Thames	313	(11)
South-East Thames	284	(6)
South-West Thames	312	(10)
Wessex	287	(7)
Oxford	262	(4)
South-Western	229	(1)
West Midlands	349	(14)
Mersey	452	(17)
North-Western	412	(16)
Wales	237	(2)
Scotland	336	(12)
Northern Ireland	260	(3)

bag and mask, 4 per cent (19) had more than ten and one unit had as many as 36. This variation is shown in more detail in Table 3.21.

The provision in terms of annual deliveries per bag and mask is similar to that of the neonatal resuscitation table and radiant heater (Figure 3.13). The very wide distribution only partly reflects the tendency for small units which have a bag and mask to appear relatively well provided. The commonest provision for units with caseloads over 500 annual deliveries is between 300 and 400 deliveries per bag and mask (Figure 3.13). But even with units grouped by

TABLE 3.21   Bag and mask
Frequency distribution of number of bags and masks in delivery areas

	No. bags and masks						
	0	1	2	3–5	6–10	11–20	21+
All institutional delivery areas ($n = 528$)	14	172	96	167	59	19	1
Unit size							
Small 1–500 ($n = 217$)	9	146	46	15	1	0	0
Medium 501–2000 ($n = 148$)	2	15	38	76	16	1	0
Large 2001–4000 ($n = 129$)	3	7	8	69	32	9	1
Very large 4001+ ($n = 25$)	0	0	1	6	9	9	0

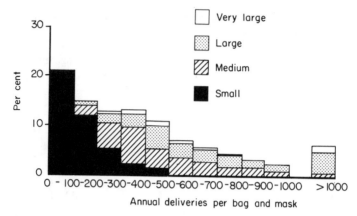

Figure 3.13 Bag and mask: frequency distribution of annual deliveries per bag and mask (see caption to Figure 3.1)

caseload size there are still surprisingly wide differences in provision (Figure 3.14). For example, 10 per cent of units in the 2001–4000 annual deliveries group delivered as few as 250 mothers per bag and mask whereas at the other end of the distribution 10 per cent of units delivered over 1100 mothers per bag and mask, each year.

As for the other items of paediatric equipment, there is about a two-fold difference in the range of regional provision (Table 3.22). Northern Ireland

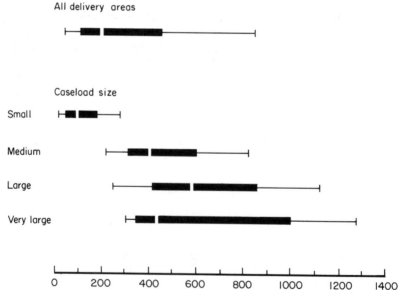

Figure 3.14 Bag and mask profile—variation in annual deliveries per bag and mask (see caption to Figure 3.2)

TABLE 3.22   Bag and mask
Regional variation in average number of annual deliveries per bag and mask (with rank position in parentheses)

Region	Average annual deliveries per bag and mask	
Northern	485	(16)
Yorkshire	399	(9)
Trent	392	(8)
East Anglia	408	(11)
North-West Thames	452	(12)
North-East Thames	469	(15)
South-East Thames	407	(10)
South-West Thames	460	(13)
Wessex	390	(6=)
Oxford	324	(3)
South-Western	378	(4)
West Midlands	519	(17)
Mersey	390	(6=)
North-Western	463	(14)
Wales	312	(2)
Scotland	388	(5)
Northern Ireland	266	(1)

and Wales showed the lowest number of deliveries per bag and mask, the West Midlands and the Northern regions, the highest. Generally speaking, regions well provided with bag and mask are also well provided with neonatal laryngoscopes. In other words, there is little evidence that the variation in the regional provision of bag and mask reflects the greater use of endotracheal intubation for resuscitation in some regions.

ANAESTHETIC EQUIPMENT

Oxygen for the mother

Of the total number of delivery areas, 97 per cent had at least one oxygen source (either piped or cylinder) and these were responsible for over 98 per cent of all deliveries. Variation in the actual numbers in the units is shown in Table 3.23; one unit had as many as 37 oxygen sources.

Figure 3.15 is the frequency distribution of annual deliveries per oxygen source. Most units with caseloads of over 500 deliveries per year had between 100 and 400 annual deliveries per source of oxygen. The smaller units again appear relatively well provided (second line on Figure 3.16) although most of these only had a single source. Variations between units in relative provision are fairly similar in the three largest standard groups based on caseload size

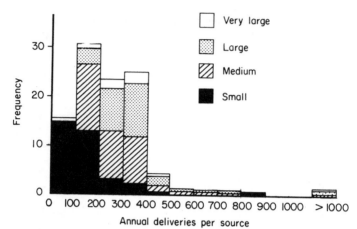

Figure 3.15   Oxygen source — frequency distribution of annual deliveries per oxygen source (see caption to Figure 3.1)

(Figure 3.16): 10 per cent of these units deliver more than 500 mothers annually per oxygen source. To put it another way, although the usual provision for a unit with an annual caseload of 1500 deliveries is five or six oxygen sources, some units may have only two or even fewer.

The regional provision of sources of oxygen for the mother is relatively uniform—almost all regions having a source of oxygen per 200–300 annual deliveries (Table 3.24).

Oxygen may be needed very rapidly in and just after labour for either fetal or maternal reasons. It is not satisfactory to await a porter with a cylinder when oxygen is needed in an emergency. Oxygen must be available everywhere a woman has a baby. It seems this is nearly always so in Britain.

TABLE 3.23   Oxygen for the mother
Frequency distribution of oxygen sources for the mother in delivery areas

| | No. of sources of oxygen | | | | | | |
	0	1	2	3–5	6–10	11–20	21+
All institutional delivery areas ($n = 528$)	13	115	94	95	126	72	13
Unit size							
Small 1–500 ($n = 217$)	11	105	73	26	2	0	0
Medium 501–2000 ($n = 148$)	0	5	18	56	56	12	1
Large 2001–4000 ($n = 129$)	2	2	2	9	64	44	6
Very large 4001+ ($n = 25$)	0	0	0	1	3	15	6

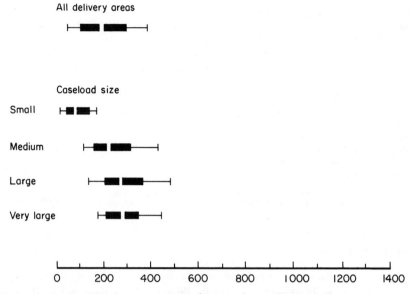

Figure 3.16   Profile of oxygen source (see caption to Figure 3.2)

TABLE 3.24   Oxygen for the mother
Regional variation in average number of annual deliveries per source of oxygen (with rank position in parentheses)

Region	Average number of deliveries per oxygen source	
Northern	249	(14)
Yorkshire	245	(12)
Trent	244	(11)
East Anglia	206	(3)
North-West Thames	205	(2)
North-East Thames	211	(4)
South-East Thames	217	(6)
South-West Thames	275	(16)
Wessex	213	(5)
Oxford	248	(13)
South-Western	233	(9)
West Midlands	281	(17)
Mersey	251	(15)
North-Western	227	(7)
Wales	192	(1)
Scotland	229	(8)
Northern Ireland	234	(10)

TABLE 3.25   Anaesthetic machines
Availability of at least one anaesthetic machine in delivery areas (%) and to women who
labour in the delivery areas (% 1983 deliveries)

	Delivery areas (%)	Deliveries (%)
All institutional delivery areas ($n = 528$)	79	96
Unit size		
Small 1–500 ($n = 217$)	56	59
Medium 501–2000 ($n = 148$)	92	94
Large 2001–4000 ($n = 129$)	98	98
Very large 4001+ ($n = 25$)	100	100
General practitioner units ($n = 197$)	54	52
Consultant-covered units ($n = 315$)	95	98

Anaesthetic machines

Seventy-nine per cent of delivery areas reportedly had at least one anaesthetic
machine and these units were responsible for 96 per cent of all deliveries (Table
3.25. There was wide variation in the annual deliveries per machine (Figure
3.17).

Virtually all the units with fewer than 500 annual deliveries have either no
machine or only one. Large units (more than 2000 deliveries per year), in
contrast, had a variable number. This is particularly true for the very large units
(more than 4000): four had only one machine whereas three had more than
five. Surprisingly, there were two of the large units (2001–4000 deliveries)
which did not appear to have a machine in the delivery area. This may have
reflected the close proximity of an operating theatre with its anaesthetic

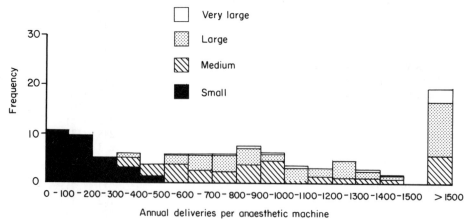

Figure 3.17   Anaesthetic machine — frequency distribution of annual deliveries per
machine (see caption to Figure 3.1)

TABLE 3.26   Anaesthetic machines
Regional variation in availability of at least one anaesthetic machine in delivery areas
and to women in labour in the delivery areas (with rank position in parentheses)

	Number delivery areas	delivery areas (%)	1983 deliveries (%)	Average annual deliveries per machine
Northern	28	93	97	780 (4)
Yorkshire	31	87	99	1059 (14)
Trent	35	74	92	1050 (13)
East Anglia	16	63	82	940 (8)
North-West Thames	22	95	100	916 (6)
North-East Thames	29	90	99	921 (7)
South-East Thames	27	93	95	1049 (12)
South-West Thames	17	94	99	1123 (16)
Wessex	31	87	95	854 (5)
Oxford	22	64	95	952 (9)
South-Western	37	57	89	966 (10)
West Midlands	41	78	94	992 (11)
Mersey	10	100	100	1485 (17)
North-Western	30	73	96	1060 (15)
Wales	37	84	98	725 (2)
Scotland	70	74	98	703 (1)
Northern Ireland	27	67	92	757 (3)

machines which was not actually part of the delivery area, but no information about this was collected in the survey.

There was a two-fold regional range in the annual deliveries per machine (Table 3.26). As for other equipment these figures must be interpreted in conjunction with those for the absolute availability. The two regions—Mersey and South-West Thames—with the largest number of deliveries per machine are also those with the highest proportion of deliveries with access to a machine. This, in turn, reflects the fact that they also have fewer GP units than any other region.

Anaesthetic ventilators

Forty-eight per cent of units were reported to have an anaesthetic ventilator in the delivery area; these units were responsible for 77 per cent of all deliveries.

The availability of an anaesthetic ventilator in the delivery area for the standard caseload groupings is shown in Table 3.27. Generally speaking, only a minority of delivery areas with fewer than 1000 deliveries per year had an anaesthetic ventilator compared with about 80 per cent of all other units.

Sixty-seven per cent of units with a ventilator had only one. For this reason, availability in terms of deliveries per ventilator is not very meaningful.

TABLE 3.27   Anaesthetic ventilator
Availability of at least one anaesthetic ventilator in delivery areas (%) and to women who labour in the delivery areas (% 1983 deliveries)

	Delivery areas (%)	Deliveries (%)
All institutional delivery areas ($n = 528$)	48	77
Unit size		
Small 1–500 ($n = 217$)	13	15
Medium 501–2000 ($n = 148$)	66	72
Large 2001–4000 ($n = 129$)	82	84
Very large 4001+ ($n = 25$)	72	71
General practitioner units ($n = 197$)	12	12
Consultant-covered units ($n = 315$)	71	77

Overall, 77 per cent of deliveries took place in units with a ventilator in the delivery area. In two-thirds of the regions the equivalent figure was between 65 and 85 per cent, with a regional range from 40 per cent in Wessex to 99 per cent in North-West Thames (Table 3.28).

Anaesthetic machines and ventilators are equipment needed for safe general anaesthesia. Since general anaesthesia may be needed in an emergency within minutes, there are items most labour wards may require at short notice. In some units, all Caesarean sections, even when emergency, have to be performed in an operating theatre away from the labour ward; in these units an anaesthetic machine and a ventilator will be available in the theatre but away from the labour ward itself. However, Caesarean sections are not the only indications for a general anaesthetic in labour; other operative deliveries and manual removals of the placenta also demand prompt general anaesthesia (though not so often controlled ventilation).

ECG monitor for mother

Forty-two per cent of delivery areas were reported to have an ECG monitor and these units were responsible for 65 per cent of all deliveries.

Absolute availability in the four standard caseload size groupings is shown in Table 3.29. It can be seen that it is unusual for units with a caseload of 500 or less to have an ECG monitor in the delivery area. About one in two units with between 500 and 2000 annual deliveries were reported to have one compared with three out of four of the larger units.

TABLE 3.28   Anaesthetic ventilator
Regional variation in availability of at least one anaesthetic ventilator in delivery areas
and to women who labour in the delivery areas (with rank and position in parentheses)

	Number of delivery areas in region	Delivery areas with ventilator (%)	Deliveries with access to a ventilator (%)
Northern	28	71	87 (2=)
Yorkshire	31	42	70 (12)
Trent	35	74	62 (13)
East Anglia	16	31	49 (15)
North-West Thames	22	82	99 (1)
North-East Thames	29	62	80 (7)
South-East Thames	27	70	76 (9)
South-West Thames	17	53	60 (14)
Wessex	31	32	40 (17)
Oxford	22	18	46 (16)
South-Western	37	30	71 (11)
West Midlands	41	51	85 (4)
Mersey	10	80	77 (8)
North-Western	30	57	81 (5=)
Wales	37	49	81 (5=)
Scotland	70	40	87 (2=)
Northern Ireland	27	41	74 (10)

TABLE 3.29   ECG monitor
Availability of at least one ECG monitor in delivery areas (%) and to women who labour
in the delivery areas (% 1983 deliveries)

	Delivery areas (%)	Deliveries (%)
All institutional delivery areas ($n = 528$)	42	65
Unit size		
Small 1–500 ($n = 217$)	16	11
Medium 501–2000 ($n = 148$)	51	55
Large 2001–4000 ($n = 129$)	70	72
Very large 4001+ ($n = 25$)	80	79
General practitioner units ($n = 197$)	15	7
Consultant-covered units ($n = 315$)	60	68

TABLE 3.30   ECG monitor
Regional variation in availability of at least one ECG monitor in delivery areas and to
women who labour in the delivery areas (with rank position in parentheses)

	Number of delivery areas in region	Delivery areas with ECG monitor (%)	Deliveries with access to ECG monitor (%)
Northern	28	61	84 (2)
Yorkshire	31	42	60 (11)
Trent	35	43	62 (10)
East Anglia	16	31	49 (14=)
North-West Thames	22	59	71 (7)
North-East Thames	29	48	67 (8)
South-East Thames	27	30	30 (16=)
South-West Thames	17	29	30 (16=)
Wessex	31	35	49 (14=)
Oxford	22	23	52 (13)
South-Western	37	32	66 (9·)
West Midlands	40	43	74 (6)
Mersey	10	80	86 (1)
North-Western	30	60	80 (4)
Wales	37	43	59 (12)
Scotland	70	43	81 (3)
Northern Ireland	27	44	75 (5)

Eighty-four per cent of units with a monitor had only one machine, hence estimates of relative provision based on annual deliveries per monitor are not very useful.

Regional variation is shown in Table 3.30. The median is 66 per cent of deliveries with access with a range from 30 to 86 per cent.

TABLE 3.31   Cardiac arrest trolley
Availability of at least one cardiac arrest trolley in delivery areas (%) and to women who labour in the delivery areas (% 1983 deliveries)

	Delivery areas (%)	Deliveries (%)
All institutional delivery areas ($n = 528$)	48	77
Unit size		
Small 1–500 ($n = 217$)	33	36
Medium 501–2000 ($n = 148$)	68	69
Large 2001–4000 ($n = 129$)	83	85
Very large 4001+ ($n = 25$)	80	81
General practitioner units ($n = 197$)	30	29
Consultant-covered units ($n = 315$)	75	80

TABLE 3.32 Cardiac arrest trolley
Regional variation in availability of at least one cardiac arrest trolley in delivery areas
and to women in labour in the delivery areas (with rank position in parentheses)

	Number of delivery areas in region	Availability (%) of cardiac arrest trolley in delivery areas	Availability (%) women in labour with access to cardiac arrest trolley
Northern	28	61	70 (12)
Yorkshire	31	55	73 (10)
Trent	35	60	85 (5=)
East Anglia	16	44	65 (15=)
North-West Thames	22	59	94 (2)
North-East Thames	29	48	71 (11)
South-East Thames	27	59	65 (15=)
South-West Thames	17	82	84 (7)
Wessex	31	48	50 (17)
Oxford	22	50	89 (3)
South-Western	37	51	88 (4)
West Midlands	40	48	66 (14)
Mersey	10	90	96 (1)
North-Western	30	57	85 (5=)
Wales	37	62	80 (8)
Scotland	70	49	78 (9)
Northern Ireland	27	52	67 (13)

Cardiac arrest trolley

Fifty-eight per cent of units were reported to have a cardiac arrest trolley in the delivery area and these units were responsible for 77 per cent of all deliveries. These proportions rose to just over 80 per cent in units with caseloads of 2000 annual deliveries or more (Table 3.31). Almost all (95 per cent) of the units with a cardiac arrest trolley had only one machine.

Table 3.32 describes the regional variation in the absolute availability of a cardiac arrest trolley in the delivery area. In most regions between 70 and 90 per cent of women labour in a delivery area with a cardiac arrest trolley; the regional extremes were 50 per cent and 96 per cent.

To some extent, the availabilities of a cardiac arrest trolley and of ECG monitor mirror each other; each would be needed rarely, but in a hurry in a crisis. Both are an indication of the readiness of an obstetric unit to cope with emergencies of the mother and the availability of this equipment probably reflects the combined interest of the obstetrician and anaesthetist in this aspect of emergency cover.

TABLE 3.33   Regional rank order for six pieces of obstetric equipment

Region	Real-time ultrasound	FHM	pH meter	Infusion pump	Delivery bed	Birth chair
Northern	12=	10	7	5	12	13
Yorkshire	14	5	10=	2	6	1
Trent	7=	9	5	11	7	9
East Anglia	10	1	13=	7	9	3=
North-West Thames	16	3	2	3=	4	15=
North-East Thames	4=	11	17	14	13	11
South-East Thames	11	7	9	10	10	10
South-West Thames	7=	8	10=	9	11	6
Wessex	4=	15	8	15	1	15=
Oxford	1	16	3	17	3	17
South-Western	6	17	4	12	14	8
West Midlands	17	14	13=	16	15	12
Mersey	7=	6	6	8	17	2
North-Western	15	13	1	13	16	3=
Wales	12=	2	13=	6	5	14
Scotland	3	4	12	3=	2	5
Northern Ireland	2	12	16	1	8	7

Geographical variation in provision of equipment

To simplify the comparison of the provision of equipment in the English regions and the Celtic kingdoms, their rank positions for the fifteen pieces of equipment have been summarized in Tables 3.33, 3.34 and 3.35.

As has been stressed earlier, these rankings must be interpreted with caution. It is not known what provision is optimal, only what is usual. Furthermore, some types of equipment are more important than others yet get equal weighting in these tables. When interpreting Tables 3.33 to 3.35 the overall natures of the regions—urban or rural—and hence the types of units in them—consultant covered or GP—should also be taken into account. To some extent, variations between regions can be explained by the economy of scale of larger units, discussed more below, and this may sometimes give an impression of underprovision—the obstetric delivery bed is an example of this. On the other hand, in the case of equipment for which a single item is sufficient (for example, the cardiac arrest trolley), regions with predominantly large units may appear relatively well provided.

Such factors, however, only partly explain the observed variation. When the equipment is grouped into its three broad categories (Table 3.36), regional patterns of provision emerge. Some regions such as Scotland, Northern Ireland and North-West Thames appear to be well provided with all types of equipment. Others, paticularly West Midlands, and to a lesser extent South-West

TABLE 3.34 Regional rank order for four pieces of paediatric equipment

Region	Neonatal resuscitation table	Neonatal radiant heater	Neonatal larygoscope	Bag and mask
Northern	14	13	15	16
Yorkshire	12	12	9	9
Trent	10	6	13	8
East Anglia	3	4=	5	11
North-West Thames	6	3	8	12
North-East Thames	11	10	11	15
South-East Thames	9	7	6	10
South-West Thames	8	15	10	13
Wessex	5	8	7	6=
Oxford	16	17	4	3
South-Western	4	4=	1	4
West Midlands	15	16	14	17
Mersey	13	11	17	6=
North-Western	17	14	16	14
Wales	2	2	2	2
Scotland	7	9	12	5
Northern Ireland	1	1	3	1

TABLE 3.35 Regional rank order for five pieces of anaesthetic equipment

Region	O$_2$ for mother	Anaesthetic machine	Anaesthetic ventilator	ECG monitor	Cardiac arrest trolley
Northern	14	4	2=	2	12
Yorkshire	12	14	12	11	10
Trent	11	13	13	10	5=
East Anglia	3	8	15	14=	15=
North-West Thames	2	6	1	7	2
North-East Thames	4	7	7	8	11
South-East Thames	6	12	9	16=	15=
South-West Thames	16	16	14	16=	7
Wessex	5	5	17	14=	17
Oxford	13	9	16	13	3
South-Western	9	10	11	9	4
West Midlands	17	11	4	6	14
Mersey	15	17	8	1	1
North-Western	7	15	5=	4	5=
Wales	1	2	5=	12	8
Scotland	8	1	2=	3	9
Northern Ireland	10	3	10	5	13

TABLE 3.36 Overall regional rank order (1–17) for three main categories of equipment surveyed

Region	Obstetric equipment	Paediatric equipment	Anaesthetic equipment
Northern	14	15	4
Yorkshire	2	11	10
Trent	7	8=	12
East Anglia	3=	4	14
North-West Thames	3=	8=	1
North-East Thames	10=	13	5=
South-East Thames	9	6	16
South-West Thames	8	12	17
Wessex	13	5	15
Oxford	12	10	13
South-Western	15	3	9
West Midlands	17	17	11
Mersey	5=	14	8
North-Western	16	16	5=
Wales	10=	2	3
Scotland	1	7	2
Northern Ireland	5=	1	7

Thames and North-Western regions, appear to be underprovided with equipment. Trent and Oxford also have consistent rankings but which are near the middle of the range for all three main categories. Other regions have high rankings for one or two of the main categories but low for others. South-Western region, for example, appears underprovided for obstetric equipment but well provided with paediatric equipment, possibly a tribute to the work on neonatal care pioneered in that region for the last 25 years.

SERVICES

Blood storage area with rhesus negative blood

Although only 54 per cent of units reported having rhesus negative blood available either in the delivery area or on the premises, these tended to be the larger units and they were responsible for 79 per cent of all deliveries (Tables 3.37 and 3.38; see also Figure 3.18 on page 95). Of the remainder, 16 per cent of units reported that rhesus negative blood was not available but, strikingly, these places were responsible for only 1 per cent of all labours.

The availability for the four main caseload size groupings is shown in the middle of Table 3.37. For all units with more than 1500 deliveries per year, rhesus negative blood was reported to be available somewhere although in 19 per cent it was only available off the premises. The proportion of units with

TABLE 3.37   Percentage of units reporting blood storage area with rhesus negative blood available by caseload size and type of unit

	Available			Not available	Not known
	In delivery area	On premises	Elsewhere		
Unit areas	18	36	27	16	2
Caseload size:					
Small 1–500	4	21	36	37	2
Medium 501–2000	18	50	28	3	3
Large 2001–4000	36	44	18	0	2
Very large 4000+	58	31	8	0	4
General practitioner units	4	15	36	41	3
Consultant-covered units	28	47	22	1	2

rhesus negative blood available somewhere on the premises rose from 25 per cent of the small units up to 90 per cent of the very large units.

The bottom of Tables 3.37 and 3.38 contrasts the non-availability of rhesus negative blood in GP units (41 per cent) with its non-availability in other units (only 1 per cent) (Table 3.37). This meant that while almost all women

TABLE 3.38   Blood storage area with rhesus negative blood available by percentage of deliveries

	Available			Not available	Not known
	In delivery area	On premises	Elsewhere		
All delivery areas	35	44	18	1	2
Unit size:					
Small 1–500	3	27	44	23	2
Medium 501–2000	19	51	26	2	2
Large 2001–4000	38	43	17	0	2
Very large 4000+	58	30	8	0	4
General practitioner units	4	22	44	26	4
Consultant-covered units	36	43	18	0	2

TABLE 3.39   Blood storage area with rhesus negative blood, regional variation

	Available (% deliveries)			Not available	Not known
	In delivery areas	On premises	Elsewhere		
Northern	32	28	35	0	5(1)
Yorkshire	28	31	39	2	0
Trent	32	55	11	2	0
East Anglia	40	56	1	3	0
North-West Thames	23	40	36	0	0
North-East Thames	29	64	7	0	0
South-East Thames	24	58	16	2	0
South-West Thames	19	64	16	2	0
Wessex	25	58	11	6	0
Oxford	40	27	30	3	0
South-Western	36	35	11	3	15(1)
West Midlands	39	40	20	0	1
Mersey	50	33	8	0	9
North-Western	28	43	28	0	1
Scotland	59	18	21	2	1
Wales	22	55	17	6	0
Northern Ireland	37	41	9	2	12(2)
Others	38	27	25	0	10(1)

Figures in parentheses are numbers of delivery areas in that region for which no data are available.

delivering in consultant units had this service, 26 per cent of those in GP units did not have it (Table 3.38).

The availability of a blood storage area with rhesus negative blood by geographical region is shown in Table 3.39. One striking variation is in the proportion of deliveries for which rhesus negative blood is not available on the hospital premises; this applied to only 4 per cent of deliveries in East Anglia compared with over 35 per cent in the Northern, Yorkshire and North-West Thames regions. The highest regional proportions of deliveries with no blood available were reported from Wessex and Wales, both regions with a relatively high proportion of small units.

Operating theatres

Operating theatres of two types were distinguished in the confidential survey: those exclusively for the use of the obstetricians and those shared with other specialities. For each type, an enquiry was made about the theatre's location. Table 3.40 describes operating theatre availability in terms of a hierarchy, the elements of which have been made mutually exclusive. From the table it can be seen that two-thirds of deliveries take place in the one-third of

TABLE 3.40   Operating theatre availability reported by percentage of units and percentage of deliveries

		Institution (%)	Deliveries (%)
Available			
In delivery area	Exclusive	36	64
	Shared	2	3
In hospital	Exclusive	11	13
	Shared	19	14
Elsewhere	Exclusive	4	1
	Shared	3	1
Not available		23	3
Not known		2	0

units with a theatre available exclusively for obstetrics. Conversely, 23 per cent of delivery areas were reported to have no theatre available, but these units were responsible for only 3 per cent of all deliveries.

The operating theatre availability in the four standard caseload size groupings is shown in Table 3.41. Over 50 per cent of small units reportedly had no theatre available and this was the case in two-thirds of the units with fewer than 100 deliveries per year, in one-half of the units with 100–300 deliveries, and in one-third of the units with 300–500 deliveries. In contrast, this did not apply to any unit with more than 1000 deliveries per year. All units with more than 2000 annual deliveries, except one, had an operating theatre in the hospital and for 75 per cent of these the theatre was in the delivery area.

TABLE 3.41   Percentage of units reporting operating theatre availability by hospital caseload size

	Caseload size groups			
	1–500	501–2000	2001–4000	4001+
Available				
In delivery area				
– exclusive	5	52	70	73
– shared	0	3	4	0
In hospital				
– exclusive	8	9	13	23
– shared	20	26	12	0
Elsewhere				
– exclusive	7	2	1	0
– shared	3	5	0	0
Not available	52	2	1	0
Not known	5	1	0	4

TABLE 3.42 Operating theatres availability reported by percentage of deliveries. Regional variations

	Available		Not available
	In hospital	Elsewhere	
Northern	97	1	2
Yorkshire	93	5	2
Trent	97	0	3
East Anglia	96	0	4
North-West Thames	97	3	0
North-East Thames	98	0	2
South-East Thames	94	4	2
South-West Thames	98	0	2
Wessex	97	0	3
Oxford	96	1	3
South-Western	NK	NK	NK
West Midlands	96	1	3
Mersey	100	0	0
North-Western	99	0	1
Wales	92	6	2
Scotland	94	4	2
Northern Ireland	96	1	3

NK = not known

As would be expected there was a marked difference between GP and other units in terms of theatre availability. There was no theatre available to 43 per cent of women delivering in GP units compared with just over 1 per cent delivering in units with consultant cover.

Table 3.42 shows operating theatre availability to women who labour in the health authority regions. There was some variation between the regions in the proportion for which this was only available 'elsewhere'; as might be expected this tended to reflect how rural a region is. For one region it was reported that a theatre was not available for 4 per cent of deliveries (East Anglia) while North-West Thames and Mersey reported no deliveries for which a theatre was unavailable. While the latter has no GP units, the former has several, yet all women were considered to have an operating theatre available.

Recovery area for mothers

The availability of a recovery area for mothers was not recorded for 10 per cent of units. This problem was not peculiar to the smallest units.

Overall, about 30 per cent of units are likely to have a recovery area for mothers in the delivery area and these units will deliver about 50 per cent of mothers (Tables 3.43 and 3.44). For a further 30 per cent of units this facility is available elsewhere and for the remaining 40 per cent (where about 25 per cent of mothers are delivered) no recovery area is available.

TABLE 3.43 Availability of recovery area for mothers reported as percentage of delivery areas by hospital caseload size and by type of unit

	Available			Not available	Not known
	In delivery area	On premises	elsewhere		
All delivery areas	26	21	4	39	10
Unit size:					
Small 1–500	7	16	6	60	11
Medium 501–2000	26	32	3	28	11
Large 2001–4000	50	20	1	19	9
Very large 4001+	65	15	0	15	4
General practitioner units	7	10	6	64	12
Consultant-covered units	39	26	2	23	10

The availability in the standard caseload size groups is shown in the middle of Tables 3.43 and 3.44. The proportion of units with recovery for mothers in the delivery area increases from 7 per cent to 65 per cent as the caseload increases. Recovery for mothers was recorded as not available for 64 per cent of GP units as opposed to 23 per cent of other units (Table 3.43).

TABLE 3.44 Availability of recovery area for mothers reported as percentage of deliveries by hospital caseload size and by type of unit

	Available			Not available	Not known
	In delivery area	On premises	elsewhere		
All delivery areas	46	22	2	22	8
Unit size:					
Small 1–500	7	21	6	56	10
Medium 501–2000	29	31	3	25	11
Large 2001–4000	55	19	1	19	8
Very large 4001+	65	14	0	16	4
General practitioner units	8	14	6	60	12
Consultant-covered units	48	22	1	20	8

TABLE 3.45 Availability of recovery area for mothers reported as percentage of delivery areas. Regional variation

	Available			Not available	Not known
	In delivery area	On premises	Elsewhere		
Northern	36	18	4	21	21
Yorkshire	32	16	3	32	16
Trent	34	9	0	54	3
East Anglia	19	31	0	37	12
North-West Thames	41	14	5	27	14
North-East Thames	24	34	0	21	21
South-East Thames	22	33	0	33	11
South-West Thames	35	35	6	23	0
Wessex	17	3	0	65	14
Oxford	18	23	4	45	9
South-Western	16	11	5	65	3
West Midlands	29	15	5	41	10
Mersey	30	40	0	20	10
North-Western	33	17	0	30	20
Wales	24	19	5	40	11
Scotland	28	17	8	39	7
Northern Ireland	15	26	4	41	15

Figures for the availability of a recovery area for mothers for the health authority regions are given in Tables 3.45 and 3.46. The relatively high proportion of units for which this information was not recorded makes the interpretation difficult. These tables do, however, provide some evidence of variation between the regions in provision of recovery areas for mothers. At the extremes, this facility was unavailable to (at most) 16 per cent of women in the Oxford region compared with 53 per cent of women in the South-Western region.

Ward clerk

The availability of a ward clerk for the delivery area was explored with the following question:

IS A WARD CLERK AVAILABLE FOR THE DELIVERY AREA AT ANY TIME IN THE 24 HOURS UNDER REVIEW?

Three per cent of units did not reply and because no assumption can be made about these places they appear as 'not recorded' on all tables.

Overall, 29 per cent of units answered yes to this question and these units

TABLE 3.46 Availability of recovery area for mothers reported as percentage of deliveries. Regional variation

	Available			Not available	Not known
	In delivery area	On premises	elsewhere		
Northern	48	25	0	9	17
Yorkshire	60	11	2	19	8
Trent	68	6	0	26	0
East Anglia	28	36	0	23	13
North-West Thames	53	9	3	24	10
North-East Thames	22	33	0	17	28
South-East Thames	30	35	0	29	6
South-West Thames	32	44	0	23	0
Wessex	31	27	0	41	0
Oxford	49	34	0	8	8
South-Western	43	2	1	53	1
West Midlands	46	11	4	26	13
Mersey	40	35	0	16	9
North-Western	54	14	0	23	8
Wales	45	31	5	13	5
Scotland	60	23	4	8	4
Northern Ireland	36	24	4	30	6

were responsible for 45 per cent of all deliveries (Table 3.47). The proportion of deliveries for which a ward clerk was available rose from 20 per cent in the 1–500 caseload size group to 59 per cent in units with more than 4000 deliveries

TABLE 3.47 Availability of ward clerk by annual caseload size

	Delivery areas (%)			Deliveries (%)		
	Available	Not available	Not recorded	Available	Not available	Not recorded
Total survey	29	68	3	45	52	3
Unit size 1–500	13	84	3	20	76	4
501–2000	31	67	2	32	66	2
2001–4000	48	50	2	51	47	2
4001+	58	38	4	59	37	4
General practitioner units	13	84	3	22	74	4
Consultant-covered units	39	58	3	47	51	2

TABLE 3.48   Ward clerks. Regional variation

	Delivery areas (%)			Deliveries (%)		
Region	Available	Not available	Not recorded	Available	Not available	Not recorded
Northern	29	71	0	42	58	0
Yorkshire	40	55	6(2)	48	36	16
Trent	20	77	3(1)	47	52	0
East Anglia	19	81	0	32	68	0
North-West Thames	45	55	0	62	38	0
North-East Thames	21	62	17(5)	30	64	7
South-East Thames	41	56	4(1)	42	55	4
South-West Thames	12	82	6(1)	18	76	7
Wessex	32	65	3(1)	69	30	0
Oxford	32	68	0	37	63	0
South-Western	14	84	3(1)	34	59	7
West Midlands	44	56	0	57	43	0
Mersey	50	50	0	54	46	0
North-Western	60	40	0	69	31	0
Wales	19	81	0	28	72	0
Scotland	15	82	3(2)	32	67	1
Northern Ireland	30	70	0	53	47	0

Figures in parentheses are the numbers of units for which no data are available.

each year. The equivalent figure for GP units was 22 per cent and for consultant-covered units, 47 per cent.

Figures for the health authority regions are given in Table 3.48. Comparison is made difficult by the non-respondents. Considering the regions with complete data (in fact including other regions missing data as all yes or all no does not change this range), the proportion of deliveries which took place in a delivery area with a clerk available ranged from 28 per cent in Wales to 69 per cent in the North-Western region.

CONCLUSIONS

Despite the undoubted problems of interpreting survey data such as these, it is possible to draw some conclusions. The survey has confirmed the importance of considering provision of equipment and services in terms both of availability in delivery areas and of availability to women in labour. A blood storage area with rhesus negative blood, for example, is not available in one-third of delivery areas yet these are responsible for only 1 per cent of all deliveries. Similarly, an operating theatre was reported as not available in 23 per cent of delivery areas but only 3 per cent of deliveries take place in these units.

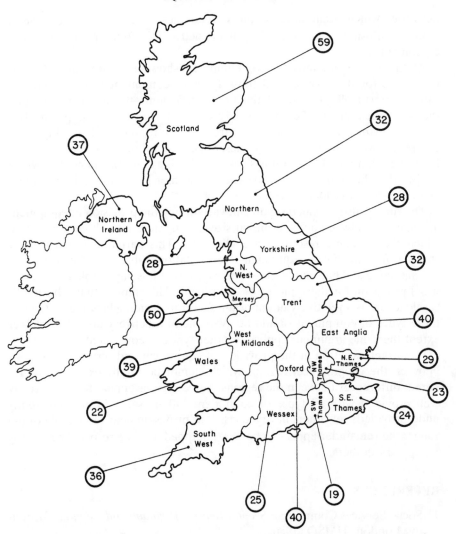

Figure 3.18 Percentage of units with blood storage in delivery area (by regions)

When viewed from these two perspectives the striking differences in provision almost entirely reflect the units with very small caseloads. The provision of equipment in the small units often appears anomalous in comparison with larger ones. Equipment which is standard in larger units may not be available at all in the smaller units; conversely, when it is available in smaller units there often appears to be a relative overprovision because of the small numbers of deliveries which occur in these units. Examples of this are the fetal heart monitor, infusion pump, obstetric delivery bed and the four types of paediatric equipment.

All the services and most types of equipment show an *economy of scale*. This is obvious for the services and those types of equipment (for example the cardiac arrest trolley) for which one item is sufficient—the larger the caseload the larger the number of deliveries covered by that service or equipment. But an *economy of scale* was also evident from the more frequently used types of equipment when the provision was described in terms of annual deliveries per item of equipment. This contrasts with the findings for midwifery staff which suggest that the number of midwives per 100 women in labour tends to increase as the hospital caseload increases.

The survey also revealed significant variation in the provision of equipment and services between units of similar size, raising questions about the ways in which the available resources are allocated. This variation is particularly striking for paediatric equipment—resuscitation table, overhead heater, laryngoscope and bag and mask—to an extent that it is impossible to discern a usual provision for these pieces of equipment. This implies that a hospital's caseload size is a relatively unimportant factor in deciding how many items of these types of equipment should be available in a delivery area. To a lesser extent the same argument applies to other types of equipment.

Important variation in the provision of equipment and services also exists between the geographical regions which cannot be totally explained by inherent differences between the regions. Some regions appear to be relatively well provided with all types of equipment; others seem to be consistently underprovided; yet others have a consistent provision near the middle of the range; the remainder appear to be well equipped in some respects but poorly equipped in others.

REFERENCES

1. Social Services Committee. *Second Report: Perinatal and Neonatal Mortality*. London: HMSO, 1980.
2. Maternity Services Advisory Committee. *Maternity Care in Action*—Part II. *Care During Childbirth—a guide to good practice and a plan for action*. London: HMSO, 1984.

APPENDIX

TABLE 3A.1   Continuous fetal heart monitor
Cumulative frequency distribution of delivery areas by annual deliveries per monitor
with subdivision into caseload size groups

	lowest	10th	25th	50th	75th	90th	highest
	\multicolumn{7}{c}{Annual deliveries per monitor}
All units with a monitor	15	185	293	374	493	640	1696
Unit size							
1–500	15	71	121	158	263	376	462
501–2000	131	222	278	350	453	595	1696
2001–4000	203	300	339	427	545	755	1278
4001+	294	315	365	408	515	638	713

TABLE 3A.2   Infusion pumps
Cumulative frequency distribution of delivery areas by annual deliveries per pump with
subdivision into caseload size groups

	lowest	10th	25th	50th	75th	90th	highest
	\multicolumn{7}{c}{Annual deliveries per pump}
All units with a pump	15	149	238	340	472	680	2477
Unit size							
1–500	15	33	79	146	198	285	448
501–2000	59	184	238	318	409	575	1970
2001–4000	88	285	340	433	555	790	2088
4001+	207	268	363	477	640	765	2477

TABLE 3A.3   Obstetric delivery beds
Cumulative frequency distribution of delivery areas by annual deliveries per bed with subdivision into caseload size groups

	lowest	10th	25th	50th	75th	90th	highest
All units with an obstetric delivery bed	4	50	118	267	400	560	1538
Unit size							
1–500	4	20	50	82	119	221	383
501–2000	134	200	252	340	437	560	945
2001–4000	182	250	316	408	544	720	1538
4001+	226	234	288	374	510	690	1070

TABLE 3A.4   Neonatal resuscitation table
Cumulative frequency distribution of delivery areas by annual deliveries per table with subdivision into caseload size groups

	lowest	10th	25th	50th	75th	90th	highest
All units with a table	1	65	158	357	649	975	2668
Unit size							
1–500	1	28	65	124	202	271	477
501–2000	132	290	352	481	662	855	1667
2001–4000	221	335	465	710	1010	1336	2668
4001+	339	390	492	730	1230	1650	2249

TABLE 3A.5   Neonatal overhead radiant heater
Cumulative frequency distribution of delivery areas by annual deliveries per heater with subdivision into caseload size groups

	lowest	10th	25th	50th	75th	90th	highest
All units with a heater	3	65	167	353	603	942	2889
Unit size							
1–500	3	29	62	119	194	290	477
501–2000	150	249	313	465	622	907	1943
2001–4000	221	335	244	585	885	1290	2889
4001+	299	330	390	642	1175	1830	2249

TABLE 3A.6   Neonatal laryngoscope
Cumulative frequency distribution of delivery areas by annual deliveries per laryngo-scope with subdivision into caseload size groups

	lowest	10th	25th	50th	75th	90th	highest
All units with neonatal laryngoscope	1	42	114	239	375	587	1339
Unit size							
1–500	1	18	44	90	153	230	448
501–2000	113	172	223	288	405	565	862
2001–4000	159	216	283	401	603	975	1334
4001+	171	230	342	432	574	1075	1339

TABLE 3A.7   Bag and mask
Cumulative frequency distribution of delivery areas by annual deliveries per bag and mask with subdivision into caseload size groups

	lowest	10th	25th	50th	75th	90th	highest
All units with a bag and mask	1	49	120	310	556	850	2141
Unit size							
1–500	1	20	50	97	187	279	477
501–2000	101	218	302	401	596	814	1725
2001–4000	110	250	416	579	852	1110	2718
4001+	247	300	342	530	991	1270	2141

TABLE 3A.8   Oxygen for the mother
Cumulative frequency distribution of delivery areas by annual deliveries per oxygen source with subdivision into caseload size groups

	lowest	10th	25th	50th	75th	90th	highest
All units with oxygen source	3	44	98	191	293	392	2085
Unit size							
1–500	3	17	46	78	141	172	460
501–2000	38	142	177	242	328	442	1340
2001–4000	98	155	212	277	374	499	2085
4001+	176	188	211	286	357	455	1071

TABLE 3A.9   Anaesthetic machines
Frequency distribution of delivery areas by number of anaesthetic machines with sub-division into major caseload size groups

	0	1	2	3	4	5	6	7	8	9	NK
All units (n = 528)	110	223	110	46	19	11	3	1	0	1	4
Unit size											
1–500 (n = 217)	91	118	3	1	0	0	0	0	0	0	4
501–2000 (n = 148)	12	65	54	15	1	1	0	0	0	0	0
2001–4000 (n = 129)	2	34	45	25	17	4	1	1	0	0	0
4001+ (n = 25)	0	4	6	5	1	6	2	0	0	1	0
Others (n = 9)	5	2	2	0	0	0	0	0	0	0	0

TABLE 3A.10   Anaesthetic ventilator
Frequency distribution of delivery areas by number of anaesthetic ventilators with sub-division into major caseload size groups

	0	1	2	3	4	5	6	7	NK
All (n = 528)	271	171	57	19	3	3	0	1	3
Unit size									
1–500 (n = 217)	185	29	0	0	0	0	0	0	3
501–2000 (n = 148)	49	75	21	3	0	0	0	0	0
2001–4000 (n = 129)	22	62	28	15	2	0	0	0	0
4001+ (n = 25)	7	5	7	1	1	3	0	1	0
Others (n = 9)	8	0	1	0	0	0	0	0	0

Birthplace
G.V.P. Chamberlain
© 1987 John Wiley & Sons Ltd

CHAPTER 4

Midwifery Facilities

PHILIPPA GUNN

INTRODUCTION

The staffing of the institutional place of birth by midwives, student midwives and nursing staff is considered in this chapter; midwives' attendance at home deliveries is examined in Chapter 8. The survey investigated the number of midwives providing for the mother's care and the seniority of these midwives as a reflection of their experience and skills.

Midwives have a variety of functions in addition to their clinical role at the place of birth. The extent of these will vary according to the type and size of unit and these were considered when analysing the results; other major variables were the different workloads and their distribution over the 24-hour period.

The midwife in charge of the delivery area on any shift takes responsibility for its organization and coordinates all aspects of the facilities offered. She needs to have detailed knowledge of the Health Service and maternity unit policies and is responsible for their implementation; the demands of this role will vary depending on the number of visiting staff. Medical cover may be a large number of general practitioners in the small units while in larger units cover is provided by obstetricians from within the hospital.

Anaesthetists, paediatricians and occasionally physicians may also be involved in care and midwives must act to facilitate the work of all these staff. The midwife in charge has to know which doctors responsible for a speciality are on call at any one time and where they may be found, often a great test of the midwife's resourcefulness.

Another load on the midwife's time is in the organization, ordering and checking of equipment and supplies although in some units she may be assisted by a ward clerk in some of the paper work. Checking of equipment and the arrangement for its swift repair is essential work in any ward or department and especially in an intensive care area such as the labour ward. In general, the larger units providing care for the higher risk mother normally incorporate in the unit more technical apparatus.

Teaching student midwives, nurses or medical students is another aspect which can make a considerable demand on the midwife's time.

The Maternity Services Advisory Committee in its report[1] stated that 'The midwife is the key person caring for the woman in labour'. It was recommended that there should be sufficient midwives allocated to the labour area to allow each midwife to care for one mother even though she may not be with her all the time in early labour. To implement these recommendations the obvious fluctuation in the numbers of women in labour at any time had to be considered. In the delivery area an even greater proportion of trained midwifery staff to other staff would normally be anticipated. In the Central Management Services Study[2] it was shown that most trained midwifery resources were devoted to the delivery areas and that the ratio of trained midwives to student and other nurses was highest in the delivery area. Areas of work undertaken by the other staff in the delivery area are limited and student nurses are present as observers.

DIFFERENT MIDWIFERY AND NURSING WORKLOADS

The style and size of the delivery area in which the midwife works varied among the units; for example one-quarter of the units did not have a central delivery area. The questionnaire specified that only midwives in the delivery area were to be recorded. It was clear that many midwives were also providing care for antenatal or postnatal women and even for medical and surgical patients. This must be remembered when drawing conclusions about the ratios of staff to women in labour. In Chapter 2, it is shown that the proportion of women in labour to ante- and postnatal women is highest in the larger units whereas the small units are shown to have far larger numbers of postnatal mothers in the delivery area.

The pattern of work over the 24 hours and between the four days was discussed in Chapter 2. It was noted that there were more deliveries, women in labour and additional procedures occurring in the morning in comparison to the remainder of the day and again more during the day than at night. It also showed that a higher proportion of abnormal deliveries, anaesthetic and paediatric procedures were undertaken in the larger units.

MIDWIVES AND NURSING STAFF

The survey examined ten grades of midwifery and nursing staff which comprised of six grades of trained midwives, student midwives and three grades of other nursing staff (Chapter 2). The following data are presented in three groups.

Trained midwifery staff

The midwife is qualified in the management of normal labour, which includes monitoring its progress, and in the detection of complications arising in the mother of the fetus. She is responsible for carrying out normal deliveries and for the care of the infant at birth. In an emergency she would also carry out appropriate treatment until the arrival of a doctor. These aspects of care are the province and the responsibility of the midwife and cannot be delegated to other nursing staff.

While normal labour and delivery are the domain of the midwife, in the higher risk group of women with more complicated labours, she also assumes responsibility for providing nursing as well. This happens with induction of labour, epidural and general anaesthesia, intravenous infusions and operative deliveries. All these procedures increase demands on the midwife's time, for medical staff rely on the support of the midwives in providing the equipment, assisting and supporting the mother during these events.

Some midwives also undertake other specific procedures, for example the application of a scalp electrode, establishing intravenous infusions and carrying out forceps or breech deliveries. In a study of the role and responsibilities of the midwives carried out in 1979 by Robinson a number of these procedures were surveyed[3]. The range varied from 16 per cent of midwives undertaking low forceps deliveries (in an emergency) to 60.9 per cent of midwives applying scalp electrodes for fetal heart monitoring. Increasingly, procedures such as applying scalp electrodes and suturing perineums are considered the normal extension of the role of the midwife. Further aspects about the different grades of trained midwives are discussed in Chapter 2.

Student midwives

Student midwives are present in the delivery area for at least one-sixth of their total training and carry out many of the midwifery tasks under the supervision of a trained midwife. Their role is further discussed in Chapter 1. The English National Board considers a student midwife's contribution to the midwifery establishment to be one-half of a full-time equivalent trained midwife.

Other nursing staff

The staff in this group were mostly nursing auxiliaries, some theatre trained nursing staff and student nurses. The student nurses were present in a supernumerary status, the theatre trained nursing staff gave assistance during operations and nursing auxiliaries provided support for the midwives in the delivery area. The Central Management Services in its report on the study of hospital-based midwives[2] reported that the 'midwifery and nursing and attendant duties' accounted for 66 per cent of the nursing auxiliary's time and that

TABLE 4.1   Numbers of midwives and nurses in labour ward

	August	September	October	November
11 am	(*n* = 530)	(*n* = 523)	(*n* = 519)	(*n* = 522)
Midwife	1779	1501	1755	1760
Student midwife	339	282	381	287
Other nursing staff	802	548	743	783
3 pm	(*n* = 530)	(*n* = 523)	(*n* = 520)	(*n* = 522)
Midwife	2212	1920	2239	2157
Student midwife	417	342	518	376
Other nursing staff	833	589	817	815
7 pm	(*n* = 530)	(*n* = 523)	(*n* = 520)	(*n* = 522)
Midwife	1345	1233	1334	1290
Student midwife	275	208	292	217
Other nursing staff	536	440	540	546
11 pm	(*n* = 529)	(*n* = 521)	(*n* = 517)	(*n* = 520)
Midwife	1335	1304	1341	1326
Student midwife	167	125	155	161
Other nursing staff	407	400	417	410

she spent 11 per cent of her time on communication. This compared with the midwives who spent 43–50 per cent of their time in midwifery nursing and attendant duties and 38–40 per cent in communication.

MIDWIVES AND NURSES AVAILABLE

The total number of staff available is shown in Table 4.1 and Figure 4.1.

Trained midwives made up the majority at all times of day and for all four months. They formed a higher proportion of the total staff by two to one, occasionally outweighing the number of student midwives and other nursing staff together. The numbers of staff recorded varied little over the three midweek days although on Saturday there was a slight fall in numbers.

Effects of time of day

On each of the four days, there was a peak in the number of staff recorded at 3 pm; this suggests an overlap of staff between the morning and evening shifts which occurs in some units between 1 pm and 4 pm. However, the increase of staff in the afternoon over the morning figures is less than one-third which further suggests that only a small proportion of the staff remain in the delivery area all afternoon. While some staff may have been employed part-time or work a half-day as part of a full-time rota, such a period of the day is frequently the only time possible to give staff time off to make up for overtime worked.

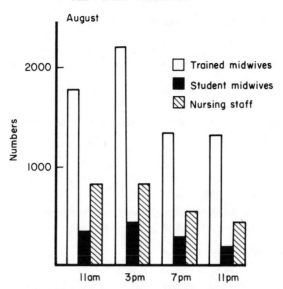

Figure 4.1   Total numbers of midwives at four survey times in August

Depending on the nature of the delivery area, the opportunity of having additional staff available will enable other activities to take place such as in-service and staff training, meetings, antenatal classes or tours of the unit. Further, jobs requiring midwives to spend additional time in the delivery area such as the ordering of supplies and equipment are frequently left until the afternoon overlap.

These figures do not show up the variations in workload over the 24-hour period and between the four days. Furthermore, the midwives recorded in this table were sometimes available to care for antenatal, postnatal and other general patients. Many were in units in which there were no women in labour at the sample time and for this reason it is helpful to look at the ratio of trained staff, student midwives, and other nursing staff to women in labour in those units in which there was such activity.

Effects of number of women in labour

In Figure 4.2 and Table 4.2, the mean ratio of midwives and nursing staff to women in labour is considered by the month and time of day. In the analysis, figures and tables are shown only for the first month, August. The other months' figures are discussed only if they deviated from these. Similarly, only one of the four times of day has been used: 7 pm is a time when it is unlikely that visiting midwives would be working.

TABLE 4.2   Mean ratios of midwives, student midwives and other nurses to 100 women in labour

	August	September	October	November
11 am				
Midwife	218.5	187.7	196.9	207.6
Student midwife	44.4	42.1	43.7	37.6
Other nursing staff	91.3	65.5	80.4	93.2
3 pm				
Midwife	291.1	265.4	285.5	278.2
Student midwife	55.9	53.9	69.0	56.8
Other nursing staff	103.0	72.2	96.2	103.0
7 pm				
Midwife	192.6	191.6	178.6	184.2
Student midwife	46.4	39.0	46.3	36.2
Other nursing staff	70.0	58.0	67.1	75.3
11 pm				
Midwife	219.9	204.2	198.3	201.3
Student midwife	27.9	18.6	23.8	29.4
Other nursing staff	53.6	58.3	52.5	59.5

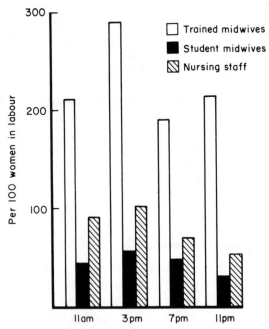

Figure 4.2   Mean ratio of midwives, student midwives and other nurses to 100 women in labour at four survey times in August

In a few units, situations obviously arose in which, despite standard midwifery staffing levels, it seems the number of women in labour was unusually low at that time. As a result, the distribution of staff to women is highly skewed as these extreme cases are far from the mean. The use of the median is frequently preferred to describe such data; however in these instances it has proved to be less informative. The small number of midwives and women in labour wards means that the ratio of midwives to women in labour usually takes one of very few values (1, 1.5, 2, etc.) and so the median is that value taken by many observations. As a result distributions with a noticeable difference in the mean can have the same median. The mean therefore becomes a better measure of location for analysing and comparing such data.

In Figure 4.2 the major groups of trained staff are evident and there continues to be an increase of staff during the afternoon overlap which is more noticeable among those in labour. A closer look at the type of unit shows certain trends in distribution.

Effect of type of unit

In Table 4.3 and Figure 4.3 the ratio of staff to women in labour is analysed by type of unit. The data for August have been used and the units grouped as

TABLE 4.3   Mean ratio of trained midwives, student midwives and other nursing staff by hospital group (August) to 100 women in labour

	Consultant Con. and private Con. and GP	GP unit	Other
11 am			
Midwife	220.7	204.6	187.5
Student midwife	49.2	12.5	—
Other nursing staff	94.6	71.8	37.5
3 pm			
Midwife	304.2	200.5	190.0
Student midwife	63.2	5.0	—
Other nursing staff	104.5	97.7	60.0
7 pm			
Midwife	200.5	127.3	83.3
Student midwife	51.7	—	—
Other nursing staff	69.9	64.0	150.0
11 pm			
Midwife	228.5	125.3	216.6
Student midwife	30.5	4.7	—
Other nursing staff	50.8	71.4	125.0

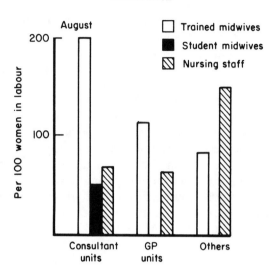

Figure 4.3   Mean ratios of midwives, student midwives and other nurses to 100 women
in labour by type of hospital in August

described earlier are those with consultant cover, separate, general practitioner units and a small group of hospitals for the Armed Services, private
hospitals and other units. There is a higher ratio of midwives and nursing staff
to women in labour at all times of the day in the consultant group compared
with the GP and other units. It should be noted that the number of units in the
other group is very small and there were no student midwives reported in this
group.

The profile of the geography and planning of the delivery area was discussed
in Chapter 2. It showed that there existed within these different groupings of
units, arrangements of workload related to that geography. Integrated delivery
areas were in existence in all the types and sizes of hospital although in different
proportions to the central delivery area within each group. In general, the very
large units had one central delivery area. Those units where a series of delivery
areas was run alongside either postnatal or antenatal beds were mostly in the
small- and medium-sized units. A few units also provided all-purpose rooms
into which women were admitted, delivered and then remained until after their
discharge whether six hours or six days later. The analysis of midwives
according to these arrangements has compared rates of those working in a
central delivery area against those fitting into any other of these categories
(Table 4.4). In general, units without central services were smaller and often
looked after a lower risk group of women. Unlike the remaining data, a
different trend is noted between the weekday and weekend figures and
therefore both are discussed.

On the first day of the survey, a Wednesday, there were at all times more

TABLE 4.4 Mean ratios of trained midwives, student midwives and other nursing staff to 100 women in labour by type of delivery area (August)

	Central	Other than central
11 am		
Midwife	219.9	212.4
Student midwife	46.0	33.4
Other nursing staff	91.0	93.5
3 pm		
Midwife	293.3	282.5
Student midwife	57.9	42.9
Other nursing staff	102.1	107.9
7 pm		
Midwife	198.3	159.7
Student midwife	51.0	18.6
Other nursing staff	67.8	81.5
11 pm		
Midwife	225.2	186.8
Student midwife	28.9	20.1
Other nursing staff	51.5	66.6

midwives available for each woman in labour in units with central services than in the other group. This pattern was observed at the four times of the day and on each of the other weekdays. In units without central services there were, however, more support staff available.

On the second day of the survey, a Saturday, the reverse was observed. With the exception of 7 pm, there was an increase in the ratios of midwives to women in those units without central services and the figures rose above those for units with a central delivery area.

Effects of size of unit

Analysis of numbers of midwives and nurses by size of unit is shown in Table 4.5. It shows that there were generally more trained midwives for every woman in labour the larger the size of unit, particularly at 7 pm and 11 pm. An exception to this trend was the very large units which at 11 am were seen to have the fewest trained midwives per woman in labour. Student midwives and other nursing staff also show a general increase in numbers as the size of unit increases and there were very few student midwives recorded in the small units (Figure 4.4).

It appears that more midwives are available in consultant units with specialist medical cover. This applies also with increasing size of unit because of the

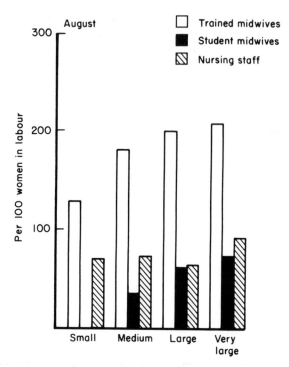

Figure 4.4   Mean ratio of midwives, student midwives and other nurses to 100 women in labour by size of hospital in August

increase in workload rather than the fewer midwives per woman in labour as might be expected with less fluctuation of activity in the big units. Some might conclude that the greater availability of midwifery and nursing staff in the larger units follows the needs of the higher risk group of women who deliver in these units and the higher proportion of complicated deliveries.

Effects of activity in unit

In Table 4.6 the data are analysed by unit activity using the Caesarean section rate in 1983 as some measure of the workload borne in that unit. Those units carrying out less than 5 per cent or no Caesarean sections had fewest midwives available. However, the groups of units with more than 5 or 10 per cent of deliveries by Caesarean section had similar staffing levels. There continues to be a wide variation of ratios of midwifery and nursing staff to women in labour even within the groupings and therefore minimum levels may give a clear picture of deficiencies particularly in the small units.

TABLE 4.5   Mean ratios of trained midwives, student midwives and other nursing staff to 100 women in labour by size of unit (August)

	Small	Medium	Large	Very large	Not grouped
11 am					
Midwife	184.8	230.9	226.8	167.8	240.0
Student midwife	8.8	39.1	61.3	47.2	—
Other nursing staff	68.6	98.9	92.7	90.0	37.5
3 pm					
Midwife	204.2	313.6	296.8	300.5	255.0
Student midwife	4.2	38.8	82.2	84.2	—
Other nursing staff	91.4	111.6	90.8	144.1	92.5
7 pm					
Midwife	129.7	182.7	209.6	227.3	133.3
Student midwife	—	35.3	61.7	73.0	—
Other nursing staff	71.4	73.1	63.3	92.8	54.0
11 pm					
Midwife	133.3	200.8	242.8	278.8	222.2
Student midwife	4.0	15.0	35.1	74.3	—
Other nursing staff	68.0	48.8	51.5	70.6	33.3

TABLE 4.6   Mean ratios of trained midwives, student midwives and other nursing staff to 100 women in labour by Caesarean section rate (August)

Proportion of deliveries by Caesarean section	0–5%	5–10%	<10%
11 am			
Midwife	195.8	231.0	214.7
Student midwife	12.5	40.8	55.3
Other nursing staff	65.6	95.7	93.8
3 pm			
Midwife	206.5	292.4	310.7
Student midwife	4.5	50.3	71.9
Other nursing staff	95.4	102.4	105.2
7 pm			
Midwife	137.8	193.7	205.0
Student midwife	—	39.5	60.8
Other nursing staff	59.6	70.3	72.2
11 pm			
Midwife	125.3	213.3	241.2
Student midwife	4.0	26.6	33.7
Other nursing staff	60.0	59.0	49.4

TABLE 4.7   Minimum levels of trained midwives by delivery group, no. of units and % of active units (August)

Ratio to 100 women in labour	Small		Medium		Large		Very large	
	No.	%	No.	%	No.	%	No.	%
11 am								
≤ 50	1	3.0	4	3.6	2	1.7	1	4.0
≤ 100	12	36.3	21	18.9	21	18.4	5	20.0
≤ 150	3	9.0	20	18.0	29	25.4	7	28.0
> 150	17	51.5	66	59.4	62	54.3	12	48.0
(No one in labour)	(185)		(38)		(15)		(1)	
3 pm								
≤ 50	1	2.9	—	—	1	0.8	1	4.1
≤ 100	9	26.4	15	14.7	12	10.2	1	4.1
≤ 150	2	5.8	11	10.7	21	17.9	1	4.1
> 150	22	64.7	76	74.5	83	70.9	21	87.5
(No one in labour)	(184)		(47)		(12)		(2)	
7 pm								
≤ 50	2	7.4	2	2.3	3	2.5	—	—
≤ 100	16	59.2	30	35.2	29	24.3	6	24.0
≤ 150	1	3.7	7	8.2	17	14.2	3	12.0
> 150	8	29.6	46	54.1	70	58.8	16	64.0
(No one in labour)	(191)		(64)		(10)		(1)	
11 pm								
≤ 50	1	4.0	6	6.4	2	1.7	—	—
≤ 100	17	68.0	21	22.5	22	19.4	2	8.6
≤ 150	—	—	8	8.6	22	19.4	5	21.7
> 150	7	28.0	58	62.3	67	59.2	16	69.5
(No one in labour)	(193)		(56)		(16)		(3)	

Critical levels of midwifery staff

Another way of assessing midwifery staffing levels would be to consider the ratio of midwives to each woman in labour below an arbitrary cut-off point. This would point out the extremes of low staffing. The percentage of units with 50 midwives or fewer per 100 women in labour (i.e. one midwife looking after two women) and 100 or fewer midwives per 100 women in labour (i.e. one midwife per labouring mother) in August is shown in Table 4.7 for the four times of day and by the delivery size group. Less than 10 per cent of units fell into the lowest category in any group and the percentage of units with a ratio of less than one to one showed a fall with increasing size of unit; it emphasizes the point that half of the small units have only one midwife or less per women in labour at 7 pm and 11 pm.

TRAINED MIDWIFERY STAFF

The grades of trained staff available in the delivery area give a further indication of facilities provided. The details of these different grades of midwives and their role in the delivery area are discussed in Chapter 2. In Table 4.8 the different grades of trained midwifery staff per woman in labour are shown and in Figures 4.5 and 4.6, the ratios for a weekday and a weekend.

The two grades of midwives which predominate are sisters and staff midwives; there were slightly more sisters than staff midwives at all times of day and for both months. The next available grade of trained midwife was the nursing officer. Her availability accounted for only one-quarter of that of the midwifery sister and she was on average twice as likely to be available in two daytime periods as in the night for both the weekend and during the week.

TABLE 4.8   Total number of trained midwives (August)

	Total no.
11 am	
Nursing officer	219
Midwifery sister	779
Community midwife	71
Staff midwife	687
Bank midwife	12
Agency midwife	11
3 pm	
Nursing officer	204
Midwifery sister	1009
Community midwife	74
Staff midwife	905
Bank midwife	8
Agency midwife	12
7 pm	
Nursing officer	73
Midwifery sister	613
Community midwife	45
Staff midwife	593
Bank midwife	10
Agency midwife	11
11 pm	
Nursing officer	76
Midwifery sister	649
Community midwife	33
Staff midwife	531
Bank midwife	18
Agency midwife	28

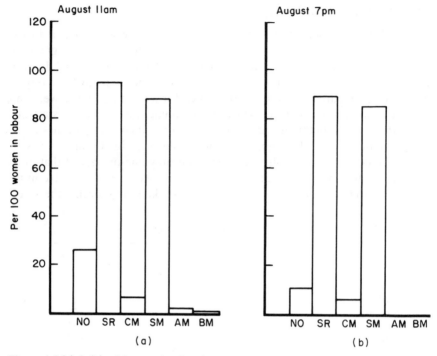

Figure 4.5 (a) & (b)   Mean ratio of various grades of trained midwife per 100 women in labour at two times in August

NO — nursing officer
SR   — midwifery sister
CM — community midwife
SM   — staff midwife
AM — agency midwife
BM — bank midwife

Of the permanent midwives, the community midwife contributed least to the staffing in the place of birth and her presence showed little variation over the four times of day and by weekend or weekday.

There were minimal numbers of agency and bank midwives employed and the highest figure was at 11 pm for each month with a total of 46 midwives at 11 pm in August and 60 at 11 pm in September. Although the current national shortage of midwives may necessitate the use of locum midwives in hospitals, it appears that units strive to avoid their use in the delivery and high dependency area. Their use in the antenatal and postnatal wards could be expected to be higher.

Effect of size of unit

Some further explanation of the use of different grades of trained midwives can be found when examining these staff by unit grouped by size of unit. Table 4.9 and Figure 4.7 show the grades of trained staff at 11 am and 7 pm in August. The same trend in the higher proportion of midwifery sisters and staff midwives continues to be shown with other grades of midwives continues to be shown with other grades of midwives providing relatively few of these facilities. In the smaller unit midwifery sisters provided a far higher proportion of the staff than staff midwives, particularly on the Saturday. There were also fewer nursing officers available in the smaller units. During the day, the ratio of these senior midwives to women in labour is highest in the medium sized units and their relative availability decreases in all size units in the evening and at night.

Community midwives provided most of their in-hospital services in the smaller units. There was some variation but no trends are noted in their presence in these units either by time of day or day of the week. In the three larger types of unit community midwives were hardly present and their availability in these units is equally distributed over 24 hours.

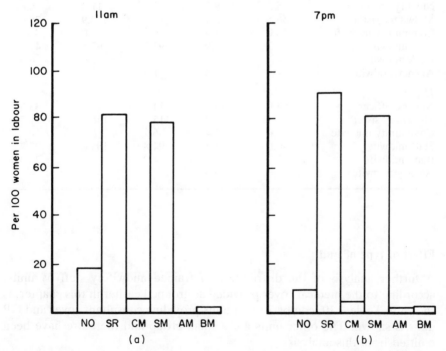

Figure 4.6 (a) and (b)   Mean ratio of various grades of trained midwife per women in labour at two times in September (for key see Figure 4.5)

TABLE 4.9 Mean ratio of different grades of trained midwives by size of unit (August)

	Small	Medium	Large	Very large	Not grouped
11 am					
Nursing officer	23.5	31.5	24.3	15.9	25.0
Midwifery sister	64.2	101.0	101.9	82.9	97.5
Community midwife	17.6	6.4	3.6	3.4	12.5
Staff midwife	73.5	91.1	94.9	64.6	80.0
Bank midwife	—	0.3	0.1	0.8	25.0
Agency midwife	5.8	0.4	1.8	—	—
3 pm					
Nursing officer	18.5	28.7	26.1	21.4	12.5
Midwifery sister	104.2	139.0	130.9	140.9	90.0
Community midwife	11.4	6.8	4.9	5.1	17.5
Staff midwife	67.1	136.9	130.1	133.0	122.5
Bank midwife	—	0.3	2.5	—	12.5
Agency midwife	2.8	1.7	2.1	—	—
7 pm					
Nursing officer	5.3	8.7	12.9	11.8	6.6
Midwifery sister	56.5	85.1	93.1	120.9	78.6
Community midwife	16.0	4.4	5.5	1.0	—
Staff midwife	51.7	80.9	95.2	92.5	41.3
Bank midwife	—	1.1	1.1	1.0	6.6
Agency midwife	—	2.3	1.6	—	—
11 pm					
Nursing officer	4.0	10.6	14.8	19.8	33.3
Midwifery sister	81.3	91.7	115.1	146.8	77.7
Community midwife	8.0	2.4	6.7	6.5	—
Staff midwife	40.0	85.3	94.8	105.6	77.7
Bank midwife	—	1.2	4.0	—	33.3
Agency midwife	—	9.3	7.0	—	—

Effect of type of unit

A further analysis of the distribution of trained midwifery staff by units, according to the medical cover provided as grouped earlier in this chapter, is shown in Table 4.10; comparison of units providing consultant cover and GP units is shown. The other units are a small group and therefore have been omitted from this analysis.

Sisters and staff midwives were available in equal numbers in the consultant group but the GP units were generally staffed by a higher proportion of sisters at all times of day and in all four months.

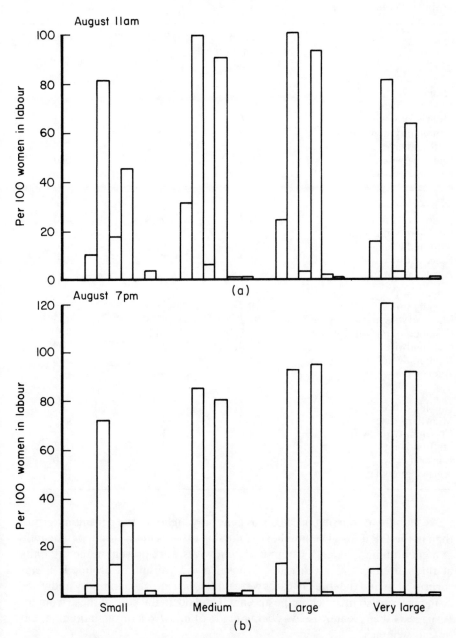

Figure 4.7 (a) and (b)   Mean ratio of various grades of trained midwife (same column order as 4.5) at two times in August by size of unit

TABLE 4.10   Mean ratios of trained midwives by 100 women in labour by type of hospital (August)

	Consultant Con. and private Con. and GP	GP unit	Other
11 am			
Nursing officer	25.8	28.1	37.5
Midwifery sister	98.1	78.1	62.5
Community midwife	3.8	28.1	—
Staff midwife	91.6	64.0	62.5
Bank midwife	0.2	—	25.0
Agency midwife	1.0	6.2	—
3 pm			
Nursing officer	26.7	18.3	10.0
Midwifery sister	134.2	98.8	150.0
Community midwife	5.5	16.6	—
Staff midwife	134.5	63.3	20.0
Bank midwife	1.3	—	10.0
Agency midwife	1.7	3.3	—
7 pm			
Nursing officer	10.7	8.0	16.6
Midwifery sister	92.2	57.3	16.6
Community midwife	3.8	24.0	—
Staff midwife	90.0	38.0	33.3
Bank midwife	1.0	—	16.6
Agency midwife	1.7	—	—
11 pm			
Nursing officer	13.9	—	25.0
Midwifery sister	107.4	77.7	158.3
Community midwife	4.0	19.0	—
Staff midwife	93.4	28.5	8.3
Bank midwife	2.4	—	25.0
Agency midwife	7.1	—	—

Availability of nursing officers was generally higher in the consultant group than in the GP units. The numbers of nursing officers in this group fell heavily at night and the weekend. Community midwives were present in the GP units at three or four times the rate of those in the consultant group. It is not surprising to find that the GP cases were under the care of community midwives as they were also involved in the antenatal and postnatal care of these women. It suggests that greater use was being made of midwives through domino and on-call schemes.

Midwifery agency and bank staff were used at all times in the consultant group of units but were rarely used in the GP units.

TEACHING THE STUDENT MIDWIFE

The English National Board recommends that the ratio of trained midwives to student midwives should be two midwives to one student in order to provide satisfactory supervision and training. This figure is calculated for the whole maternity unit establishment, although a variation between the different clinical areas would be anticipated with a higher ratio in the delivery area and a conversely lower ratio in the antenatal and postnatal wards. Students must gain their experience in units sufficiently large to provide both training schools and sufficient workloads of women having babies. Hence they are less likely to be present in units doing fewer deliveries.

Effect of the size of unit

In Table 4.5 the distribution of the number of student midwives reported is shown by size of unit. The numbers are shown for August, figures for the other months are similar and indicate a similar trend in the fall on the Saturday as there was for trained midwives. As previously shown there were very few student midwives in the smaller units at 11 am and 3 pm and only one at 7 pm and 11 pm.

No student midwives were reported in the 'not grouped' size units in August although a few were available in the other months. The majority of student midwives were present in large and very large group of units and student midwives were almost absent from the small units.

In the earlier tables a large number of units were presented including some without student midwives on duty, and so we were unable to demonstrate the ratio of trained midwifery staff to student midwives within individual units. In Figure 4.8 only those units with a student midwife on duty are examined and are related to the four sizes of delivery unit.

It is obvious that the student midwives gained their experience in the larger and medium sized units. During the day and evening, a higher ratio of student midwives to each woman in labour existed in the medium sized and larger units. However, at 11 pm there was greater evidence of student midwives in the larger units. In contrast, the mean ratio of midwives to provide instructional supervision to students receiving it increases with size of unit. However, at 11 am there were fewest midwives and students in the large unit. A similar trend was seen on each of the days of the week at 7 pm, with no significant variation in supervision on the Saturday.

Effect of the type of unit

When examined by type of unit (which relates to the medical cover given as described early in the chapter) the distribution of midwifery students is even

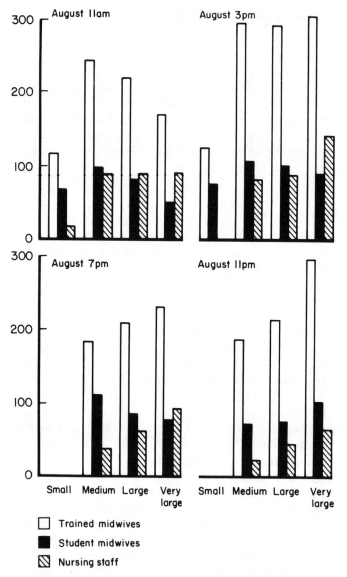

Figure 4.8   Mean ratio of trained midwives, student midwives and nurses per 100 women in labour by size of unit at four survey times in August

more marked as shown in Table 4.3. Over 95 per cent of midwifery students were reported to work in units with a consultant cover rather than those of general practitioners.

Effect of the time of day

The tables show the availability of students by time of day. As with trained midwives, the numbers of students were highest in the afternoon during the overlap while the numbers on duty at night were half those of the day figures.

Minimum ratios of trained staff to student midwives

A further approach to analysing the supervision provided by trained staff over student midwives is to consider the number of units in which there were fewer than two midwives per student on duty. In Figure 4.8, the minimum levels are expressed in terms of the ratio of trained staff to students for the month of August. The highest proportion of units with these minimum ratios was the medium-sized ones for most times surveyed in that day. In general, the number of units with less than one midwife per student was very few throughout those surveyed.

OTHER NURSING STAFF

Midwives were asked to record the number of support staff in the delivery area;

TABLE 4.11   Total numbers of other nursing staff by delivery group (August)

	Small	Medium	Large	Very large	Not grouped
11 am					
Theatre trained					
nursing staff	7	4	29	24	0
Student nurse	21	71	87	18	2
Other staff	171	163	153	49	3
3 pm					
Theatre trained					
nursing staff	11	3	24	20	1
Student nurse	25	86	118	29	3
Other staff	157	155	136	61	4
7 pm					
Theatre trained					
nursing staff	4	1	12	9	0
Student nurse	15	41	61	15	3
Other staff	134	111	90	37	3
11 pm					
Theatre trained					
nursing staff	5	0	10	5	0
Student nurse	1	0	0	0	0
Other staff	138	108	108	29	3

TABLE 4.12   Total numbers of other nursing staff by delivery group (November)

	Small	Medium	Large	Very large	Not grouped
11 am					
Theatre trained					
nursing staff	11	6	30	8	0
Student nurse	12	85	73	19	4
Other staff	184	146	154	42	8
3 pm					
Theatre trained					
nursing staff	8	5	16	13	0
Student nurse	8	101	106	28	8
Other staff	172	136	162	44	5
7 pm					
Theatre trained					
nursing staff	9	1	6	6	0
Student nurse	5	47	48	14	6
Other staff	134	111	123	30	6
11 pm					
Theatre trained					
nursing staff	7	1	7	6	0
Student nurse	0	1	0	0	0
Other staff	128	106	117	26	10

these were classified as auxiliary nursing staff, theatre trained nursing staff and student nurses. The role played by these staff in the delivery area is discussed in Chapter 2.

In Tables 4.11 and 4.12 the total numbers of other nursing staff recorded for the four times of day are shown for August and November. Over half of the support staff included in this group are nursing auxiliaries. While some theatre trained nursing staff are available in the small and medium sized units at all times of the day, a far larger number were available in the large and very large units as might be expected. Student nurses were also more commonly found in the larger units.

The numbers of auxiliaries were lowest in the evening and at night for each month as were those of the trained midwifery staff. The numbers of theatre trained nursing staff were even fewer and student nurses were virtually absent with only one being recorded in the whole country at 11 pm in August (Wednesday) and again in November (Thursday). The numbers of each group recorded over the three weekdays are similar and lowest on the Saturday. Both theatre trained nursing staff and student nurses show the greatest decrease in numbers in their availability over the weekend.

REGIONAL VARIATIONS

In Chapter 2, the distribution of maternity units throughout the United Kingdom was examined. It showed the difference in the number of deliveries carried out and the sizes and types of services according to the region. Variation in the distribution of units will affect the use of midwifery resources and the number of midwives and nursing staff available for any mother.

To examine the availability of midwifery and nursing staff by region, the numbers per 100 women in labour have been used. The mean for each region is shown in Tables 4.13 to 4.16 for August at 11 am, 3 pm, 7 pm and 11 pm. Analysis by region has been performed using the DHSS coding for England including Scotland, Wales and Northern Ireland as one region each.

The mean of midwives per 100 women in labour at 7 pm ranges from 148 in Scotland to 239 in Mersey; the variation continues to be wide, for each part of the country may need a differing range of maternity services and sizes of hospitals. Scotland is the largest of the regions and has a number of small hospitals while Mersey region has no GP units but is the smallest region with several very large units. Thus it is able to provide high ratios of midwife to woman in labour. Regions with a higher proportion of small units will distort the

TABLE 4.13   Mean ratios of midwives, student midwives and nursing staff to 100 women in labour by region at 11 am—August

	No.	Trained midwives	Student midwives	Other nursing staff
Northern	17	243	35	134
Yorkshire	17	222	39	117
Trent	18	182	65	69
East Anglia	8	201	41	49
North-West Thames	15	259	43	133
North-East Thames	21	219	48	101
South-East Thames	22	238	44	62
South-West Thames	13	214	47	88
Wessex	15	168	48	104
Oxford	9	222	36	81
South-Western	13	190	44	106
West Midlands	24	195	40	87
Mersey	8	303	52	108
North-Western	22	239	48	77
Wales	17	202	24	91
Scotland	25	173	62	86
Specials	2	121	25	53
Northern Ireland	17	295	36	79
Others	5	230	0	30

TABLE 4.14 Mean ratios of midwives, student midwives and nursing staff to 100 women in labour by region at 3 pm—August

	No.	Trained midwives	Student midwives	Other nursing staff
Northern	19	302	31	125
Yorkshire	16	276	65	103
Trent	15	293	62	111
East Anglia	8	349	68	106
North-West Thames	14	356	72	129
North-East Thames	22	332	89	112
South-East Thames	22	251	29	48
South-West Thames	12	291	34	71
Wessex	15	267	69	123
Oxford	9	216	50	85
South-Western	15	316	44	161
West Midlands	24	281	45	82
Mersey	9	332	72	135
North-Western	24	337	77	93
Wales	14	272	16	123
Scotland	24	246	86	97
Specials	1	250	0	300
Northern Ireland	13	277	41	86
Others	6	208	0	50

TABLE 4.15 Mean ratios of midwives, student midwives and nursing staff to 100 women in labour by region at 7 pm—August

	No.	Trained midwives	Student midwives	Other nursing staff
Northern	14	209	27	95
Yorkshire	11	155	26	78
Trent	20	170	45	65
East Anglia	7	208	23	82
North-West Thames	14	209	37	51
North-East Thames	21	186	40	83
South-East Thames	19	198	48	46
South-West Thames	11	166	18	53
Wessex	12	165	27	79
Oxford	11	165	41	75
South-Western	16	171	44	81
West Midlands	24	220	44	47
Mersey	10	239	82	75
North-Western	19	236	64	76
Wales	14	219	16	118
Scotland	23	147	105	42
Specials	2	155	25	50
Northern Ireland	12	234	48	68
Others	2	83	0	150

TABLE 4.16 Mean ratios of midwives, student midwives and nursing staff to 100 women in labour by region at 11 pm—August

	No.	Trained midwives	Student midwives	Other nursing staff
Northern	16	228	15	72
Yorkshire	14	213	10	42
Trent	18	161	12	34
East Anglia	6	392	25	79
North-West Thames	15	244	43	58
North-East Thames	16	244	26	39
South-East Thames	22	233	16	51
South-West Thames	12	180	30	25
Wessex	9	220	48	18
Oxford	9	259	72	92
South-Western	14	201	33	71
West Midlands	25	215	45	52
Mersey	9	244	40	64
North-Western	18	271	16	47
Wales	16	213	15	61
Scotland	23	181	27	57
Specials	2	150	50	33
Northern Ireland	9	196	29	42
Others	4	216	0	125

TABLE 4.17 Percentage of units with less than one midwife to woman in labour—August

Region	11 am	3 pm	7 pm	11 pm
Northern	13.4	3.1	30.0	19.2
Yorkshire	33.3	10.2	34.3	39.3
Trent	35.5	14.4	30.5	30.9
East Anglia	34.2	6.0	32.2	41.9
North-West Thames	22.3	10.7	35.5	35.2
North-East Thames	17.0	11.7	35.4	35.2
South-East Thames	33.3	17.0	38.6	24.3
South-West Thames	19.1	11.1	34.8	26.6
Wessex	32.0	18.8	52.2	29.2
Oxford	42.8	23.0	42.1	34.2
South-Western	30.1	15.5	41.3	53.5
West Midlands	37.1	20.5	52.0	31.2
Mersey	14.7	13.5	30.5	34.2
North-Western	30.4	11.4	32.9	28.1
Wales	41.9	26.7	37.5	40.0
Scotland	36.3	18.4	42.3	40.9
Specials	25.0	14.2	42.8	40.0
Northern Ireland	23.7	11.3	22.2	22.2
Others	22.7	4.7	27.2	55.5

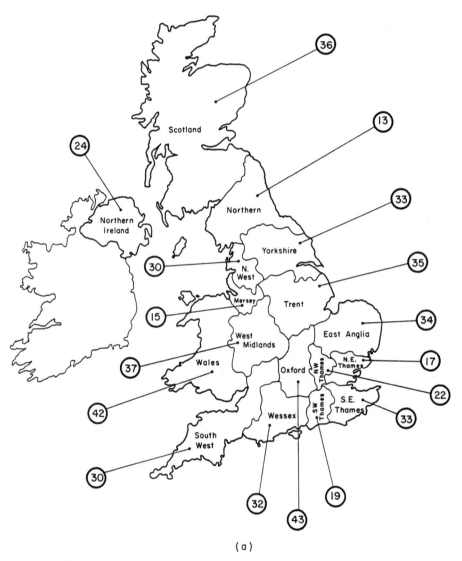

(a)

Figure 4.9 (a)   Percentage of units with less than one midwife per 100 women in labour
by regions in August—11 am

mean and will average fewer midwives per woman between units even though
these small units will account for few deliveries.

At 3 pm only 3.1 per cent of units in the Northern region and 6 per cent in
East Anglia had one or fewer midwives per woman in labour and this figure
rose to 23 per cent of units in Oxford and 26.7 per cent of units in Wales (Table
4.14).

At 7 pm, 22 per cent of units in Northern Ireland and 30 per cent of units in

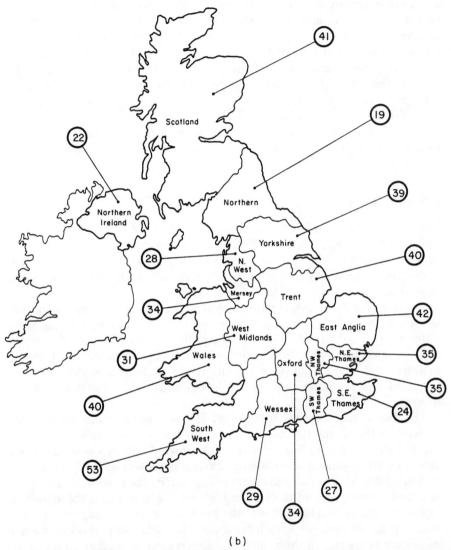

(b)

Figure 4.9 (b)   Percentage of units with less than one midwife per 100 women in labour
by regions in August—11 pm

the Northern region had minimal levels while over half the units in Wessex and
West Midlands, 52.2 per cent and 52.0 per cent, had one or fewer midwives per
woman in labour. The Northern region also had the fewest units with low levels
of midwifery staffing at 11 am and at 11 pm (Tables 4.15 and 4.16; see also
Figure 4.9).

Student midwives were trained in all regions. The mean of the numbers per woman in labour are also distorted by small units where student midwives were absent since no training was undertaken. However, the average ratio of students to women was highest in Scotland (105.5) and Mersey (80.5), while lowest ratios were 16.6 in Wales and 18.1 in South-West Thames.

Another way of assessing midwifery and nursing services by region is to consider the critically low levels as discussed earlier in this chapter. In Table 4.17, the percentage of units in each region with one or fewer midwives per woman in labour is shown for the four months together and for each of the four times a day. Each region conforms with the national figures in having least units with minimum numbers of midwives at 3 pm and the highest numbers at 7 pm and 11 pm.

CONCLUSIONS

The total numbers of midwifery and nursing staff allocated to the delivery area suggest that the English National Board's recommendations for ratios between different groups of staff are met at least at the place of birth. Of the trained midwifery staff, there is an equal proportion of experienced midwives, shown in the ratios of midwifery sisters to staff midwives.

The results of the analysis of the ratios of midwives and other nursing staff to women in labour describe the facilities available to any mother delivering in the different type and size of units or in any of the regions. These relate only to those women in labour, this figure correlating closest to the total annual delivery rate. These data do not relate to the additional workload of the antenatal and postnatal cases in the labour ward, approximately half the women.

The data cannot show the role of staff in those units in which there was no activity on the survey day nor their workload during such inactive periods. Nevertheless, in the smaller units when labour ward activity was irregular, the ratio of staff to women was lowest and minimum levels were highest.

Availability of midwives and other nursing staff increases with the size of unit and the decreasing proportion of normal deliveries to be conducted by midwives.

Student midwives add further to the establishment in the larger units. The majority are in large or very large units where the proportion of normal midwifery is lowest. In these units the supervision of student midwives by trained midwives in terms of total numbers is highest.

REFERENCES

1. Report of the Maternity Services Advisory Committee. London: HMSO, 1982.
2. Central Management Services. *A Study of Hospital-based Midwives.* London: HMSO, 1984.
3. Robinson, S. *The Role and Responsibilities of the Midwife.* Chelsea College, London, 1979.

Birthplace
G.V.P. Chamberlain
© 1987 John Wiley & Sons Ltd.

CHAPTER 5

Obstetric Facilities

Naren Patel

INTRODUCTION

In the Second Report of The House of Commons Social Services Committee (1980) it was stated that 'Labour wards should be regarded as an intensive care area in which staffing and equipment are optimal'[1]. This chapter will deal almost entirely with the provision of obstetric staffing with a short section on medical students and on the obstetrical flying squad. The grade of obstetrician and discussion about their availability will be found in Chapter 3. The numbers and sizes of units and their distribution within the UK, detailed in Chapter 2, are outlined in Tables 5.1 and 5.2 while the obstetrical workload is shown in Table 5.3.

The survey examined the availability of obstetric staffing at 11 am and 11 pm on each of the four days. Data were collected about the whereabouts of the medical staff in four localities — in the delivery area, in the hospital, on call, available within 20 minutes or longer. The questions asked are to be found in Chapter 1. The data are analysed in several different ways looking at the whole survey by the size of the units (number of deliveries per year), by types of units (consultant, GP, private), and by regions. Comparisons were made about the

TABLE 5.1 Number and percentage of the units in each category

Total units	(n) 531	(%) 100
Deliveries		
Small 1–500	217	41
Medium 501–2000	149	29
Large 2001–4000	129	25
Very large >4000	26	5

TABLE 5.2   The number of each of the four types of obstetric units by regions

Regions	Consultant unit	Consultant & GP unit	Other	GP unit
Northern	16	5	0	7
Yorkshire	13	8	0	10
Trent	10	9	0	16
East Anglia	6	3	1	6
North-West Thames	13	5	0	2
North-East Thames	11	10	2	7
South-East Thames	13	8	2	4
South-West Thames	8	8	0	1
Wessex	9	2	0	19
Oxford	5	5	0	12
South-Western	4	8	1	23
West Midlands	16	7	0	18
Mersey	5	5	0	0
North-Western	13	8	0	9
Wales	15	6	0	16
Scotland	25	9	0	38
Specials	2	0	0	0
Northern Ireland	11	4	1	11
Others	0	3	13	0
TOTALS	195	113	20	199

availability of staffing on each of the four days. For the sake of brevity, often data are presented for one month only when there were no recognizable differences but comparative data from two different sampling times of 11 am and 11 pm are most often presented. The availability of all the various grades of

TABLE 5.3   Obstetric workload on each of the four survey days

Total deliveries	No.	Total %	No.	August %	No.	September %	No.	October %	No.	November %
SINGLETONS										
– Normal deliveries	6117	(75.2)	1539	(74.9)	1432	(77.4)	1653	(74.4)	1439	(74.4)
– Vaginal breech	131	(1.6)	22	(1.0)	24	(1.2)	42	(1.8)	43	(2.1)
– Vaginal operative cephalic	890	(10.9)	226	(11.0)	219	(11.8)	234	(10.5)	211	(10.5)
– Emergency Caesarean	585	(7.1)	140	(6.8)	150	(6.8)	166	(7.4)	129	(6.4)
– Elective Caesarean	335	(4.1)	110	(5.3)	24	(1.2)	91	(4.1)	110	(5.4)
TWIN DELIVERIES	96	(1.1)	17	(0.8)	18	(0.9)	34	(1.5)	27	(1.3)
TOTALS	8154	(100)	2054	(100)	1867	(100)	2219	(100)	2013	(100)

TABLE 5.4 Numbers of obstetricians reported on August survey day in all units

Grade	Delivery area	In hospital	On premises	On call <20 min	On call >20 min	Total
11 am						
Consultant	42	299	341	149	47	537
Senior registrar	26	80	106	13	10	129
Registrar post-MRCOG	33	133	166	20	8	194
Registrar pre-MRCOG	40	120	160	17	8	185
SHO	176	390	566	40	11	617
GPO	19	68	87	1513	333	1933
Other[a]	8	29	37	17	3	57
11 pm						
Consultant	7	15	22	282	50	354
Senior registrar	19	26	45	36	7	88
Registrar post-MRCOG	36	51	87	24	4	115
Registrar pre-MRCOG	33	69	102	18	2	122
SHO	156	176	332	27	6	365
GPO	10	7	17	1009	211	1237
Other[a]	0	3	3	12	0	15

[a] Clinical assistants or associate specialists.

staff has not been analysed separately on each occasion. Here, as in Chapters 6 and 7, the editors have provided full data of medical staffing as appendix tables 1–8.

TOTAL NUMBERS OF OBSTETRICIANS ON DUTY

The full details of obstetricians available on each day of the study at 11 am and 11 pm are grouped in the tables in the appendix to this chapter (Tables 5A.1 to 5A.8).

Table 5.4 shows the numbers of obstetricians at the 11 am and 11 pm sample points arranged by their proximity to the place of birth. Those in the labour area and in the hospital (columns 1 and 2) are added together to make column 3 — those on the premises and therefore on immediate call for the labour ward. Again the special position of the GP, who goes in only when his own patients are in labour, is remembered. The clinical assistant and associated specialist grade are very small, comprising only 2.0 per cent of all the obstetricians or 3.3 per cent of the hospital obstetricians reported. This probably reflects their major use in outpatients, wards and gynaecological operating theatres rather than in the labour room.

Table 5.5 gives some impression of the proportion of the total obstetrical workforce on duty for the labour ward. The difference between 11 am and 11 pm can be seen. About two-thirds of the daytime staff numbers in all grades are

TABLE 5.5   Total obstetricians on duty for delivery area at 11 am and 11 pm. All survey days

	August		September		October		November	
	11 am	11 pm	11 am	11 pm	11 am	11 pm	11 am	11 pm
Consultant	537	354	362	354	501	349	461	376
Senior registrar	179	88	104	85	137	90	141	105
Registrar	379	237	243	234	344	251	319	235
SHO	617	365	310	355	484	331	507	362

on duty at night and this has implications for the rest of the work to be done. The consultants and senior registrars are mostly on call from home and would only be brought in to hospital for problems. The majority of the registrars and SHOs live in and often are at work for much of the night. Their proportions are smaller, otherwise the next day's elective work would be done by a tired team.

The numbers of doctors available at each grade are shown in Figures 5.1 and 5.2 for 11 am and 11 pm respectively. The drop at the weekend (September) is noticeable for all grades in the daytime; this is not apparent at 11 pm when the clustering of those on duty every month is much tighter at all grades.

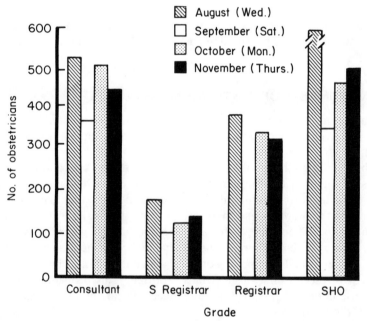

Figure 5.1   Numbers of obstetricians by various grades available for delivery area at 11 am on the four days of survey

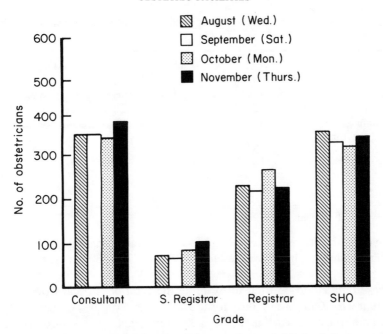

Figure 5.2   Numbers of obstetricians by various grades available for delivery area at 11 pm on the four days of survey

Number covering for the labour ward

In the daytime, 70 per cent of the consultants covered the labour ward in August, 47 per cent in September (a weekend), 66 per cent in October and 60 per cent in November. Hence, on weekdays probably two-thirds of all consultants are on call for the labour ward in addition to the rest of their workload. At 11 pm the respective percentages were 46, 46, 47 and 49 so just under half of all the obstetric and gynaecological consultants are on call at night for the labour ward.

Senior registrars show a different pattern. At 11 am, the numbers of appointed staff on duty for labour wards were 179, 104, 137 and 141 implying that in the daytime the majority of senior registrars cover the labour wards. At night time these reduce to 88, 85, 90 and 105 but two-thirds are still on duty for the labour wards.

Registrars are in training. They were on duty in the daytime in 77, 69, 70 and 62 per cent of units; at night, they were on duty 48, 47, 51 and 47 per cent of the time. This reflects the greater amount of fixed 'off duty' the registrars get but it does not add up to the wide implementation of a 1 : 3 rota of night duties recommended.

The senior house officers (SHOs) performed less cover for women in labour.

TABLE 5.6 Number and percentage of doctors on call who were on the premises (August)

	11 am			11 pm		
	n on premises	Total	(%)	*n* on premises	Total	(%)
Consultant	341	537	63.5	22	354	6.2
Senior registrar	80	129	62.0	45	88	51.1
Registrar	326	381	85.6	189	237	79.7
SHO	566	617	91.7	332	365	91.0
GPO	68	1933	3.5	17	1237	1.4
Other[a]	37	57	64.9	3	15	20.0

[a] Mostly clinical assistants and associate specialists.

In daytime, the proportion of the total workforce covering was 49, 29, 40 and 42 per cent while at night this was reduced to 29, 28, 27 and 30 per cent, more like a 1 : 3 rota.

These data could be used to examine the total obstetrical workforce in a different way. Of those on duty for the labour area on the August day (11 am and 11 pm) the proportion actually on the premises can be assessed (Table 5.6). It might be expected that registrars and SHOs would have a high representation both by day and night while consultants and senior registrars, being on call, might not be present in the evening sample on the premises. The GP will only be there when needed as previously explained and the remaining group was very small. These findings are shown diagrammatically in Figure 5.3.

A further analysis of those on the premises is made later in Chapter 9.

OBSTETRIC STAFF IN AND ON CALL FOR DELIVERY AREA

Table 5.7 illustrates the proportions of consultants and senior house officers in the delivery area at 11 am and 11 pm on each of four survey days. The

TABLE 5.7 Percentage of the total obsetric units with consultants and SHOs in the delivery area at 11 am and 11 pm on each of the four survey days

	Consultants (%)		SHOs (%)	
	am	pm	am	pm
August	8	1	34	30
September	7	1	29	24
October	5	1	34	26
November	7	2	35	24
Mean	7	1.3	33	26

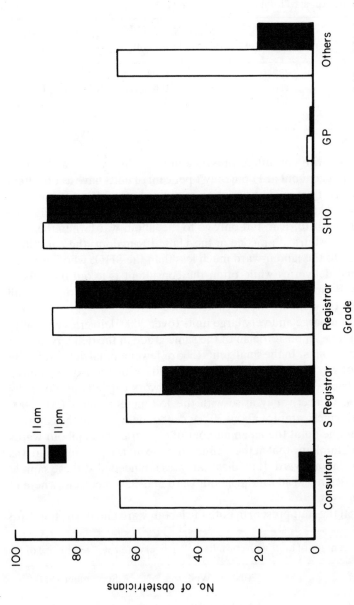

Figure 5.3   Numbers of obstetricians by various grades who were on the premises at 11 am and 11 pm (August)

TABLE 5.8   Numbers of obstetricians of any grade in the delivery area reported by
unit by size of unit. August 11 am and September 11 am. Total number (n) and mean

Size of unit	No. of units in August	August (Wed)		September (Sat)	
		n	*mean*/unit	n	*mean*/unit
1–500	222	19	0.08	22	0.18
501–2000	150	95	0.6	101	0.7
2001–4000	130	177	1.4	153	1.2
>4000	25	53	2.1	46	1.8

percentage of units with consultant presence in the delivery area at 11 am is
approximately 7 per cent but at 11 pm only 1 per cent of units have a consultant
actually in the delivery area. The variation in senior house officer presence is
much less marked: 33 per cent at 11 am and 26 per cent at 11 pm. This might be
expected for senior obstetrical staff only go to the labour ward when the need
arises. In current obstetrical practice in the United Kingdom, the consultant
tends to be called to the labour ward much less than the SHO, who has many
tasks with normal deliveries while often the consultant is asked only about
major problems. Perhaps more important is the presence of obstetricians of all
grades in total in the delivery area (Table 5.8).

This shows that in large and very large units (over 2000 deliveries annually)
there was on average an obstetrician of the same grade in the delivery area at
each of the sample points. In the small units (500 or fewer annual deliveries) the
mean presence of any obstetrician was very low but, as previously explained,
this might have been expected with the pattern of work carried out mostly by
GP obstetricians. Concern may arise with the 150 medium units (501–2000
deliveries a year) which cater for about 30 per cent of deliveries in the country.
Here, at each sample point the mean number of obstetricians in labour wards
was less than one, implying that at these times in some units no obstetrician was
specifically in the labour ward. If medical care was not needed at these sample
times, the obstetrician on call for the labour ward may have been elsewhere in
the hospital premises.

If we accept that the staff present in both the labour ward and the hospital are

TABLE 5.9   Percentage of units with consultant in delivery area at 11 am by size of unit

Size of unit	August (Wed)	September (Sat)
1–500	0.4	0.0
501–2000	6.0	9.0
2001–4000	20.0	15.0
>4000	25.0	8.0

TABLE 5.10   Percentage of units with consultant in hospital at 11 am by size of unit

Size of unit	August (Wed) (%)	September (Sat) (%)
1–500	12	4
501–2000	87	21
2001–4000	90	19
>4000	108	36

readily available for the care of the labouring women, then the pattern is somewhat different. As an example, compare Tables 5.9 and 5.10. During weekdays at the sampling time of 11 am nearly 65 per cent of the units have a consultant available, either in the delivery area or in the hospital. On a Saturday, the figures are reduced but the comparison remains the same (4 per cent) at 11 pm.

Figure 5.4 shows that this pattern exists for all the grades of doctors. It also shows the difference in staffing levels between day and night. Staffing is somewhat different in the general practitioner units. Because of the obvious commitments of general practice there are large numbers of GPs available on call within 20 minutes of the GP units but fewer numbers are actually present on the premises or in the delivery area. Unless he has one of the patients he has contracted to deliver actually in the unit in labour, there is no reason why a GP should be at the place of delivery.

The figures for the availability of different grades of staff on each of the four survey days at the two survey times for the other months are very similar to those for August (Figure 5.4) excepting for the daytime at the weekend (Figure 5.1). During the day (11 am) 54 per cent of the units had consultants available on immediate call and 88 per cent had SHOs available on call. During the night the grade most commonly available was the SHO. At night (11 pm) 4 per cent of the units had consultants available on the premises compared with 60 per cent of the units with SHOs available.

EFFECTS OF THE SIZE OF UNIT

When the availability of the staffing for the whole survey is examined, including the large number of small units delivering a relatively small percentage of the total deliveries (40 per cent of units accounting for 5 per cent of deliveries), the figures are diluted as these units are not staffed permanently on a 24-hour basis. It is therefore useful to look at staffing according to the size of the units. The large and very large units, delivering more than 2000 babies per year, had some obstetric staff available in the delivery area at 11 am and the larger of the units often had two doctors available. The small units showed a

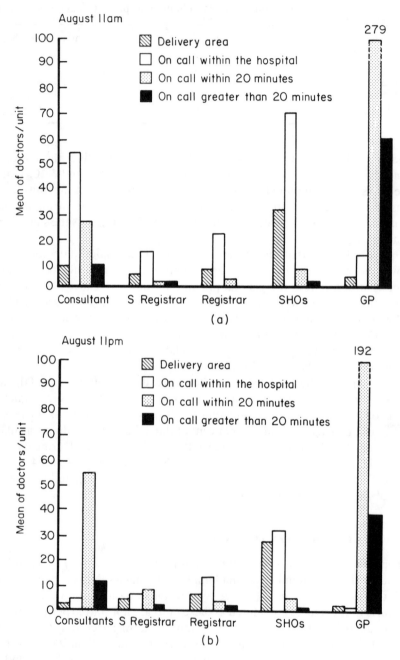

Figure 5.4 Ratios of units reporting the availability of obstetricians of various seniorities (August) (a) 11 am   (b) 11 pm

TABLE 5.11   Percentage of units with consultant in delivery area at 11 am by size of unit

	August (Wed)	September (Sat)	October (Mon)	November (Thur)
1–500	0.4	0.0	0.9	2.2
501–2000	6.0	9.0	9.0	3.0
2001–4000	20.0	15.0	6.0	17.0
>4000	25.0	8.0	12.0	12.0

pattern where only 1 in 10 units had a doctor available in the delivery area. The figures show the same kind of staffing availability on Saturday at 11 am (Table 5.8).

The availability of consultants in the delivery area by size of unit is compared on the four study days (Table 5.11). There appears to be a wide variation in the percentage of units with consultant presence even in large and very large hospitals which probably reflects the need and work pattern. If the consultant is not required in the delivery area, he may well be present in the hospital carrying out other duties as shown in the previous section of this chapter.

Nonetheless, it does appear that the small and medium units again fair badly. The majority of the small and medium units appear to have a lower availability of consultants in the delivery area at 11 am on weekdays and on Saturdays. The percentage of those units having a consultant in the delivery area varies from 3 per cent to 9 per cent. More of the large and very large units had a consultant available in the delivery area. This is not the case on a Saturday but at that time most of the units have a consultant on call within 20 minutes. This is interesting when the workload in the delivery areas on weekdays and Saturdays is compared (Table 5.11).

Analysis of the data for the medium units indicates that only 5 per cent have a consultant further than 20 minutes away on call.

Figures 5.5–5.7 illustrate the availability of various grades of staff in three groups of units on the August study day. For the reasons given, units delivering less than 500 women a year are not considered here. To a larger extent they are analysed in Chapter 9. The grade mostly available for the delivery area is a senior house officer but the middle and senior grades are available within the hospital, probably involved with other duties such as clinics or in the operating theatre. On weekdays, 90 per cent of the units have a consultant available either in the delivery area or hospital at 11 am, the figure for Saturday being 30 per cent.

The large units, presumably with their larger staff numbers, are able more easily to provide staff in the delivery area at registrar and SHO grades. There is access to a consultant available in the hospital in nearly all of these units on

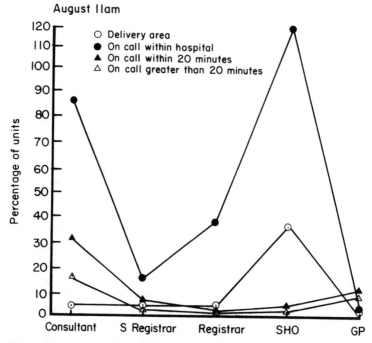

Figure 5.5   Percentage of medium sized units (501–2000 deliveries a year) showing availability of obstetrician by grade (August 11 am)

weekdays at 11 am while at the weekend 40 per cent of the units are so provided.

Table 5.12 shows the availability of the most senior doctor for duty in the delivery area or in the hospital by size of unit. In the small units at 11 am, 55 per cent had no doctor of any grade in the hospital; 26 per cent of deliveries were covered by consultants; and 14 per cent by general practitioners.

In the medium units only 4 per cent of the delivery areas were not covered by a doctor in the delivery area or hospital. Large and very large units with over

TABLE 5.12   Most senior doctor available in the delivery area or hospital – percentage of deliveries covered – 11 am August – by size of unit

Size of units	Con- sultant	Senior registrar	Registrar	SHO	GP	None	Total (%)
1–500	26	—	—	5	14	55	100
501–2000	74	9	7	5	1	4	100
2001–4000	75	5	13	6	—	—	99
>4000	91	7	2	—	—	—	100

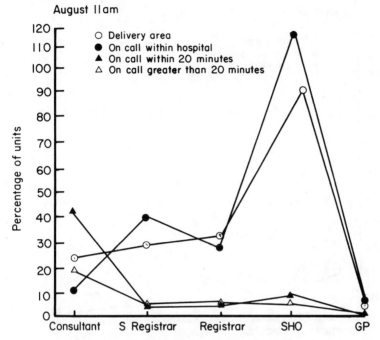

Figure 5.6   Percentage of large sized units (2001–4000 deliveries a year) showing availability of obstetrician by grade (August 11 am)

2000 deliveries were better staffed. The larger the unit, the more likely that a consultant would be available in the delivery area or in the hospital. In units delivering more than 4000 per year 91 per cent of the deliveries had a consultant on the premises.

The position in the daytime at the weekend is shown by comparing Tables 5.12 and 5.13. Beyond one medium unit reporting no doctor at all available, the total cover by hospital size is similar to that on a weekday. However, the shift inside the grades already referred to is again seen. The units with a consultant,

TABLE 5.13   Most senior doctor available in the delivery area or hospital – percentage of deliveries covered – 11 am September – by size of unit

Size of units	Con-sultant	Senior registrar	Registrar	SHO	GP	None	Total (%)
1–500	3	3	17	—	11	64	98
501–2000	28	14	36	14	3	5	100
2001–4000	33	11	49	6	—	1	100
>4000	39	27	34	—	—	—	100

August 11am

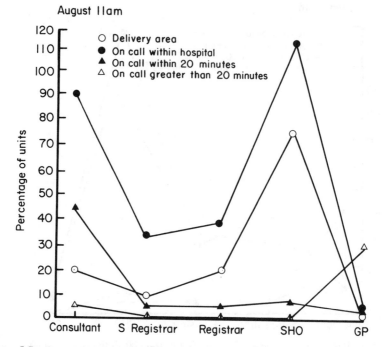

Figure 5.7 Percentage of very large sized units (4000+ deliveries a year) showing availability of obstetrician by grade (August 11 am)

as the most senior obstetrician to turn to immediately, are halved but senior registrar numbers are greatly increased particularly in the large and very large units (5 to 11 per cent and 7 to 27 per cent respectively). Many more units report registrars as being the most senior doctor on call and this applies to small, medium, large and very large units (0 to 17, 7 to 36, 13 to 49 and 2 to 34 per cent respectively), a more than three-fold increase.

A similar comparison can be made of units between day and night by comparing Tables 5.12 and 5.14 showing respectively 11 am and 11 pm data for

TABLE 5.14   Most senior doctor available in the delivery area or hospital and percentage of deliveries covered – 11 pm August – by size of unit

Size of units	Con-sultant	Senior registrar	Registrar	SHO	GP	None	Total (%)
1–500	7	—	—	7	7	79	100
501–2000	9	7	34	45	—	4	99
2001–4000	10	24	55	8	—	4	101
>4000	6	38	56	—	—	—	100

TABLE 5.15 Most senior doctor available for delivery area only by type of unit. August 11 am (figures relate to percentages of units)

Type of unit	None	Con-sultant	Senior registrar	Registrar	SHO	GP	Total (%)
Consultant/ Con. + GP	70	1	1	10	18	—	100
GP units	99	—	—	—	—	1	100
Other	83	8	—	—	—	—	91

August. Here the shift goes even further so that the registrars are the most senior obstetrician on the premises in over four-fold of the large and very large units.

EFFECTS OF THE TYPE OF UNIT

While the number of doctors available on call solely for the delivery area is confined to a small number of hospitals, senior obstetric cover is available for the majority of the women in labour, particularly in consultant units. If an obstetrician was reported as being on duty for the labour ward, he may have been performing another task at the time such as an outpatient clinic. The more senior the doctor, the more likely that would be.

Analysis of the data from the confidential enquiry was carried out to determine the most senior doctor available solely for the delivery area according to the type of unit. The question asked was 'Are there any obstetricians on duty for the Delivery Area with no other responsibilities for other areas of the maternity unit?'

Of the consultant and consultant/general practitioner units, 70 per cent had no doctor available solely for the delivery area at 11 am and 1 per cent of the units had a consultant available (Table 5.15). In 28 per cent of the units there was a registrar or senior house officer solely available in the delivery area. In the general practitioner unit 99 per cent of the units had no doctor available in the delivery area but these units do deliver low risk cases and only account for 5 per cent of the total deliveries.

At 11 pm 82 per cent of the consultant units did not have a doctor solely on duty for the delivery area (Table 5.16). A registrar or a SHO was available in 16 per cent of the units. No doctor was available in 96 per cent of the GP units.

The picture was different when examined against the percentage of deliveries covered by these staff in the hospital. Table 5.17 shows that on 1 August at 11 am 78 per cent of total deliveries in the UK were covered by a consultant available either in the delivery area or in the hospital in the consultant units. Another 16 per cent of women delivering in these units had a senior registrar or

TABLE 5.16   Most senior doctor available for delivery area only by type of unit. August 11 pm (figures relate to percentages of units)

Type of unit	None	Con-sultant	Senior registrar	Registrar	SHO	GP	Total (%)
Consultant/ Con. + GP	82	1	1	7	9	—	100
GP units	96	4	—	7	—	—	100
Other	100	—	—	—	—	—	100

registrar immediately available. In only 5 per cent was the most senior doctor available in the hospital a senior house officer who may or may not have been experienced and 1 per cent seemed to have no doctor solely on duty to cover them.

In the general practitioner units, 68 per cent of the deliveries had no doctor available on immediate call in the hospital; in 24 per cent of the deliveries a general practitioner was available in the delivery area or hospital, which may reflect the usage of the unit for if one of his patients was not in labour, the general practitioner obstetrician (GPO) would have no reason to be there.

Compared with weekdays, on Saturday at 11 am only 33 per cent of deliveries in consultant units have a consultant available in the hospital (Table 5.18). The middle grades, senior registrar or registrar, are available on the premises for 56 per cent of deliveries in these units.

At 11 pm on 1 August the senior registrar and registrar consultant units were available to cover 67 per cent of the deliveries (Table 5.19). There was a higher percentage of deliveries covered by SHOs (19 per cent) at this time. Only 4 per cent of the units did not have a doctor available in the hospital whereas 79 per cent of the GP units did not have a doctor available. This fits with the probable load, as the larger the unit the more likely there would be someone in labour in that hospital who needed attention. In GP units if no one was in labour, there would be no doctor there.

TABLE 5.17   Most senior doctor in delivery area or hospital – percentage of deliveries covered – 11 am August

Unit type	None	Con-sultant	Senior registrar	Registrar	SHO	GP	Total (%)
Con./Con. + GP + Private	1	78	7	9	5	—	99
GP	68	8	—	—	—	24	100
Other	33	50	—	—	—	—	83

TABLE 5.18 Most senior doctor available in delivery area or hospital – percentage of deliveries covered – 11 am September by type of unit

Unit type	None	Con-sultant	Senior registrar	Registrar	SHO	GP	Total (%)
Con./Con. + GP	1	33	14	42	7	1	98
GP	67	5	—	15	—	13	100
Other	—	—	100	—	—	—	100

TABLE 5.19 Most senior doctor available in delivery area or hospital – percentage of deliveries covered – 11 pm August by type of unit

Unit type	None	Con-sultant	Senior registrar	Registrar	SHO	GP	Total (%)
Con./Con. + GP	4	9	20	47	19	—	99
GP	79	8	—	4	4	4	99
Other	—	50	17	—	16	17	100

AVAILABILITY OF OBSTETRICIANS PER HUNDRED WOMEN IN LABOUR

In smaller units delivering only a few patients a day it is unnecessary to have a doctor present all the time; the larger units make it possible for a doctor to be available as he or she could be supervising several deliveries a day. Examination of figures for the number of obstetricians (all grades) present in the delivery area shows a striking uniformity on the four study days and between 11 am and 11 pm. There are, on average, 41 doctors (range 36–48) per 100 women in labour, nearly one doctor for every two women in labour at both times throughout the four days (see Table 5.20).

The grade of obstetrician available per 100 women in labour is shown in

TABLE 5.20 Percentage of all grades of obstetricians in delivery area on all four days of survey per 100 women in labour

	11 am	11 pm
August	43	48
September	44	41
October	36	39
November	39	38

TABLE 5.21   Obstetricians by grade available for the delivery area – rate per 100 women in labour

	Consultant and senior registrar		Registrar and SHO	
	11 am	11 pm	11 am	11 pm
August	9	5	31	42
September	8	4	32	34
October	5	3	29	34
November	6	5	30	31

Table 5.21 and the number of consultants and senior registrars in the delivery area per 100 women in labour on the four study days at 11 am and 11 pm. On average during the day, one senior doctor is available for every 14 women in labour compared to one for every 25 women at night time. Registrars and senior house officers are much more readily available. During day and night one doctor (SHO) is available for every three women in labour.

Even among the very large units delivering over 4000 deliveries per year, 42 per cent had no doctor in the delivery area at the sample time but 15 per cent of these units had two doctors solely on duty for the delivery area only.

TABLE 5.22   Presence of obstetricians in the delivery area by regions. Rate per 100 women in labour at 11 am and 11 pm – August

	Consultant		All registrars		Senior house officer		GPs	
	am	pm	am	pm	am	pm	am	pm
Northern	2.5	—	12.5	25.0	32.5	28.5	—	—
Yorkshire	7.4	—	1.8	9.7	24.0	21.9	1.8	4.8
Trent	3.1	—	7.9	18.1	15.8	25.0	4.7	—
East Anglia	—	—	16.6	30.0	25.0	50.0	—	—
North-West Thames	6.0	—	21.2	11.4	36.3	31.4	—	2.8
North-East Thames	5.0	—	11.6	18.4	15.0	47.3	—	—
South-East Thames	8.9	—	5.3	9.3	19.6	18.6	1.7	—
South-West Thames	10.0	3.8	16.6	19.2	23.3	19.2	3.3	—
Wessex	2.5	—	2.5	26.6	12.5	53.3	—	6.6
Oxford	—	—	11.3	12.5	11.3	33.3	4.5	—
South-Western	3.4	—	17.2	8.0	51.7	20.0	6.8	8.0
West Midlands	4.0	2.0	13.5	16.3	17.5	20.4	2.7	2.0
Mersey	9.0	—	22.7	18.1	36.3	18.1	—	—
North-Western	6.4	—	4.8	11.5	27.4	30.7	3.7	—
Wales	—	—	17.7	13.6	11.1	22.7	—	—
Scotland	12.9	4.5	12.9	21.1	22.0	30.3	1.2	—
Specials	—	—	9.0	33.3	9.0	33.3	—	—
Northern Ireland	4.0	7.1	8.0	21.4	10.0	64.2	4.0	—
Others	—	16.6	14.2	—	57.1	33.3	28.5	50.0

TABLE 5.23 Presence of obstetricians in the hospital by regions. Rate per 100 women in labour at 11 am and 11 pm – August

	Consultant		All registrars		Senior house officer		GPs	
	am	pm	am	pm	am	pm	am	pm
Northern	45.0	—	50.0	28.5	57.5	42.8	2.5	—
Yorkshire	40.7	2.4	25.9	21.9	37.0	26.8	1.8	—
Trent	30.1	2.2	34.9	18.1	36.5	18.1	—	—
East Anglia	33.3	10.0	20.8	30. 0	50.0	60.0	4.1	—
North-West Thames	51.5	5.7	51.5	34.2	27.2	22.8	15.1	—
North-East Thames	30.0	—	40.0	31.5	36.6	15.7	26.6	—
South-East Thames	26.7	—	44.6	27.9	55.3	41.8	—	—
South-West Thames	43.3	3.8	70.0	23.0	36.6	34.6	—	—
Wessex	37.5	—	47.5	33.3	55.0	53.3	27.5	—
Oxford	18.1	—	27.2	29.1	38.6	20.8	9.0	—
South-Western	55.1	8.0	48.2	24.0	68.9	44.8	34.4	—
West Midlands	33.7	—	33.7	22.4	45.9	22.4	—	2.04
Mersey	22.7	4.5	45.4	27.2	54.4	27.2	—	—
North-Western	41.9	—	45.1	53.8	59.6	92.3	2.2	3.8
Wales	57.7	4.5	62.2	50.0	91.1	63.6	8.8	—
Scotland	23.3	4.5	37.6	15.1	46.7	13.6	14.2	3.0
Specials	18.1	—	9.0	16.6	9.0	—	—	—
Northern Ireland	34.0	7.1	20.0	14.2	32.0	42.8	2.0	—
Others	157.1	16.6	42.8	50.0	42.8	66.6	28.5	50.0

OBSTETRIC STAFF BY REGION

The availability of different grades of obstetrician varies from region to region. The differences may reflect the populations, size of units or geography. The distribution of the different types of units in the regions will also have some influence on the staffing available. Tables 5.22 to 5.25 show the breakdown of the staff of different grades, available at the two sampling times on 1 August, in the delivery area, in the hospital or on call within 20 minutes of the delivery area or more than 20 minutes from the hospital; the figures are shown as a rate per 100 women in labour.

The units with a consultant actually in the labour ward at 11 am range from 13 per cent in Scotland and 10 per cent in South-West Thames to 0 per cent in Oxford, East Anglia and Wales. The mean rate of consultants in the labour ward at 11 am and 11 pm is 4.5 and 1.8 respectively, per 100 women in labour.

The mean rate of consultant availability within hospital rises to 42 per 100 women in labour at 11 am (Table 5.23). This is a better measure of immediate cover and evens out some of the extremes seen in Table 5.22. The numbers of consultants per 100 women in labour range from 58 per cent in Wales to 18 per cent in Oxford and the special hospitals (private and service sector). The

TABLE 5.24 Availability of obstetricians within 20 minutes of the delivery area by regions. Rate per 100 women in labour at 11 am and 11 pm – August

	Consultant		Registrars		Senior house officer		GPs	
	am	pm	am	pm	am	pm	am	pm
Northern	15.0	60.7	2.5	10.7	2.5	—	105.0	117.8
Yorkshire	16.6	51.2	9.2	14.6	16.6	4.8	157.4	168.2
Trent	9.5	38.6	6.3	6.8	1.5	4.5	206.3	188.6
East Anglia	25.0	90.0	4.1	30.0	—	—	362.5	340.0
North-West Thames	27.2	48.5	9.0	17.1	18.1	—	72.7	82.5
North-East Thames	20.0	39.4	6.6	15.7	1.6	—	98.3	115.7
South-East Thames	16.0	37.2	5.3	13.9	3.5	9.3	58.9	2.3
South-West Thames	23.3	42.3	—	15.3	3.3	7.6	53.3	69.2
Wessex	12.5	80.0	7.5	20.0	7.5	13.3	232.5	500.0
Oxford	6.8	41.6	4.5	20.8	—	—	284.0	425.0
South-Western	44.8	44.0	10.3	12.0	24.1	40.0	606.8	268.0
West Midlands	14.8	44.8	5.4	14.2	5.4	20.4	404.0	442.8
Mersey	40.9	59.0	9.0	—	—	—	—	—
North-Western	4.8	73.0	—	33.3	—	—	70.9	192.3
Wales	22.2	63.6	11.1	36.3	4.4	4.5	35.5	86.3
Scotland	9.0	33.3	10.3	15.1	1.2	1.5	261.0	162.1
Specials	—	16.6	—	—	—	—	—	—
Northern Ireland	22.0	107.1	4.0	21.9	4.0	14.2	158.0	407.1
Others	185.7	333.3	—	—	—	—	57.1	66.6

TABLE 5.25 Availability of obstetricians more than 20 minutes from the delivery area by regions. Rate per 100 women in labour at 11 am and 11 pm – August

	Consultant		All registrars		Senior house officer		GPs	
	am	pm	am	pm	am	pm	am	pm
Northern	5.0	14.2	—	—	—	—	12.5	10.7
Yorkshire	7.4	7.3	—	—	—	—	22.2	7.3
Trent	1.5	4.5	1.5	—	—	—	55.5	63.6
East Anglia	12.5	10.0	—	—	—	—	—	40.0
North-West Thames	6.0	2.8	3.0	—	9.0	—	—	—
North-East Thames	3.3	7.8	—	—	—	—	1.6	2.6
South-East Thames	1.7	11.6	1.7	—	1.7	—	30.3	—
South-West Thames	6.6	7.6	3.3	3.8	—	3.8	120.0	—
Wessex	20.0	26.6	15.0	13.3	5.0	—	72.5	26.6
Oxford	6.8	8.3	11.3	12.5	2.2	4.1	90.0	125.0
South-Western	33.3	—	10.3	4.0	—	—	179.3	264.0
West Midlands	4.05	6.1	—	—	—	4.0	33.7	75.5
Mersey	—	9.0	—	—	—	—	—	—
North-Western	1.6	11.5	—	3.8	—	3.8	66.1	119.2
Wales	15.5	27.2	11.1	9.0	—	—	46.6	9.0
Scotland	5.1	4.5	3.8	3.0	5.1	1.5	7.7	3.0
Specials	—	—	—	—	—	—	—	—
Northern Ireland	—	—	—	—	—	—	—	—
Others	—	100.0	—	—	—	—	—	—

TABLE 5.26 Consultants available in delivery area or hospital by regions. Rate per 100 women in labour at 11 am and 11 pm – August

	11 am	11 pm
Mean (n = 19)	70.4	8.0
Northern	78.0	0
Yorkshire	96.0	9.3
Trent	81.0	5.0
Wessex	60.0	0
East Anglia	79.0	10.0
Oxford	88.0	0
North-West Thames	70.0	17.0
North-East Thames	75.0	0
South-Western	48.0	8.0
North-Western	85.0	0
South-East Thames	79.0	0
West Midlands	59.0	8.0
South-West Thames	70.0	4.0
Mersey	50.0	0
Scotland	78.0	41.0
Wales	73.0	5.0
Ireland	90.0	7.0
Others (private etc.)	43.0	50.0
Specials	36.0	0

TABLE 5.27 Senior registrar (as the most senior grade) available in the delivery area or hospital by regions. Rate per 100 women in labour at 11 am and 11 pm – August

	11 am	11 pm
Mean (n = 19)	6.0	23.0
Northern	5.0	21.0
Yorkshire	0.0	19.0
Trent	10.0	23.0
East Anglia	0.0	20.0
North-West Thames	10.0	11.0
North-East Thames	0.0	16.0
South-East Thames	0.0	26.5
South-West Thames	0.0	19.0
Wessex	0.0	33.0
Oxford	0.0	14.0
West Midlands	0.0	29.0
South-Western	24.0	28.0
Mersey	32.0	28.0
North-Western	5.0	8.0
Wales	22.0	23.0
Scotland	10.0	0.0
Specials	0.0	100.0
Northern Ireland	2.0	7.0
Other	0.0	17.0

TABLE 5.28   Registrars (as the most senior grade) available in the delivery area or hospital by regions. Rate per 100 women in labour at 11 am and 11 pm – August

	11 am	11 pm
Mean (*n* = 19)	8.3	42.0
Northern	10.0	46.0
Yorkshire	2.0	60.0
Trent	0.0	59.0
East Anglia	21.0	20.0
North-West Thames	0.0	43.0
North-East Thames	21.0	68.0
South-East Thames	12.0	26.0
South-West Thames	17.0	69.0
Wessex	18.0	27.0
Oxford	6.0	76.0
West Midlands	14.0	35.0
South-Western	10.0	28.0
Mersey	14.0	64.0
North-Western	3.0	50.0
Wales	0.0	41.0
Scotland	10.0	27.0
Specials	0.0	0.0
Northern Ireland	0.0	50.0
Other	0.0	0.0

Celtic kingdoms are 58 per cent (Wales), 34 per cent (N Ireland) and 23 per cent (Scotland) while in the Thames regions the numbers of consultants per 100 women in labour were 52, 30, 27 and 43 respectively (see Table 5.23).

Those on call outside the hospital premises are shown in Tables 5.24 and 5.25. The regions with a larger proportion of consultants more than 20 minutes away are mostly those with widespread populations, for example South-Western, Wessex and East Anglia.

Another way to examine the breakdown of the staff availability in the regions is shown in Tables 5.26–5.28 where the grade of staff and percentage of women in labour catered for by each grade is tabulated by the most senior grade of staff available on call in the delivery area or hospital. In August, at 11 am the consultant availability ranged from 96 per cent of the women in labour covered in Yorkshire to 48 per cent in South-Western region, with the mean for all regions being 70 per cent (Figures 5.8 and Table 5.26). At 11 pm the mean was 8 per cent and the range from 41 per cent in Scotland to 0 per cent in seven regions not having a consultant on the premises. This, of course, records over the workload on that day, at that time in the different regions.

The senior registrar, as the most senior grade available for women in labour, showed very different figures during the day compared with the night cover

TABLE 5.29   SHOs (as the most senior grade) available in the delivery area or hospital by regions. Rate per 100 women in labour at 11 am and 11 pm – August

	11 am	11 pm
Mean (n = 19)	7.0	20.0
Northern	5.0	29.0
Yorkshire	0.0	12.0
Trent	0.0	0.0
East Anglia	0.0	50.0
North-West Thames	15.0	29.0
North-East Thames	0.0	13.0
South-East Thames	7.0	42.0
South-West Thames	0.0	8.0
Wessex	5.0	20.0
Oxford	3.0	10.0
West Midlands	20.0	8.0
South-Western	0.0	20.0
Mersey	5.0	9.0
North-Western	0.0	38.0
Wales	4.0	14.0
Scotland	4.0	20.0
Specials	64.0	0.0
Northern Ireland	0.0	36.0
Other	0.0	17.0

(Table 5.27). The mean percentage of women in labour covered by this grade during the day is 6 per cent with a range of 32 per cent in Mersey to eight regions (excluding specials and others) not having a senior registrar as the senior grade of doctor on call. At 11 pm on the same day, the mean rises to 23 per cent with a range from 29 per cent in West Midlands to only one region, Scotland, not having a senior registrar as the senior ranking obstetrician available for the labour ward.

The mean percentage of women for whom at 11 am a registrar was the most senior grade of doctor available in the hospital was 8.3 per cent, the range being 21 per cent in East Anglia and NE Thames to four regions with registrar grade not being the most senior grade available in hospital (Table 5.28).

Table 5.29 shows the percentage of women in labour where the most senior doctor on duty for the labour ward is the senior house officer. In West Midlands 20 per cent of women in labour are covered by a SHO as the most senior doctor at 11 am. At night time the mean figure is three times that of the daytime. Mersey is one of the regions not having a lot of small units or split sites. Nonetheless, a significant percentage of women in labour have a SHO as the most senior cover available in the hospital in the daytime.

Since this is a question with ranked answers, one can conclude that in the

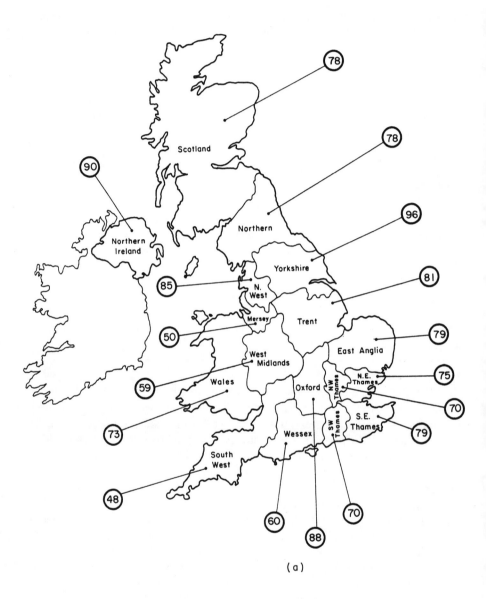

(a)

Figure 5.8 (a)   Percentage of women in labour for whom a consultant obstetrician was available in either the delivery area or the hospital (by regions)—11 am

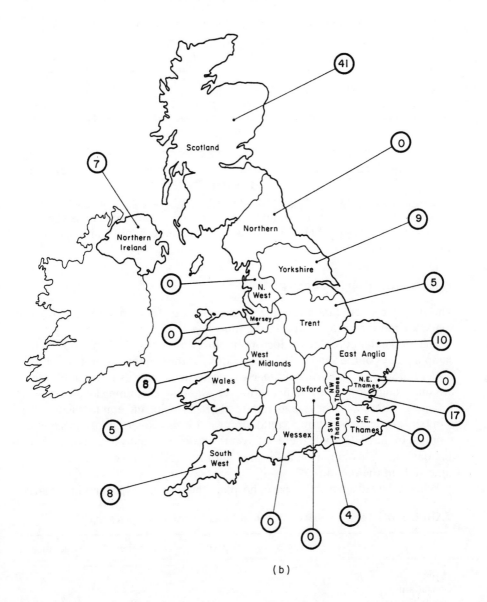

(b)

Figure 5.8 (b)   Percentage of women in labour for whom a consultant obstetrician was available in either the delivery area or the hospital (by regions)—11 pm

TABLE 5.30   Most senior obstetrician available on the premises

	Morning (%)	Night (%)
Consultant	70	8
Senior registrar	6	23
Registrar	8	42
SHO	7	20
	91	93

United Kingdom, the senior obstetrician on the premises on call to deal with problems in the labour ward is as shown in Table 5.30.

In the daytime, the majority of women are under the aegis of a consultant; at night that immediate cover is senior registrar or more commonly registrar, and in one-fifth of cases the SHO. The consultant and other seniors are on call but do not live in the unit.

LOCUM OBSTETRIC STAFF

The survey collected data relating to the number of locum staff serving two weeks or more employed during the four days.

The total numbers of locum doctors employed are shown in Table 5.31 by the sampling days of the survey. When one looks at the requests for locums at the back of the *British Medical Journal* each week the numbers shown in this table are surprisingly low. The enquiry, however, was only examining locums in post for more than two weeks and not in short-term locum employment. The numbers are small but show a trend for fewer locums covering for the summer months. In the SHO grade there are over three times as many locums at night as the daytime. This might be associated with the greater involvement of part-time staff in the daytime.

When assessed against the size of hospital, there were few locums in the large

TABLE 5.31   Total numbers of locum doctors by grade on each survey day

	August	September	October	November
11 am				
Consultant	8	6	3	5
Senior registrar	1	0	0	4
Registrar	7	10	3	2
SHO	9	9	4	4
11 pm				
Consultant	5	3	2	4
Senior registrar	0	0	0	1
Registrar	6	10	3	0
SHO	27	30	16	29

TABLE 5.32 Obstetrical flying squad available according to the type of units

Type of unit	No. of institutions		
	Yes	No	Not known
NHS consultant unit	145	47	1
Combined GP and consultant unit	77	33	2
Combined consultant unit and privat unit	3	3	0
Other units	18	190	2

and very large units. The greatest numbers in all grades in relation to numbers of units were in the 501–2000 deliveries a year group of hospitals.

OBSTETRICAL FLYING SQUAD

Table 5.32 illustrates the type of units and the availability of flying squads. Forty-seven of the NHS consultant and 33 of the combined consultant/GP units did not operate a flying squad service; altogether 83 out of 311 consultant-led units (27 per cent) provided no flying squad.

Examination of the information on obstetrical flying squads is shown by regions in Table 5.33 and Figure 5.9. Assessing the numbers of squads as

TABLE 5.33 Regional provision of obstetrical flying squads: (a) by all consultant and combined units in region; (b) by 1000 women delivering; (c) by numbers of home deliveries

	Number	Con/Con + GP units providing squad (%)	No. squads/ 1000 deliveries (1984 data)	No. squads/ home delivery
Northern	18	56	0.5	3.6
Yorkshire	15	71	0.3	2.2
Trent	18	95	0.3	3.6
East Anglia	8	89	0.3	0.9
North-West Thames	17	94	0.4	2.1
North-East Thames	17	81	0.3	2.4
South-East Thames	18	86	0.4	1.5
South-West Thames	12	75	0.3	6.0
Wessex	11	00	0.3	11.0
Oxford	12	00	0.4	4.0
South-Western	12	00	0.3	3.0
West Midlands	18	78	0.3	1.5
Mersey	8	80	0.3	8.0
North-Western	18	86	0.3	9.0
Wales	11	52	0.3	2.2
Scotland	23	68	0.3	11.5
Northern Ireland	10	67	0.2	10.0

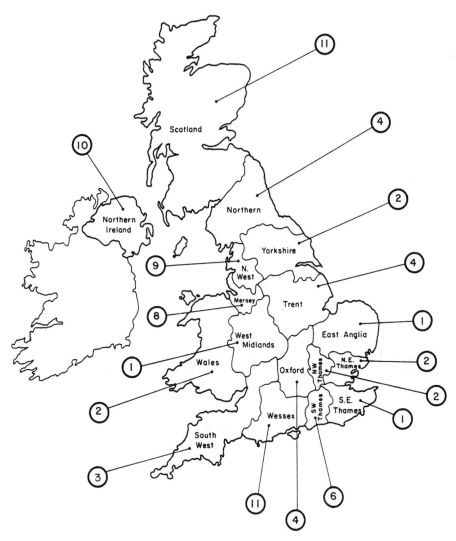

Figure 5.9   Number of obstetrical flying squads per home delivery (by regions)

a proportion of all units is perhaps not as useful as examining them by those hospitals which might be expected to run such a service — the consultant and combined consultant/GP units. In three regions, all such units provided the facility while in two others all but one unit did so. A distinctly lower percentage was seen in the Northern and all three Celtic regions (56, 52, 68 and 67 per cent respectively) while where the need might be thought to be less, the four Metropolitan regions around London, there was a 94, 81, 86 and 75 per cent cover.

Re-examination of the data in Table 5.33 was made by the numbers of deliveries in hospital, and perhaps even more relevant for flying squads, in the home. In the former, a more uniform pattern of provision is shown. In the home deliveries, however, a wide range occurred with the East Anglian region reporting one-third of the provision of that in North-East and North-West Thames regions and other regions with comparatively closely gathered populations.

Eighteen other units said they provided a flying squad service; while these may have been in the sparser populated areas, it was possibly a misunderstanding of the question so that while we were looking for the providers, they were responding as consumers. None of the Armed Service hospitals nor the two private sector units reported providing this service.

MEDICAL STUDENTS

Medical students are based in obstetric units attached to teaching hospitals and increasingly in the district hospitals. Table 5.34 shows their distribution by survey days. A high proportion are on the delivery areas in the night time but the Saturday reduction of other staff is seen in this group too. Also, there are fewer students present in the traditional holiday months. Numbers are too few for extensive analysis but checks on each of the four survey days showed the students to be mostly at the medium sized and large hospitals (35 and 60 per cent respectively) and fewer were represented at the small or very large units (5 and 20 per cent respectively).

TABLE 5.34   Total number of medical students at 11 am and 11 pm on four survey days

	August	September	October	November
Medical students at 11 am				
in delivery area	58	42	79	90
in hospital	75	24	88	106
>20 minutes	9	5	9	6
<20 minutes	4	0	0	0
TOTAL	146	71	176	202
Medical students at 11 pm				
in delivery area	35	46	66	71
in hospital	41	19	81	53
<20 minutes	5	4	6	10
>20 minutes	0	0	8	1
TOTAL	81	69	161	135

CONCLUSIONS

The arrangements for obstetrical staffing of the Units in the United Kingdom are described. The large numbers of smaller units skews towards the distribution at all grades. There were an average of 41 obstetricians (range 36–48) available per 100 women in labour at both morning and evening sample times on all four days of the survey. A registrar or SHO was available for 1 in 3 women in labour in the day or night while one senior doctor (consultant or senior registrar) was available for 14 women in labour in the day and one for each 25 at night. Fifteen per cent of the very large units had two obstetricians solely on duty for the labour ward at all times. The proportions were lower in smaller units.

A reduction of doctors in the hospital was seen on the Saturday of the Survey but there was a proportional increase on call for the delivery units so cover was maintained; most doctors on call were within 20 minutes of the unit.

Regional variations showed a wide range of consultants on call from 58 per 100 women in labour in Wales to 18 in Oxford. Even inside the four Thames regions, a variation from 27 to 52 consultants per 100 women in labour was seen. When re-examined by the most senior grade of obstetricians available to labouring women, in all regions 70% had a consultant at 11 am and 8% at 11 pm. At night time, three times as many units have an SHO as the most senior obstetrician available.

Obstetrical flying squads were examined; 27% of consultant units do not provide one. Using home deliveries as an indicator of a potential need for a Flying Squad, a wide range of availability occurred with for example East Anglia having a relatively low provision of service.

REFERENCE

1. House of Commons Second Report of the Social Services Committee 1979–1980. *Perinatal and Neonatal Mortality*. London: HMSO, 1982.

APPENDIX

TABLE 5A.1   Place of birth
Obstetricians by size of unit at 11 am – August

Group (No. of dels 1983)	Con-sultant	Senior registrar	Regi-strars	Associate specialist and clinical assistants	GP	Senior house officer
	No.	No.	No.	No.	No.	No.
In delivery area						
1–500	1	0	0	1	12	5
501–2000	9	6	17	4	2	56
2001–4000	27	12	40	3	3	93
4001+	6	8	16	0	1	22
Not grouped	2	0	2	0	1	0
TOTAL	45	26	75	8	19	176
In hospital						
1–500	24	1	17	5	52	30
501–2000	130	25	109	11	5	178
2001–4000	117	44	107	11	10	149
4001+	27	10	17	2	0	29
Not grouped	4	0	4	0	1	3
TOTAL	302	80	254	29	68	289
Within 20 min						
1–500	34	2	14	8	1343	10
501–2000	47	7	15	7	99	20
2001–4000	58	3	8	2	44	9
4001+	11	1	1	0	0	2
Not grouped	0	0	0	0	40	0
TOTAL	150	13	38	17	1526	41
Greater than 20 min						
1–500	13	6	12	2	265	5
501–2000	20	3	2	1	15	5
2001–4000	7	0	1	0	38	0
4001+	5	1	1	0	0	1
Not grouped	2	0	0	0	30	0
TOTAL	46	10	16	3	348	11

TABLE 5A.2   Place of birth
Obstetricians by size of unit at 11 pm – August

Group (No. of dels 1983)	Con- sultant	Senior registrar	Regi- strars	Associate specialist and clinical assistants	GP	Senior house officer
	No.	No.	No.	No.	No.	No.
In delivery area						
1–500	0	0	2	0	5	3
501–2000	2	2	10	0	0	45
2001–4000	3	11	40	0	5	78
4001+	1	5	17	0	0	27
Not grouped	1	1	0	0	0	2
In hospital						
1–500	3	1	5	0	7	14
501–2000	6	8	53	2	0	89
2001–4000	6	13	59	1	0	64
4001+	0	4	2	0	0	8
Not grouped	2	0	2	0	0	2
TOTAL	17	26	121	3	7	177
Within 20 min						
1–500	43	6	9	4	700	4
501–2000	110	13	22	6	58	19
2001–4000	109	12	8	1	33	3
4001+	20	5	2	1	0	1
Not grouped	2	0	1	0	42	27
TOTAL	284	36	42	12	833	27
Greater than 20 min						
1–500	14	4	5	0	194	3
501–2000	17	1	0	0	5	2
2001–4000	13	2	1	0	0	0
4001+	2	0	0	0	0	0
Not grouped	3	0	0	0	20	0
TOTAL	49	7	6	0	219	6

TABLE 5A.3 Place of birth
Obstetricians by size of unit at 11 am – September

Group (No. of dels 1983)	Con- sultant	Senior registrar	Regi- strars	Associate specialist and clinical assistants	GP	Senior house officer
	No.	No.	No.	No.	No.	NO.
In delivery area						
1–500	0	0	0	0	15	2
501–2000	13	4	26	3	4	51
2001–4000	19	10	46	2	3	73
4001+	2	7	14	0	1	23
Not grouped	0	1	1	0	1	2
TOTAL	34	22	87	5	24	151
In hospital						
1–500	8	2	5	2	25	10
501–2000	32	17	51	1	1	90
2001–4000	24	11	55	0	1	78
4001+	9	10	12	0	0	16
Not grouped	1	0	2	0	1	1
TOTAL	74	40	125	3	28	195
Within 20 min						
1–500	25	8	7	5	1031	5
501–2000	74	14	10	7	78	10
2001–4000	83	13	5	1	40	2
4001+	20	2	1	0	0	0
Not grouped	2	0	0	0	44	0
TOTAL	204	37	23	13	1193	17
Greater than 20 min						
1–500	17	2	5	3	150	4
501–2000	21	1	4	0	2	2
2001–4000	10	2	1	0	1	0
4001+	4	0	0	0	0	0
Not grouped	0	0	1	0	20	0
TOTAL	52	5	11	3	173	6

TABLE 5A.4   Place of birth
Obstetricians by size of unit at 11 pm – September

Group (No. of dels 1983)	Consultant	Senior registrar	Registrars	Associate specialist and clinical assistants	GP officer	Senior house
	No.	No.	No.	No.	No.	No.
In delivery area						
1–500	0	0	2	0	12	3
501–2000	2	1	9	1	1	25
2001–4000	3	10	37	1	2	77
4001+	1	6	11	0	0	22
Not grouped	0	0	0	0	0	0
TOTAL	6	17	59	2	15	127
In hospital						
1–500	2	1	2	0	8	8
501–2000	9	9	56	2	0	99
2001–4000	4	10	55	0	0	57
4001+	1	6	8	0	0	9
Not grouped	0	1	2	0	0	3
TOTAL	16	27	123	2	8	176
Within 20 min						
1–500	40	8	9	2	701	11
501–2000	95	12	22	6	43	10
2001–4000	109	10	16	0	20	9
4001+	23	2	0	0	0	0
Not grouped	3	0	0	0	43	0
TOTAL	270	32	47	8	807	30
Greater than 20 min						
1–500	19	3	4	1	119	4
501–2000	25	2	2	0	3	1
2001–4000	16	3	1	0	0	0
4001+	4	0	0	0	0	0
Not grouped	0	0	1	0	20	0
TOTAL	64	8	8	1	142	5

TABLE 5A.5   Place of birth
Obstetricians by size of unit at 11 am – October

Group (No. of dels 1983)	Con-sultant	Senior registrar	Regi-strars	Associate specialist and clinical assistants	GP officer	Senior house
	No.	No.	No.	No.	No.	No.
In delivery area						
1–500	2	0	0	0	10	2
501–2000	13	6	21	2	5	57
2001–4000	7	7	40	1	0	92
4001+	3	5	14	0	0	25
Not grouped	0	0	0	0	1	2
TOTAL	25	18	75	3	16	178
In hospital						
1–500	23	5	9	5	35	21
501–2000	126	29	92	11	6	144
2001–4000	136	41	102	9	1	102
4001+	27	13	9	1	0	23
Not grouped	11	1	10	0	0	10
TOTAL	323	89	222	26	42	300
Within 20 min						
1–500	28	1	11	4	1082	2
501–2000	44	11	13	3	81	7
2001–4000	37	7	14	0	51	2
4001+	15	4	3	0	0	1
Not grouped	3	0	1	1	50	0
TOTAL	127	23	42	8	1264	12
Greater than 20 min						
1–500	13	7	6	3	223	3
501–2000	18	0	0	0	14	1
2001–4000	5	1	1	0	0	0
4001+	4	0	4	0	0	0
Not grouped	0	0	0	0	20	0
TOTAL	40	8	11	3	257	4

TABLE 5A.6   Place of birth
Obstetricians by size of unit at 11 pm – October

Group (No. of dels 1983)	Con-sultant	Senior registrar	Regi-strars	Associate specialist and clinical assistants	GP	Senior house officer
	No.	No.	No.	No.	No.	No.
In delivery area						
1–500	0	0	0	0	9	1
501–2000	1	3	20	1	0	39
501–2000	1	3	20	1	0	39
2001–4000	3	8	40	1	0	72
4001+	1	2	16	1	0	22
Not grouped	1	1	3	0	1	2
TOTAL	6	14	79	3	10	136
In hospital						
1–500	3	1	7	0	7	11
501–2000	6	8	50	1	0	91
2001–4000	4	17	55	1	1	62
4001+	0	4	9	0	0	8
Not grouped	1	0	5	0	0	5
TOTAL	14	30	126	2	8	177
Within 20 min						
1–500	33	4	9	5	925	4
501–2000	108	12	14	6	49	10
2001–4000	109	14	16	7	20	2
4001+	16	6	1	0	0	0
Not grouped	6	0	0	1	51	0
TOTAL	272	36	40	19	1045	16
Greater than 20 min						
1–500	18	6	4	1	158	5
501–2000	18	1	4	0	5	0
2001–4000	16	2	0	0	21	0
4001+	9	1	0	0	0	0
Not grouped	0	0	1	0	20	0
TOTAL	61	10	9	1	204	5

TABLE 5A.7   Place of birth
Obstetricians by size of unit at 11 am – November

Group (No. of dels 1983)	Con-sultant	Senior registrar	Regi-strars	Associate specialist and clinical assistants	GP	Senior house officer
	No.	No.	No.	No.	No.	No.
In delivery area						
1–500	5	0	1	1	13	4
501–2000	5	1	21	3	4	50
2001–4000	21	10	46	5	1	96
4001+	3	7	16	0	0	27
Not grouped	0	0	2	0	1	3
TOTAL	34	18	86	9	19	180
In hospital						
1–500	20	5	7	2	57	19
501–2000	129	29	95	11	6	146
2001–4000	119	40	75	10	0	108
4001+	33	12	13	0	0	26
Not grouped	9	0	10	0	1	7
TOTAL	310	86	200	23	64	306
Within 20 min						
1–500	35	8	9	3	1160	5
501–2000	38	7	13	2	104	9
2001–4000	29	8	6	1	23	8
4001+	10	4	1	0	0	1
Not grouped	2	0	0	1	49	0
TOTAL	114	27	29	7	1336	23
Greater than 20 min						
1–500	16	5	4	1	248	3
501–2000	14	2	4	0	8	3
2001–4000	10	1	2	2	34	0
4001+	6	2	0	0	0	0
Not grouped	0	0	0	0	25	0
TOTAL	46	10	10	3	315	6

TABLE 5A.8 Place of birth
Obstetricians by size of unit at 11 pm – November

Group (No. of dels 1983)	Con- sultant	Senior registrar	Regi- strars	Associate specialist and clinical assistants	GP	Senior house officer
	No.	No.	No.	No.	No.	No.
In delivery area						
1–500	0	1	0	0	9	2
501–2000	4	4	11	0	1	33
2001–4000	5	10	30	1	2	66
4001+	1	6	12	0	0	24
Not grouped	0	1	0	0	0	1
TOTAL	10	22	53	1	12	126
In hospital						
1–500	2	2	6	0	6	12
501–2000	7	19	58	2	0	100
2001–4000	3	12	58	2	0	74
4001+	2	3	9	0	0	14
Not grouped	1	1	5	0	0	4
TOTAL	15	37	136	4	6	204
Within 20 min						
1–500	45	5	7	2	776	10
501–2000	109	9	16	6	40	11
2001–4000	116	19	13	2	14	7
4001+	22	6	2	0	0	0
Not grouped	5	0	0	1	53	1
TOTAL	297	39	38	11	883	29
Greater than 20 min						
1–500	23	5	6	3	129	5
501–2000	16	1	1	0	2	0
2001–4000	10	2	1	1	43	0
4001+	6	0	0	0	0	0
Not grouped	0	0	0	0	22	0
TOTAL	55	8	8	4	196	5

CHAPTER 6

Anaesthetic Facilities

Barbara Morgan

INTRODUCTION

This chapter considers the facilities that exist in the UK to provide anaesthesia in labour, an essential aspect of care. The whereabouts of the anaesthetist in every hospital where babies are born was sought; other aspects of anaesthetic facilities were examined.

The availability of anaesthesia is an important factor in reducing perinatal mortality and morbidity. During labour a fetus may unpredictably suffer a shortage of oxygen. This is an urgent medical emergency; permanent cerebral damage may be avoided or minimized by rapid delivery, often by Caesarean section. Waiting for the anaesthetist to arrive before surgical delivery can start may result in irreversible brain damage in some infants. One of the major advantages of hospital delivery is to have an anaesthetist available quickly.

When a mother needs immediate anaesthesia her well-being depends directly on the skill of an anaesthetist. The number of mothers whose deaths are attributed to anaesthesia has decreased little since the first report on the Confidential Enquiry into Maternal Deaths in 1952–1954[1]. Anaesthesia has thus become associated with an increasing proportion of maternal deaths; in the 1979–81[5] Report it was one of the three commonest causes of maternal death. Almost one-quarter of deaths associated with Caesarean section are the result of anaesthesia. All were declared in the reports to be avoidable. Seven out of the nine reports on Confidential Enquiries into Maternal Deaths condemn the practice of leaving the responsibility of obstetric anaesthesia to junior or unskilled anaesthetists. For example in the 1955–57 Report[2] tragedies could have been avoided by a more experienced anaesthetist'.

In the light of the evidence it received, the Social Services Committee[6] recommended that no anaesthetist below the grade of registrar should be responsible for obstetric patients. Professional anaesthetic associations advise against unskilled junior anaesthetists treating the obstetric patient unsupervised.

The N.H.S. grade of anaesthetist on duty for the delivery area has been used as a rough guide to skill and experience. Naturally some individuals are much more experienced and have greater skills than their grade indicates. However, as explained in Chapter 1, this would not be possible to assess in a countrywide survey.

It can be assumed that anaesthetists appointed to registrar grade and above will have acquired experience in anaesthesia. Virtually all doctors in these grades will therefore be competent to administer unsupervised anaesthesia to the mother, but those below this grade may not be so competent. General practitioners may or may not have received adequate anaesthetic training for there is no GP anaesthetic list as there is a published GP obstetric list. There is little continuing training in anaesthesia for GPs although the nature of their occupation frequently makes them into occasional anaesthetists.

Training of junior doctors is essential if their skills are to be relied upon in the acute clinical situation; often when unaided at night. Obviously, training cannot occur unless there is both a teacher and a pupil. Thus the number of units in which more than one anaesthetist is available during the day will give a measure of the number of units in which teaching can take place. But if there is only one anaesthetist, he or she can neither teach nor be taught. Teaching is likely to be done mostly during the day although the clinical demands of obstetric anaesthesia occur over the whole 24 hours. Thus the number of cases from whom the junior anaesthetist can learn skills under supervision in smaller units is limited.

An important aspect of this survey was to enquire into the availability of epidural anaesthesia and the whereabouts of the anaesthetist and essential equipment in units where epidural anaesthesia was used.

The ability of hospital obstetric practice to prevent serious injury or death to those fetuses distressed by insufficient oxygen *in utero*, may be reduced by having to wait for an anaesthetist who may be busy elsewhere. A further cause

TABLE 6.1   Number of units, number of deliveries in the previous year and those in 24 hours during the survey

Size of units by average number of deliveries	Number of units	(%)	% deliveries 1983	Number of deliveries per 24 h during survey	(%)
1–500 (small)	217	(41)	1	95	(5)
501–2000 (medium)	149	(29)	29	579	(28)
2001–4000 (large)	129	(25)	52	1041	(51)
>4000 (very large)	26	(5)	18	317	(16)
TOTAL	521	100	100	2032	100

TABLE 5.32   TABLE 6.2   Percentage of deliveries occurring at 11 am in units without an anaesthetist on the premises and percentage of all deliveries in the country

Unit size by average number of deliveries	Deliveries in each size group with no anaesthetist on premises (%)	Deliveries with no anaesthetist on premises as % of total deliveries
1–500	77	0.8
501–2000	26	7.5
2001–4000	9	4.7
>4000	4	0.7
TOTAL	116	13.7

of delay which is potentially intolerable to some infants is the shared operating theatre or one not on the labour suite. Easy access to an anaesthetist who is not likely to be giving anaesthetics to another patient elsewhere in the hospital as well as easy access to a theatre exclusively for obstetric emergencies is the ideal if perinatal mortality and morbidity are to be reduced even further. Bromage (1978)[7] states that in obstetric anaesthesia 'perfection is the only practical and acceptable goal. Less than this is too costly in terms of individual suffering and the collective toll of subnormal children falling as a charge on the State.'

THE AVAILABILITY OF ANAESTHETISTS

Children were born in 521 units during the survey. Table 6.1 shows these units grouped by number of deliveries based on their delivery figures of the previous year as well as the proportion of births that occurred in each group in the survey days. It shows that although most units (41 per cent) were small (1–500 deliveries) they delivered very few women, that medium sized units (501–2000 deliveries) made up one-third of the units and delivered one-third of the women. One-quarter of the units were large (2001–4000 deliveries) and half of all the children born were delivered in these units. Only 5 per cent of units were very large (over 4000 deliveries) and delivered 16 per cent of women. Thus about 70 per cent of children were born in the 155 units with more than 2000 deliveries per year, the remaining 30 per cent in 366 smaller units.

Fourteen per cent of the women in the country are delivered in hospitals that have no anaesthetist on the premises during the day; this proportion increases to 23 per cent at night (see Figure 6.1). Tables 6.2 and 6.3 indicate the percentage of deliveries that occur in each unit size group without an anaesthetist on the premises and the percentage of total deliveries that are not covered during the day and night.

Most women delivering in the small units have no anaesthetist available to them on the premises. It is possible that women delivering in these small units

TABLE 6.3   Percentage of deliveries occurring at 11 pm in units with no anaesthetist on premises and percentage of all deliveries in the country

Unit size by average number of deliveries	Deliveries occurring without anaesthetist on premises at night (%)	Total UK deliveries occurring without anaesthetist on premises at night (%)
1–500	94	1
501–2000	42	12
2001–4000	18	9
>4000	4	0.7
TOTAL	158	22.7

have been selected with the expectation of a normal delivery but such selection seems unlikely for the medium sized units where a quarter of mothers deliver with no anaesthetist in the building. Half of all the women in the country who deliver without an anaesthetist on the premises do so in medium sized units. However, even in units with more than 2000 deliveries a year, one in twenty women during the day and one in ten women during the night deliver without an anaesthetist on the premises.

Tables 6.4 and 6.5 show the number of units during the day and at night, respectively, in which no anaesthetist was on the premises or where anaesthetic attention was shared with other surgical disciplines in the hospital; it also shows those units in which the anaesthetist was responsible exclusively for the care of the obstetric patients. These tables indicate that as the unit size increases so does the anaesthetic provision. However, there are only 37 units in the country where an anaesthetist is available solely for the delivery suite day and night and therefore available immediately for the obstetric patient. Eighteen per cent of

TABLE 6.4   Availability of the anaesthetist at 11 am by size of units (August)

Unit size by average number of deliveries	Number of units (%) without anaesthetist on the premises		Number of units (%) with anaesthetist shared with other disciplines		Number of units (%) with anaesthetist for for the delivery area only		Total
1–500	181	(83)	37	(17)	0		218
501–2000	46	(31)	92	(62)	11	(7)	149
2001–4000	13	(10)	71	(55)	45	(35)	129
>4000	1	(4)	9	(36)	15	(60)	25
TOTAL	241	(46)	209	(40)	71	(14)	521

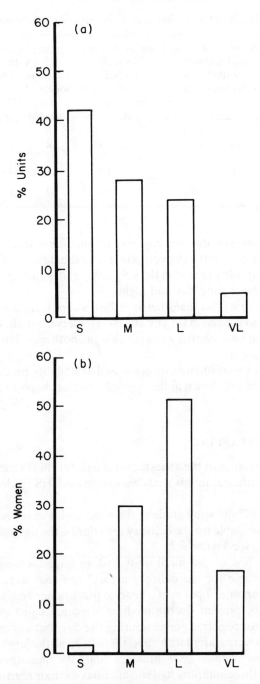

Figure 6.1 Percentage of (a) unit size and (b) deliveries with no anaesthetist present

TABLE 6.5   Availability of anaesthetist at 11 pm in units by size groups

Unit size by average number of deliveries	Number of units (%) without anaesthetist on the premises		Number of units (%) with anaesthetist shared with other disciplines		Number of units (%) with anaesthetist for for the delivery area only		Total
1–500	216	(99)	2	(1)	0		218
501–2000	70	(47)	75	(50)	4	(3)	149
2001–4000	24	(19)	84	(65)	21	(16)	129
>4000	1	(4)	12	(48)	12	(48)	25
TOTAL	311	(60)	173	(33)	37	(7)	521

all deliveries in the country are covered by this ideal level of anaesthetic attention. In 3 per cent of the deliveries in the medium sized units, 17 per cent in the large units and 46 per cent in the very large units, there is an anaesthetist present on the labour suite day and night.

Units where there was no anaesthetist in the building were the 135 small units where there was no provision for any anaesthetic service at all. In another 106 units of all sizes an anaesthetist was available in another building, usually less than 20 minutes away.

The full tables of anaesthetists by grade and availability for each survey day at 11 am and 11 pm are shown in the appendix to this chapter (Tables 6A.1 to 6A.8).

ANAESTHETIC STAFFING

The skill and experience of the anaesthetist is a factor that influences maternal safety under anaesthesia. In this study we have used NHS grades as a measure of experience.

Tables 6.6 and 6.7 show the grade of the most senior anaesthetist present in the hospital and available for the delivery area during the day and night in units of different sizes (see Figure 6.2).

Although very few of the small units had an anaesthetist present in the hospital and available for the delivery area, 7 per cent were covered by a consultant but in another 7 per cent a general practitioner anaesthetist was the most senior doctor present. In the medium sized units just over half had a consultant or senior registrar present during the day, but at night only 13 per cent of these units were staffed with anaesthetists. In all the large and very large units delivering more than 2000 infants a year, the anaesthetic availability improved so that three-quarters had consultants or senior registrars present in the hospital during the day and one-fifth did at night.

TABLE 6.6   Most senior anaesthetist in the hospital available for the delivery area at 11 am (August)

Grade of most senior anaesthetist in hospital	Number (%) of units 1–500 deliveries (small)		Number (%) of units 501–2000 deliveries (medium)		Number (%) of units 2001–4000 deliveries (large)		Number (%) of units >4000 deliveries (very large)	
Consultant	16	(7)	76	(51)	80	(62)	15	(60)
SR	2	(1)	8	(5)	10	(7)	4	(16)
Registrar	2	(1)	9	(6)	18	(14)	3	(12)
SHO	0		6	(4)	5	(4)	2	(8)
Clinical assistant	2	(1)	4	(3)	3	(2)	0	
General practitioner	15	(7)	0		0		0	
None	180	(83)	46	(31)	13	(10)	1	(4)

When considering all units with more than 500 deliveries per year, a registrar was the most senior anaesthetist in the hospital during the day in only one in ten of units and in almost half at night. However, one in fourteen units had a senior house officer or clinical assistant as the most senior anaesthetist in the hospital and available for the delivery suite during the day and in one in six units at night (Figure 6.3).

Tables 6.8 and 6.9 indicate the whereabouts of the consultant available for the delivery area during the day and night. In almost 90 per cent of units above 500 deliveries a consultant was available during the day either in the hospital or within 20 minutes of it. Very few units had consultants who were more than 20 minutes away while on duty for the labour ward. In some 15 units the midwife

TABLE 6.7   Most senior anaesthetist in the hospital and available for the delivery area at 11 pm

Grade of most senior anaesthetist in hospital	Number (%) units 1–500 deliveries		Number (%) units 501–2000 deliveries		Number (%) units 2001–4000 deliveries		Number (%) units >4000 deliveries	
Consultant	1		8	(5)	8	(6)	1	(4)
Senior registrar	2		12	(8)	18	(14)	4	(16)
Registrar	2		30	(20)	58	(45)	16	(64)
SHO	3		24	(16)	19	(15)	3	(12)
Clinical assistant	0		4	(3)	2		0	
GP	2		0		0		0	
None	216	(99)	70	(47)	24	(19)	1	(4)

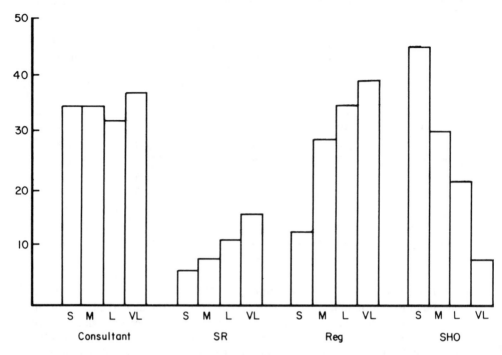

Figure 6.2   Grade of anaesthetist on premises and available for delivery area at 11 am

in charge of the labour ward even after consultation with the junior anaesthetist on call was unaware of a consultant being available.

Thirty small and 15 medium units with an anaesthetic provision had no consultant available. The availability of the consultant anaesthetist was reduced at night with over 10 per cent of all units above 500 deliveries per year declaring that no consultant was available for the labour suite.

Tables 6.10 and 6.11 show the grade of anaesthetists who, while not in the hospital, were available for the delivery suite within 20 minutes. Consultants and senior registrars available at this distance were most likely to be the senior anaesthetists covering juniors on the labour ward. In the three larger grades of units, most or all the anaesthetists less than 20 minutes away during the day were consultant or senior registrars but in 37 per cent of the medium sized units and 28 per cent of the large units an anaesthetist of registrar grade or below was less than 20 minutes away. It is possible that these were the first call anaesthetists. At night, although more anaesthetists were on call from outside the hospitals, the proportions of junior to senior staff were similar.

TABLE 6.8 Availability of consultant anaesthetist on duty for delivery suite at 11 am (August)

Whereabouts of consultant anaesthetist	No. (%) units 1–500 deliveries		No. (%) units 501–2000 deliveries		No. (%) units 2001–4000 deliveries		No. (%) units >4000 deliveries		Total (%) units	
In hospital	16	(7)	76	(51)	80	(63)	15	(60)	187	(36)
Less than 20 minutes away	27	(12)	53	(36)	43	(33)	9	(32)	132	(26)
More than 20 minutes away	10	(5)	5	(3)	3	(2)	0		18	(3)
No consultant available	165	(76)	15	(10)	0		0		180	(35)
TOTAL	218		149		126		24		517	(100)

TABLE 6.9 Availability of consultant anaesthetist on duty for delivery suite at 11 pm (August)

Whereabouts of consultant anaesthetist	No. (%) units 1–500 deliveries		No. (%) units 501–2000 deliveries		No. (%) units 2001–4000 deliveries		No. (%) units >4000 deliveries		Total (%) units	
In hospital	1	(1)	8	(5)	8	(6)	1	(4)	18	(3)
Less than 20 minutes away	37	(17)	100	(67)	93	(72)	19	(76)	249	(48)
More than 20 minutes away	16	(7)	15	(10)	14	(11)	2	(8)	47	(9)
None	164	(75)	26	(18)	14	(11)	3	(12)	207	(40)
TOTAL	218	(100)	149	(100)	129	(100)	25	(100)	521	(100)

TABLE 6.10 Grade of anaesthetists not in the hospital but available for the delivery area and less than 20 minutes away at 11 am (August)

Grade of anaesthetists	Number (%) of units 1–500		Number (%) of units 501–2000		Number (%) of units 2001–4000		Number (%) of units >4000	
Consultant	27	(21)	53	(48)	42	(57)	6	(75)
Senior registrar	6	(5)	16	(14)	11	(15)	2	(25)
Registrar	5	(4)	11	(10)	11	(15)	0	
SHO	3	(2)	24	(22)	6	(8)	0	
Clinical assistant	3	(2)	7	(6)	4	(5)	0	
GP	85	(66)	0		0		0	
TOTAL	129	(100)	111	(100)	74	(100)	8	(100)

TABLE 6.11   Grade of anaesthetists not in the hospital but available for the delivery area and less than 20 minutes away at 11 pm (August)

Grade of anaesthetists	Number (%) of units 1–500		Number (%) of units 501–2000		Number (%) of units 2001–4000		Number (%) of units >4000	
Consultant	37	(27)	100	(60)	93	(64)	19	(68)
Senior registrar	4	(3)	15	(9)	18	(12)	6	(21)
Registrar	9	(6)	27	(16)	17	(12)	2	(7)
SHO	5	(4)	16	(10)	14	(9)	0	
Clinical assistant	4	(3)	9	(5)	4	(3)	1	(4)
GP	79	(57)	1		0		0	
TOTAL	138	(100)	168	(100)	146	(100)	28	(100)

In units below 500 deliveries per year the majority of anaesthetists available were general practitioners. Less than 30 per cent of units had consultants or senior registrars available in the event of the GP anaesthetist requiring help within that unit.

Table 6.12 shows that very few anaesthetists available for the labour ward were more than 20 minutes away.

TRAINING OF JUNIOR ANAESTHETISTS

Teaching of junior anaesthetists is only possible in hospitals where two or more anaesthetists are present during the day. Table 6.13 shows that in the three larger size groups of units, this occurs in one-half to three-quarters, so that about one-third of all units with more than 2000 deliveries could do no teaching

TABLE 6.12   Grade of anaesthetist not in hospital but available for the delivery and more than 20 minutes away at 11 am and 11 pm (August)

Grade of anaesthetist	Number (%) of units 1–500		Number (%) of units 501–2000		Number (%) of units 2001–4000		Number (%) of units °>4000	
	11 am	11 pm	11 am	11 pm	11 am	11 pm	11 am	11 pm
Consultant	10	16	5	15	3	14	0	2
Senior registrar	1	2	2	2	0	0	0	0
Registrar	5	4	2	2	0	0	0	0
Registrar	5	4	0	1	0	0	0	0
SHO	1	2	0	1	0	0	0	0
Clinical assistant	1	3	0	0	0	0	0	0
GP	17	5	2	1	0	0	0	0
TOTAL	35	32	9	20	3	14	0	2

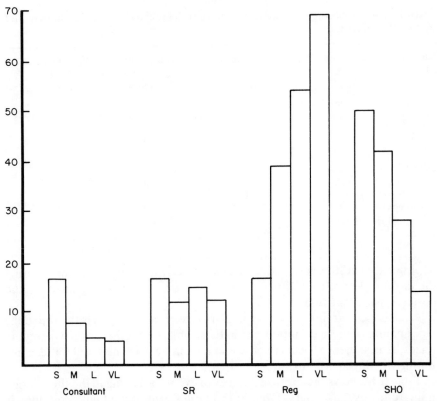

Figure 6.3   Grade of anaesthetist on premises and available for delilvery area at 11 pm

TABLE 6.13   Number of units with more than two anaesthetists in the hospital at 11 am (August)

Number of anaesthetists in hospital	Number (%) of units 501–2000 (Medium)		Number (%) of units 2001–4000 (Large)		Number (%) of units >4000 (Very large)	
One or no anaesthetist in hospital	70	(48)	46	(36)	7	(28)
Two or more anaesthetists in hospital	78	(52)	82	(64)	18	(72)
	148	(100)	128	(100)	25	(100)

TABLE 6.14   Anaesthetic workload and obstetrical events per unit in a 24-hour period
by size of unit (August)

Number of events per 24-h	Medium unit 501–2000 deliveries	Large unit 2001–4000 deliveries	Very large unit >4000 deliveries
Anaesthesia			
Epidural	0.3	1.6	3
General	0.4	0.9	1.4
Obstetrics			
Caesarean section	0.4	1.0	1.7
Twins and breech	0.07	0.15	0.28
Forceps	0.3	0.8	2.1
Normal delivery	3	6	8.5

of obstetric anaesthesia to juniors during the day. In 9 per cent of units during the day and 17 per cent at night a SHO is the anaesthetist available for the obstetric patients overall.

A further constraint to the teaching of obstetric anaesthesia is the round the clock nature of the speciality. Even in those units where there are two or more anaesthetists, there appears to be less emergency clinical material for teaching during the daytime hours.

Table 6.14 shows the average number of events occurring in the three larger unit groups over 24 hours. Even in the 52 per cent of medium sized units in which teaching can occur, on average one Caesarean section is performed every two days and one forceps delivery every three days. In the large units, more anaesthetic events occur and on average one Caesarean section is performed every 24 hours and three epidurals each 24 hours. In 72 per cent of very large units where teaching can occur three epidurals are performed daily as well as three Caesarean sections with general anaesthesia every two days approximately.

Table 6.15 shows that 573 general and epidural anaesthetics were given in the 24 hours in the UK. Other major procedures requiring anaesthesia and events that may have required the presence of the anaesthetist such as breech and twin deliveries or manual removal of the placenta are also noted.

Table 6.16 shows how these events are related to the units by their size. Although anaesthetic demands in the small units are low there is little difference in the requirements for general anaesthesia in the three larger size units (Figure 6.4). In the medium sized units however, the workload is dissipated between 149 units, which is almost the same number as the two largest groups which together comprise 154 units. Thus there were 68 general and 54 epidural

TABLE 6.15 Total anaesthetic and obstetric events in the United Kingdom in 24 hours in August

Events	Number per 24 hours Maternities = 2032	%
Anaesthesia		
General anaesthetic	232	11
Epidural block	341	17
Obstetrical		
Normal delivery	1537	75
Forceps	227	11
Caesarean section	257	12
Breeches and twins	39	2
Other major procedures	80	4

TABLE 6.16 Total obstetric and anaesthetic events per 24 hours in each size unit

Events	Number (%) small units 1–500 deliveries		Number (%) medium units 501–2000 deliveries		Number (%) large units 2001–4000 deliveries		Number (%) very large units >4000 deliveries	
Total deliveries	95		579		1041		317	
Normal delivery	86	(90)	448	(77)	779	(75)	214	(68)
Forceps	8	(8)	52	(9)	108	(10)	54	(17)
Twins and breech	0		11	(2)	20	(2)	7	(2)
Caeserean section								
Elective	0		33	(6)	58	(6)	17	(5)
Emergency	1		35	(6)	76	(7)	25	(8)
Total	1		68	(12)	134	(13)	42	(13)
Other major procedures	0		12	(2)	51	(5)	16	(5)
General anaesthesia	2	(2)	68	(12)	120	(12)	36	(11)
Epidural anaesthesia	1	(1)	54	(9)	203	(20)	77	(24)

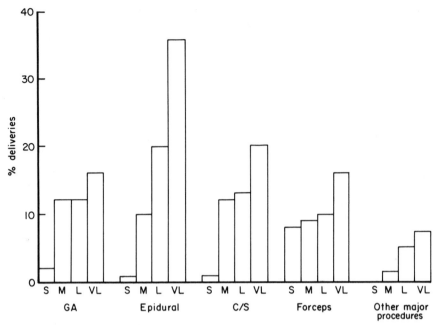

Figure 6.4   Anaesthetic demands as percentage of deliveries by unit size (S = small, M = medium, L = large, VL = very large)

anaesthetics in the 149 medium sized units but 156 general and 276 epidural anaesthetists in the 154 larger units.

The provision of immediately available safe anaesthesia in these medium units may be considered profligate of anaesthetic manpower and offering insufficient activity for the anaesthetist to maintain interest or gain adequate experience of the obstetric patient with her particular anaesthetic problems. Although units of 501–2000 size often did not have an anaesthetist immediately available for the obstetric patient (Table 6.2), mothers delivering in such units had the same anaesthetic requirements as do those in the larger units. Those in the larger units were more likely to be more experienced than those in the medium sized units (see Figures 6.5 and 6.6).

EPIDURAL SERVICE

Advances in obstetric care have resulted from the use of epidural anaesthesia, but it has created a greater anaesthetic commitment to the delivery suite. The 1973–75 Report on the Confidential Enquiries into Maternal Deaths in England and Wales[3] states: 'Epidural analgesia is entirely contra-indicated for

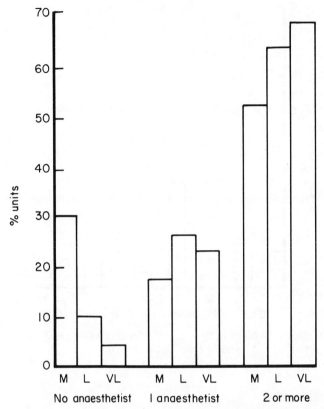

Figure 6.5   Numbers of anaesthetists available for delivery area by unit size at 11 am (M = medium, L = large, VL = very large)

safety reasons unless a trained anaesthetist is immediately available whenever the technique is in use'. The 1976–78 Report[4] states: 'It is also unsafe to use epidural analgesia in labour and for delivery if the anaesthetist is not immediately available to attend to the patient. This is not the counsel of perfection, simply a recommendation to transfer the same level of anaesthetic care to obstetric patients as that regarded as being essential in surgical practice.'

As the anaesthetist must be in constant attendance on each patient during an operation or for a group of patients in an intensive care ward, so he must be constantly available for mothers throughout the duration of the epidural blocks. The presence in the delivery suite of essential resuscitative equipment as well as an anaesthetist is a measure for the mother's safety with epidural anaesthesia, as serious complications (which may occur rarely) must be treated quickly if a catastrophe is to be avoided.

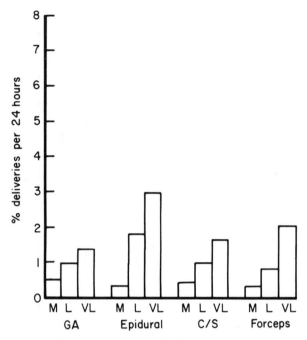

Figure 6.6   Events in 24 hours in medium (M), large (L) and very large (VL) units in August as a percentage of the deliveries that occurred.

Availability of service

There are 296 units in the United Kingdom that provide an epidural service. Only 18 of these deliver fewer than 500 babies a year while 284 or 95 per cent of all units with more than 500 deliveries a year offer an epidural service. Forty-five per cent of these (136) offer an epidural on-demand service while another 45 per cent (137) offer an epidural service when possible. There are 28 medium sized units (501–2000 deliveries) and two large units (2001–4000 deliveries per year) with no epidural service. All units over 4000 deliveries have epidural services.

Table 6.17 shows that 70 per cent of the medium sized units and 44 per cent of the large units have a limited or no epidural service while a quarter of the very big units have only a limited epidural service. The overall epidural rate is 17 per cent. Medium units have a 9 per cent epidural rate, large units a 20 per cent rate and the very large units 24 per cent (see also Figure 6.7).

Staffing

The availability of the anaesthetist is of special concern when epidural anal-

TABLE 6.17   Epidural service in the three larger sized units (August)

Availability of epidural service	Number (%) of medium units 501–2000 deliveries		Number (%) of large units 2001–4000 deliveries		Number (%) of very large units >4000 deliveries		Total availability	
Epidural on demand	45	(30)	72	(56)	19	(76)	136	(45)
Epidural when possible	76	(51)	55	(43)	6	(24)	137	(45)
No epidural service	28	(19)	2	(1)	0		30	(10)
Total units	149	(100)	129	(100)	25	(100)	303	(100)

gesia is in progress. It is not possible to have appropriate access for essential care unless the anaesthetist is immediately available for the obstetric patient with an epidural block. Anaesthetists who also have duties elsewhere in hospital are only immediately available when not busy giving other anaesthetics. Those not on the premises are quite obviously not immediately available. Table 6.18 shows the whereabouts of the anaesthetist in those units with a 24-hour epidural on-demand service and indicates that both during the

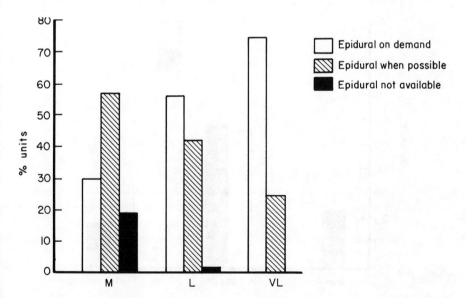

Figure 6.7   Percentage of units and their epidural service in medium (M), large (L) and very large (VL) units (August)

TABLE 6.18   Presence of anaesthetist in the 136 units with an epidural anaesthetic service on demand at 11 am and 11 pm (August)

Whereabouts of anaesthetist	Units with epidural on demand 11 am (%)	Units with epidural on demand 11 am (%)
No anaesthetist in hospital	15 (10)	33 (23)
In hospital with other duties	76 (55)	79 (58)
For delivery area duty	46 (33)	24 (18)
TOTAL	136	136

day and at night some units have no anaesthetist on the premises in spite of an epidural on-demand service (Figure 6.8).

Tables 6.19 and 6.20 show the most senior anaesthetist in the hospital in relation to the epidural service during the day and night. In more than half the units with an epidural service, a consultant anaesthetist is in the hospital during the day; however, in almost 10 per cent of units with an on-demand epidural service, the most senior anaesthetist in the hospital is a senior house officer, a clinical assistant or a GP. During the night, in almost half the units the most senior anaesthetist present in the hospital with an on-demand epidural service was a registrar.

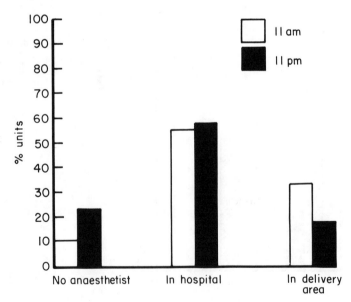

Figure 6.8   Availability of anaesthetists in percentage of units offering on-demand epidural service at 11 am and 11 pm (August)

TABLE 6.19   Most senior grade of anaesthetist in hospital at 11 am and the type of epidural service (August)

Grade of anaesthetist	Number (%) of units with epidural on available		Number (%) of units with epidural when available		Number (%) of units with epidural not available	
Consultant	83	(56)	92	(62)	13	(9)
SR	17	(11)	6	(4)	1	(0.4)
Registrar	19	(13)	12	(8)	1	(0.4)
SHO	7	(5)	5	(3)	1	(0.4)
Clinical assistant	4	(3)	2	(1)	3	(1)
GP	1	(0.6)	1	(0.6)	13	(6)
No anaesthetist available	15	(10)	30	(20)	192	(86)
TOTAL	146	(100)	148	(100)	224	(100)

In units where epidurals are done only when possible, the anaesthetic staffing is poorer with 38 per cent of units having no anaesthetist on the premises and 22 per cent having a senior house officer as the most senior anaesthetist in the hospital. The provision of this limited epidural service may be safer for the mother than an on-demand service with insufficient anaesthetic care. In units where epidurals are not available, 95 per cent have no anaesthetist present at night (see also Figure 6.9).

In an average of 73 (49 per cent) units with an on-demand epidural service, an anaesthetist was recorded as being present in the delivery suite at 11 am. An average of 24 units (16 per cent) recorded the anaesthetist present in the delivery suite in those units with a limited epidural service. The fact that the anaesthetist was present on the labour ward at any particular time may have

TABLE 6.20   Most senior grade of anaesthetist in hospital at 11 pm and the type of epidural service

Grade of anaesthetist	Number (%) of units with epidural on demand		Number (%) of units with epidural when possible		Number (%) of units with epidural not available	
Consultant	12	(8)	6	(4)	0	(0)
SR	19	(13)	15	(10)	0	(0)
Registrar	65	(44)	37	(25)	2	(1)
SHO	13	(9)	32	(22)	4	(2)
Clinical assistant	4	(3)	2	(1)	0	
GP	1	(0.6)	0		0	
No anaesthetist	34	(22)	56	(38)	212	(95)
TOTAL	148	(100)	148	(100)	218	

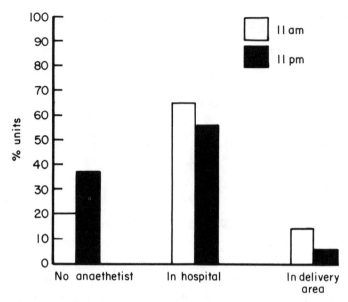

Figure 6.9   Availability of anaesthetists in percentage of units offering 'when available' epidural service at 11 am and 11 pm (August)

been coincidence as only in 48 units with an on-demand service were anaesthetists available solely for the labour ward during the day and in only 27 at night. In the units where epidurals are available only when possible, nineteen have anaesthetists available solely for the labour ward during the day and nine at night.

The availability of the anaesthetist related to the availability of the epidural service is shown in Tables 6.21 and 6.22 which indicate that the anaesthetic cover is similar during the day in both the on-demand service and in the limited service. At night, however, fewer units with a limited service have an exclusive

TABLE 6.21   Anaesthetist on call for delivery area only with epidural on-demand service 11 am and 11 pm (August)

	Number (%) units with 501–2000 deliveries		Number (%) units with 2001–4000 deliveries		Number (%) units with >4000 deliveries	
Epidural on demand	45		72		19	
Anaesthetist 11 am	5	(11)	31	(43)	12	(63)
Anaesthetist 11 pm	4	(1)	13	(18)	10	(53)

TABLE 6.22 Anaesthetist on call for delivery area only by epidural in units with an epidural service when possible 11 am and 11 pm (August)

	Number (%) units 501–2000 deliveries		Number (%) units 2001–4000 deliveries		Number (%) units >4000 deliveries	
Number units with an epidural when possible service	76		54		7	
Anaesthetist 11 am	6	(8)	12	(22)	3	(43)
Anaesthetist 11 pm	0	—	7	(13)	2	(28)

anaesthetist. These therefore declare themselves able to offer epidurals only when possible.

Emergency equipment

The facilities available in the delivery suite when an epidural service is offered are of considerable interest. Most units have epidural services but most do not have an anaesthetist immediately available for the obstetric patient. Whenever an epidural anaesthetic is in progress a mother can develop a total spinal block. This demands early diagnosis and urgent treatment by the anaesthetist if the mother is to survive unharmed. The condition may be diagnosed by the midwives before maternal cardiac arrest occurs but without the immediate availability of resuscitative equipment, essential treatment would be delayed.

TABLE 6.23 Percentage of anaesthetic facilities available in the delivery area

	Units with 501–2000 deliveries (%)	Units with 2001–4000 deliveries (%)	Units with >4000 deliveries (%)
With epidural service	81	98	100
No anaesthetic machine in delivery area	18	1	0
No ventilator in delivery area	34	17	6
No ECG monitor in delivery area	49	31	3
No cardiac arrest trolley in delivery area	32	17	2

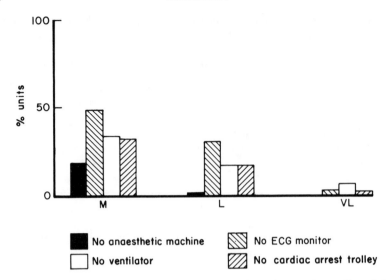

Figure 6.10   Absence of certain items of anaesthetic equipment in medium (M), large (L) and very large (VL) hospitals (August)

Bringing the cardiac arrest equipment and team from elsewhere in the hospital would cause delay. While most units have anaesthetic machines, fewer have a ventilator; many are without an ECG monitor or a cardiac arrest trolley in the delivery suite (Table 6.23 and Figure 6.10).

OTHER RELEVANT OPERATIVE FACILITIES

The operative facilities are analysed more fully in Chapter 3 but a short section is included here because of their relevance to the anaesthetist.

Obstetric operating theatre

The ideal situation of an exclusive theatre in the delivery area was found more often in the bigger units, but it is only achieved in 70 and 76 per cent, respectively in the large and very large units (Table 6.24). Clearly transferring mothers in labour to operating theatres elsewhere in the hospital must increase fetal hypoxia. The necessity for such a transfer for Caesarean section occurred at almost the same rate of about 12 per cent in all sized units. Sharing a theatre with other disciplines is unsatisfactory for it can cause unpreventable delay if another surgeon is in the middle of an operation. Although less common in the biggest units, it was still found in three (12 per cent) of the very large units performing over 4000 deliveries a year.

TABLE 6.24 Obstetric operating theatres in relation to delivery areas (August)

	Small units 1–500 deliveries number (%)		Medium units 501–2000 deliveries number (%)		Large units 2001–4000 deliveries number (%)		Very large units >4000 deliveries number (%)	
Theatre exclusive in delivery area	10	(5)	77	(52)	90	(70)	19	(76)
Theatre exclusive to obstetrics elsewhere in hospital	36	(16)	18	(12)	17	(13)	3	(12)
Theatre not exclusive to obstetrics	48	(22)	54	(36)	22	(17)	3	(12)
No theatre available	124	(57)	0		0		0	
TOTAL	218	(100)	149	(100)	129	(100)	25	(100)

Stored group O rhesus negative blood

This essential requirement in emergency obstetrics was available in most units either in the delivery suite or in the hospital, 92 per cent of the very large units, 80 per cent of the large and 68 per cent of the medium sized units. In the small units, only one-quarter had blood on the premises and more than one-third had no access to stored blood as shown in Table 6.25.

TABLE 6.25 Blood storage area with group O rhesus negative blood (August)

	Small units 1–500 deliveries number (%)		Medium units 501–2000 deliveries number (%)		Large units 2001–4000 deliveries number (%)		Very large units >4000 deliveries number (%)	
In delivery area	8	(4)	25	(18)	47	(36)	15	(60)
In hospital	45	(21)	74	(50)	57	(44)	8	(32)
Elsewhere	78	(36)	41	(28)	23	(18)	2	(8)
Not available	81	(38)	4	(3)	0		0	
Missing data	5		4		2		1	
TOTAL	219		149		129		26	

TABLE 6.26   Availability of recovery room for mothers by size of unit (August)

Mother's access to recovery room	Small units 1–500 number (%)		Medium units 501–2000 number (%)		Large units 2001–4000 number (%)		Very large units >4000 number (%)	
In delivery area	15	(7)	38	(26)	65	(50)	17	(68)
Elsewhere in hospital	47	(27)	52	(35)	27	(21)	4	(16)
Not available	130	(60)	41	(28)	25	(19)	4	(16)
Missing data	23	(10)	17	(11)	12	(9)	1	
TOTAL	217		149		129		26	

Recovery room for mothers

As shown in Table 6.26, a recovery room was not available in a number of units; almost one-fifth of the large units were without this facility. It is unsafe for any patient to be transported anywhere in the immediate post-operative period. She should therefore be cared for in a recovery room which ideally should be very close to the operating theatre. This facility must be considered essential for any patient after an anaesthetic; poor post-operative care accounted for almost one third of maternal deaths in the 1979–81 Report on the

TABLE 6.27   Numbers of units by size in each region (August)

	Small units 1–500 deliveries	Medium units 501–2000 deliveries	Large and very large units >2000 (% of all units)		Total number of units
Northern	7	14	7	(25)	28
Yorkshire	12	9	10	(32)	31
Trent	15	5	14	(41)	34
East Anglia	7	4	4	(27)	15
North-West Thames	4	9	9	(41)	22
North-East Thames	7	7	14	(50)	28
South-East Thames	4	16	7	(26)	27
South-West Thames	2	19	6	(35)	17
Wessex	16	8	6	(20)	30
Oxford	11	1	8	(40)	20
South-Western	24	5	8	(22)	37
West Midlands	15	10	16	(39)	41
Mersey	0	2	8	(80)	10
North-Western	9	7	14	(47)	30
Wales	18	13	6	(16)	37
Scotland	45	13	13	(18)	71
Northern Ireland	13	10	4	(15)	27

TABLE 6.28   Anaesthetic workload expressed as % of total load and incidence of Caesarean sections by regions (August)

	Anaesthesia		Caesarean section %	Total number of deliveries per 24 hours
	Epidural %	General %		
Northern	11	14	10	105
Yorkshire	23	8	9	132
Trent	20	6	10	163
East Anglia	27	10	16	62
North-West Thames	24	11	13	119
North-East Thames	9	9	14	160
South-East Thames	14	11	11	147
South-West Thames	20	9	11	87
Wessex	11	9	11	91
Oxford	15	10	12	85
South-Western	15	6	14	110
West Midlands	18	10	14	200
Mersey	30	16	17	74
North-Western	12	8	15	145
Wales	8	9	13	91
Scotland	18	12	20	163
Northern Ireland	6	8	8	84

Confidential Enquiry into Maternal Deaths[5] and the absence of a recovery room in the delivery area may have been a factor.

Further discussion about these facilities will be found in Chapter 3.

REGIONAL ANAESTHETIC PROVISION

Table 6.27 shows the breakdown of units in each region and the percentage of units delivering about 2000 babies a year. Most of the hospitals in the Mersey region are over 2000 delivery size; none there delivers fewer than 500 infants a year whereas in the South-Western region over half of its units deliver fewer than 500 babies a year. With the exception of Mersey all regions have half or fewer of their obstetric units in the over 2000 deliveries a year group.

Table 6.28 shows the anaesthetic workload in the different regions. The highest epidural rate occurs in Mersey and the lowest in Northern Ireland, where just under three-quarters of the units deliver less than 2000 babies a year (see also Figure 6.11). The Caesarean section rate is here used as an example of anaesthetic workload; every section needs some form of anaesthetic. In all regions except Northern the general anaesthetic rate is less than the Caesarean section rate. This is indicative of the greater use of epidural block in obstetrics, for Caesarean sections and other operative procedures. The use of epidural anaesthesia for pain relief in vaginal deliveries is indicated by the greater

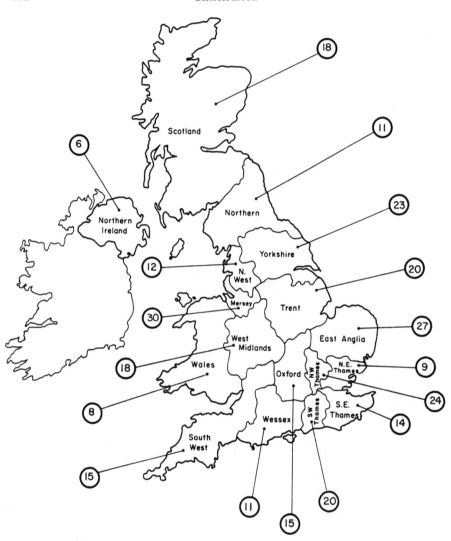

Figure 6.11   Percentage of deliveries for which an epidural anaesthetic was given (by regions in August)

incidence of this anaesthetic than Caesarean section rate alone. In most regions, the anaesthetic rate was about 30 per cent of deliveries, lowest in Northern Ireland and Northern regions, and highest in Mersey.

Table 6.29 shows that with the exception of Mersey, where there was one consultant anaesthetist for each of the premises during the day, most regions had many more units than they had consultant anaesthetists available during the day. Many of these units would have been small with no one in labour.

TABLE 6.29 The numbers of units with consultant anaesthetists reported on the premises by regions (August)

	Total no. of units	No. of consultants on premises in day
Northern	28	12
Yorkshire	31	13
Trent	34	16
East Anglia	15	6
North-West Thames	22	17
North-East Thames	28	15
South-East Thames	27	12
South-West Thames	17	12
Wessex	30	10
Oxford	20	10
South-Western	37	10
West Midlands	41	17
Mersey	10	10
North-Western	30	21
Wales	37	14
Scotland	71	17
Northern Ireland	27	19

The regional distribution indicates that many regions contain a large number of units without an immediately available anaesthetic service. The geography of some regions such as Scotland makes this pragmatic. Mersey is the exception in having few units, in almost all of which women deliver more than 2000 babies a year. This region also has the most used anaesthetic facilities.

CONCLUSIONS

The size of the units seems to be a major determinant of anaesthetic facilities. As the size of units increases, so do the availability and numbers in service grades of the anaesthetists. Provision of anaesthetic facilities in the small units is poor but then so is the demand for anaesthetic attention. It would seem sensible for women delivering in these units to have been selected as likely to have normal deliveries. More than half the units of this size have no anaesthetic provision at all; resuscitation may rely on an obstetric flying squad and transfer to a larger unit if necessary.

The greatest cause for concern is the anaesthetic provision for medium sized units (501–2000 deliveries). In these units the anaesthetic demands are similar to those in large and very large units but the availability and grade of the anaesthetist are not equivalent. The 149 units of this size delivering almost 30 per cent of women cannot be staffed with an experienced anaesthetist immediately available to the obstetric patient. Even if sufficient anaesthetists were available, it would be an extravagent waste of anaesthetic manpower to provide an exclusive obstetric service which was used, at the most, once a day.

The dissipated workload spread throughout 149 units cannot provide adequate clinical teaching for junior anaesthetists; even so these are the very units where a most junior anaesthetist is frequently likely to be responsible for anaesthesia in the delivery suite.

The provision of anaesthetic care for the 155 units delivering 70 per cent of children in the two larger sized units is such that only just over one-third have an anaesthetist immediately available and more than half share the attention of an anaesthetist with other disciplines in the hospital. One in ten units delivering more than 2000 children a year has no anaesthetist on the premises, and one in seven has a senior house officer as the most senior anaesthetist at night. To ensure that each of these large units has an anaesthetist of registrar grade immediately available would require the complete attention of over half the anaesthetic registrars in the country. This is obviously not possible and makes the provision of adequate anaesthetic care impractical even for these large units. Training of junior anaesthetists should be concentrated in units delivering over 2000 babies a year as the scarcity of procedures requiring anaesthetic attention in small units makes adequate teaching impossible.

Epidural anaesthetics are used in 284 units delivering more than 500 babies a year. To provide the 'same level of care as that regarded as essential in surgical practice' would require the exclusive attention of 852 anaesthetists if they were on a one-in-three 24-hour rota and even more to cover leave. The countrywide complement of anaesthetic registrars is 803 or 20 per cent of the total of 4013 anaesthetists of all grades.

Concentration of the obstetric patients into larger units would allow a safer provision of immediate anaesthetic care and provide a sufficient workload to justify the exclusive attention of an anaesthetist on the delivery suite for 24 hours. Concentration would also provide opportunities for teaching of junior anaesthetists and thus improve standards of skill, which may reduce the number of avoidable anaesthetic maternal deaths.

REFERENCES

1. Report on the Confidential Enquiry into Maternal Deaths in England and Wales (1952–54), London: HMSO.
2. Ibid. 1955–57, London: HMSO.
3. Ibid. 1973–75, London: HMSO.
4. Ibid. 1976–78, London: HMSO.
5. Ibid. 1979–81, London: HMSO.
6. House of Commons Third Report from The Social Services Committee (1983–84). *Perinatal and Neonatal Mortality Report.*
7. Bromage P.R. (1978). *Epidural Analgesia.*

APPENDIX

TABLE 6A.1 Place of birth
Anaesthetists by size of unit at 11 am – August

Group (No. of dels 1983)	Con- sultant	Senior registrar	Regi- strars	Associate specialist and clinical assistants	GP	Senior house officer
	No.	No.	No.	No.	No.	No.
In delivery area						
1–500	0	0	0	0	3	0
501–2000	5	1	11	4	0	7
2001–4000	33	9	34	3	0	11
4001+	10	6	14	0	0	5
Not grouped	0	0	0	0	0	0
TOTAL	48	16	59	7	3	23
In hospital						
1–500	20	5	7	2	19	5
501–2000	83	21	55	12	0	45
2001–4000	59	20	44	4	0	33
4001+	5	3	5	0	0	1
Not grouped	4	0	1	0	0	0
TOTAL	171	49	112	18	19	84
Within 20 min						
1–500	27	6	6	3	85	3
501–2000	53	16	11	7	0	24
2001–4000	41	11	11	4	0	6
4001+	6	2	0	0	0	1
Not grouped	0	0	0	0	0	0
TOTAL	127	35	28	14	85	34
Greater than 20 min						
1–500	10	1	5	1	17	1
501–2000	5	2	0	0	2	0
2001–4000	3	0	0	0	0	0
4001+	0	0	0	0	0	0
Not grouped	0	0	0	0	0	0
TOTAL	18	3	5	1	19	1

TABLE 6A.2   Place of birth
Anaesthetists by size of unit at 11 pm – August

Group (No. of dels 1983)	Con-sultant	Senior registrar	Regi-strars	Associate specialist and clinical assistants	GP	Senior house officer
	No.	No.	No.	No.	No.	No.
In delivery area						
1–500	0	2	0	0	2	1
501–2000	0	2	2	0	0	1
2001–4000	2	4	15	2	0	6
4001+	1	1	10	0	0	1
Not grouped	1	1	0	0	0	1
TOTAL	4	10	27	2	2	10
In hospital						
1–500	2	1	2	0	3	4
501–2000	8	13	36	4	0	46
2001–4000	6	16	61	3	0	28
4001+	0	3	9	0	0	4
Not grouped	1	0	0	0	0	1
TOTAL	17	33	108	7	3	83
Within 20 min						
1–500	36	5	10	2	82	6
501–2000	99	17	16	8	7	16
2001–4000	91	15	18	5	0	9
4001+	22	5	1	0	0	0
Not grouped	1	0	0	0	0	2
TOTAL	249	42	45	15	89	33
Greater than 20 min						
1–500	16	1	7	1	8	2
501–2000	15	3	1	0	0	3
2001–4000	12	2	0	5	1	0
4001+	2	0	0	0	0	0
Not grouped	2	0	0	0	0	0
TOTAL	47	6	8	6	9	5

TABLE 6A.3   Place of birth
Anaesthetists by size of unit at 11 am – September

Group (No. of dels 1983)	Con-sultant	Senior registrar	Regi-strars	Associate specialist and clinical assistants	GP	Senior house officer
	No.	No.	No.	No.	No.	No.
In delivery area						
1–500	0	0	0	0	4	1
501–2000	4	2	12	0	0	4
2001–4000	4	3	25	0	0	4
4001+	4	3	11	0	0	0
Not grouped	0	0	0	0	0	0
TOTAL	12	8	48	0	4	9
In hospital						
1–500	4	3	7	0	9	6
501–2000	14	6	43	4	0	40
2001–4000	15	15	46	2	1	32
4001+	4	4	10	1	0	1
Not grouped	1	0	0	0	0	2
TOTAL	38	28	106	7	10	81
Within 20 min						
1–500	36	5	5	2	83	3
501–2000	92	9	21	5	2	19
2001–4000	85	16	19	5	0	10
4001+	14	4	2	0	0	0
Not grouped	3	0	0	0	0	0
TOTAL	230	34	47	12	85	32
Greater than 20 min						
1–500	10	2	2	3	8	2
501–2000	17	3	1	1	1	1
2001–4000	12	0	0	0	0	0
4001+	4	0	0	0	0	0
Not grouped	0	0	1	0	0	0
	43	5	4	5	9	3

TABLE 6A.4   Place of birth
Anaesthetists by size of unit at 11 pm – September

Group (No. of dels 1983)	Con- sultant	Senior registrar	Regi- strars	Associate specialist and clinical assistants	GP	Senior house officer
	No.	No.	No.	No.	No.	No.
In delivery area						
1–500	0	0	0	0	3	1
501–2000	2	0	3	0	0	0
2001–4000	1	1	18	0	0	6
4001+	0	1	8	0	0	0
Not grouped	0	0	0	0	0	1
TOTAL	3	2	29	0	3	8
In hospital						
1–500	1	4	3	0	3	2
501–2000	3	8	43	2	0	41
2001–4000	3	17	48	2	0	46
4001+	2	3	12	0	0	2
Not grouped	2	1	0	0	0	1
TOTAL	11	33	106	4	3	75
Within 20 min						
1–500	37	3	9	4	78	5
501–2000	100	15	27	9	1	16
2001–4000	94	18	17	4	0	14
4001+	19	6	2	1	0	0
Not grouped	2	1	0	0	1	0
TOTAL	252	43	55	18	80	35
Greater than 20 min						
1–500	15	2	3	3	5	2
501–2000	15	2	1	0	1	1
2001–4000	14	0	0	0	0	0
4001+	2	0	0	0	0	0
Not grouped	1	0	0	0	0	0
TOTAL	47	4	4	3	6	3

TABLE 6A.5   Place of birth
Anaesthetists by size of unit at 11 am – October

Group (No. of dels 1983)	Con- sultant	Senior registrar	Regi- strars	Associate specialist and clinical assistants	GP	Senior house officer
	No.	No.	No.	No.	No.	No.
In delivery area						
1–500	2	0	0	0	5	0
501–2000	9	2	9	3	1	6
2001–4000	23	10	27	3	0	16
4001+	6	6	10	0	0	1
Not grouped	0	0	0	0	0	0
TOTAL	40	18	46	6	6	23
In hospital						
1–500	20	3	8	0	14	10
501–2000	91	20	59	4	1	58
2001–4000	57	15	51	4	0	24
4000+	15	4	8	0	0	4
Not grouped	8	0	5	0	0	4
TOTAL	191	42	131	8	15	100
Within 20 min						
1–500	28	4	7	3	120	1
501–2000	41	7	14	5	1	15
2001–4000	43	6	16	1	0	9
4001+	4	3	0	0	0	1
Not grouped	2	0	0	1	1	0
TOTAL	118	20	37	10	122	26
Greater than 20 min						
1–500	8	5	2	2	16	3
501–2000	3	2	3	0	1	0
2001–4000	2	0	0	0	0	0
4001+	0	0	0	0	0	0
Not grouped	0	0	1	0	1	0
TOTAL	13	7	6	2	18	3

TABLE 6A.6   Place of birth
Anaesthetists by size of unit at 11 pm – October

Group (No. of dels 1983)	Con-sultant	Senior registrar	Regi-strars	Associate specialist and clinical assistants	GP GP	Senior house officer
	No.	No.	No.	No.	No.	No.
In delivery area						
1–500	0	0	0	0	6	0
501–2000	3	2	9	0	0	4
2001–4000	2	6	19	1	0	2
4001+	0	1	10	0	0	1
Not grouped	0	0	0	0	0	0
TOTAL	5	9	38	1	6	7
In hospital						
1–500	2	3	4	0	0	4
501–2000	9	13	38	2	0	46
2001–4000	3	16	46	1	0	32
4001+	0	2	9	0	0	4
Not grouped	2	0	2	1	0	7
TOTAL	16	34	99	4	0	93
Within 20 mins						
1–500	39	3	8	5	97	5
501–2000	93	15	18	7	7	16
2001–4000	92	15	20	3	0	13
4001+	16	8	1	3	0	1
Not grouped	7	0	0	1	1	1
TOTAL	247	41	47	19	105	36
Greater than 20 min						
1–500	14	7	2	1	6	5
501–2000	18	3	2	1	3	1
2001–4000	12	1	0	0	0	0
4001+	5	1	0	0	0	0
Not grouped	0	1	1	0	0	0
TOTAL	49	13	5	2	9	6

TABLE 6A.7   Place of birth
Anaesthetists by size of unit at 11 am – November

Group (No. of dels 1983)	Con-sultant	Senior Registrar	Regi-strars	Associate specialist and clinical assistants	GP	Senior house officer
	No.	No.	No.	No.	No.	No.
In delivery area						
1–500	1	1	1	0	5	1
501–2000	10	0	8	1	1	9
2001–4000	30	5	38	2	0	13
4001+	8	4	11	0	0	4
Not grouped	0	0	1	0	0	0
TOTAL	49	10	59	3	6	27
In hospital						
1–500	24	4	8	1	12	9
501–2000	93	23	52	11	0	64
2001–4000	62	15	45	5	1	31
4001+	10	3	10	1	0	1
Not grouped	5	1	2	2	0	2
TOTAL	194	46	117	20	13	107
Within 20 mins						
1–500	26	4	4	5	113	2
501–2000	43	7	15	3	2	11
2001–4000	31	8	9	1	0	6
4001+	3	2	3	0	0	1
Not grouped	2	0	0	1	1	0
TOTAL	105	21	31	10	116	20
Greater than 20 min						
1–500	10	5	3	2	31	2
501–2000	4	2	3	2	1	1
2001–4000	1	1	1	0	0	1
4001+	2	0	0	0	0	0
Not grouped	0	0	1	0	0	0
TOTAL	17	8	8	4	32	4

TABLE 6A.8 Place of birth
Anaesthetists by size of unit at 11 pm – November

Group (No. of dels 1983)	Consultant	Senior registrar	Registrars	Associate specialist and clinical assistants	GP	Senior house officer
	No.	No.	No.	No.	No.	No.
In delivery area						
1–500	0	0	0	0	3	0
501–2000	1	2	2	0	0	2
2001–4000	0	0	16	0	0	8
4001+	0	0	9	1	0	2
Not grouped	0	0	0	0	0	0
TOTAL	1	2	27	1	3	12
In hospital						
1–500	4	2	7	1	1	4
501–2000	13	17	37	1	0	47
2001–4000	2	17	49	2	0	30
4001+	1	4	9	1	0	3
Not grouped	2	0	1	2	0	1
TOTAL	22	40	103	7	1	85
Within 20 min						
1–500	40	7	5	5	100	5
501–2000	93	11	21	5	3	21
2001–4000	95	15	19	0	0	12
4001+	19	6	5	0	0	1
Not grouped	5	0	1	1	2	0
TOTAL	252	39	51	11	105	39
Greater than 20 min						
1–500	17	2	3	2	24	2
501–2000	15	2	0	1	1	1
2001–4000	9	1	0	0	0	0
4001+	5	0	0	0	0	0
Not grouped	0	0	0	0	0	0
TOTAL	46	5	3	3	25	3

Birthplace
G.V.P. Chamberlain
© 1987 John Wiley & Sons Ltd.

CHAPTER 7

Paediatric Facilities

BRIAN SPEIDEL

INTRODUCTION

During the past fifteen years, a number of reports[1-4] published about perinatal care have dealt mainly with staffing and facilities for special and intensive care of the newborn and have been concerned with care in the delivery room only briefly. The role of the paediatrician in the delivery area is primarily the resuscitation of the asphyxiated neonate but it also involves the immediate management of the very low birthweight baby and those babies with malformations or a variety of other disorders needing immediate intervention.

The discussion document produced by the Royal College of Obstetrics and Gynaecology/British Paediatric Association Joint Committee in 1978 'Recommendations for the improvement of infant care during the perinatal period in the UK'[1] commented that flexibility was necessary in the responsibility for resuscitation in the labour wards and that all medical and nursing staff in maternity hospitals should be able to resuscitate newborn infants. The Second Report from the House of Commons Social Services Committee (1979–80)[3] was more specific and recommended that 'In all maternity units (including GP units) there should be present at every delivery where problems of resuscitation are anticipated, a trained person . . . whose sole responsibility is to resuscitate and give immediate care to the baby. This person should normally in consultant units be a paediatrician.' This report also stated that the trained person should be available within at most two minutes' call of the delivery room in case unexpected difficulties arise. These recommendations were incorporated into the British Paediatric Association's guidelines on minimum standards of neonatal care[4] submitted to the Maternity Services Advisory Committee in 1983, it being emphasized that these were minimum, not optimum standards. The guidelines state that 'At all times in all maternity units there must be someone available in the labour ward (or able to reach there within two minutes) capable of starting expert neonatal resuscitation by intubation or bag and mask'. In district general hospitals and regional intensive care units the resuscitation service should be supported by a special care baby unit under the supervision of at least two consultant paediatricians with 24-hour resident junior paediatric staff of SHO and/or registrar grade. In small maternity units the workload could not justify resident paediatric staff and the guidelines recommend that such units must not deliver high risk mothers. Nevertheless, emergencies do occur and arrangements for paediatric cover must be provided and facilities made available for transport of the sick newborn baby to a special care baby unit.

GRADES OF PAEDIATRIC STAFF

Consultants

Several comments about the NHS grades of staff are made in Chapter 3. We examine here those features which relate to paediatrics.

Much of the neonatal care in hospital in the UK is under the supervision of general paediatric consultants. The number of sessions each week devoted to the newborn service will depend upon the workload but it is thought that in a district general hospital (DGH) a consultant paediatrician may spend one-third of his time with the newborn. In large DGHs or regional centres there is an increasing number of neonatal paediatricians who spend most, if not all, their time in newborn care.

Senior registrars

These are consultants in training who are based in teaching hospitals though they will rotate to peripheral hospitals as part of their training. Most will include a period of neonatal care in the training programme but will usually have only several sessions per week for this and non-resident on-call duties.

Associate specialists

There are relatively few doctors in this grade in paediatrics, and because of their varied training and higher qualifications, it is difficult to fit them into the hierarchy of the hospital staff in a study where the data must be collected by a compact questionnaire.

Registrars

The major postgraduate qualification in paediatrics is the MRCP (Paed) diploma of the three Royal Colleges of Physicians. Most paediatric registrars will have passed Part I of this examination and many will have the full MRCP diploma which is normally a requirement for appointment to a senior registrar post. Most registrars will have some neonatal responsibilities as part of their daily programme but will often have general paediatric duties as well which may be in a different part of the hospital or even in a different hospital altogether. In larger DGHs or regional centres there are some registrar posts with full-time neonatal duties. Some registrar posts are resident when on call.

Clinical assistants

In paediatrics these tend to be doctors with domestic responsibilities who do part-time work in hospital. They are not often involved in acute neonatal work or on-call rotas, though may work in the lying-in wards with the normal baby.

General practitioners

The GP obstetrician will normally also look after the babies of his mothers, though in some GP units attached to consultant units the hospital paediatric staff may help with the neonatal care of his patients. The GP will usually be on call only for his own patients or for those of his practice colleagues.

Senior house officers

Paediatrics, especially neonatal care, is not normally a pre-registration post. The SHO performs most of the neonatal resuscitation in labour wards and the routine daily care of babies in lying-in wards and SCBUs. The SHO may have both neonatal and general paediatric duties in different parts of the same hospital or even in different hospitals. In larger units SHOs are full-time neonatal appointments and in this case will usually have previous general paediatric experience. SHO posts are resident on call and are held for six months.

PAEDIATRICIANS IN AND ON CALL FOR DELIVERY AREA

The main responsibility of the paediatric staff in the delivery room is the resuscitation of the asphyxiated baby. In general practitioner units this will be the responsibility of the GP, but in hospitals the SHO is normally the first on call for the labour wards. He will summon more senior aid if difficulties arise or in cases of multiple births. In all cases where a problem with the baby can be anticipated the paediatrician should be sent for before the baby is delivered, and there should be sufficient time for him to come from elsewhere in the hospital. The total data on availability of all grades of paediatricians on all the survey days at 11 am and 11 pm are given in the appendix tables to this chapter (Tables 7A.1–7A.8).

TABLE 7.1 Paediatricians by size of unit. Units of 1–500 deliveries (August)

	In delivery area	In hospital	<20 minutes	>20 minutes	Total (mean)
11 am Number of units 217					
Consultant	0	13	27	19	59 (0.27)
Senior registrar	0	3	3	6	12 (0.05)
Registrar	0	5	6	7	18 (0.08)
Associate specialist Clinical assistant	0	6	2	2	10 (0.05)
GP	9	33	271	70	383 (1.76)
SHO	0	21	9	12	42 (0.19)
11 pm Number of units 216					
Consultant	0	1	37	16	54 (0.25)
Senior registrar	1	2	5	4	12 (0.05)
Registrar	1	3	6	5	15 (0.07)
Associate specialist Clinical assistant	0	0	3	0	3 (0.01)
GP	4	3	222	54	283 (1.31)
SHO	3	10	8	10	31 (0.14)

In this study we have asked the whereabouts of the medical staff in four categories; either in the delivery area, or in the hospital premises, these two groups being readily available for emergency call, and either within or beyond 20 minutes' call outside the hospital. The recommendations in the opening statement of this chapter state that in all units there must be someone available for neonatal resuscitation within at most two minutes' call. Clearly only those doctors on the hospital premises can fulfil this requirement and those who have to be called even from up to 20 minutes away cannot provide an emergency neonatal resuscitation service, only being available for elective deliveries or where problems can be anticipated in good time.

TABLE 7.2 Paediatricians by size of unit. Units of 501–2000 deliveries (August)

	In delivery area	In hospital	<20 minutes	>20 minutes	Total (mean)
11 am Number of units 148					
Consultant	3	66	49	17	135 (0.9)
Senior registrar	1	13	10	2	26 (0.17)
Registrar	3	36	16	1	56 (0.38)
Associate specialist Clinical assistant	0	8	4	3	15 (0.10)
GP	0	1	11	1	13 (0.09)
SHO	13	145	31	3	192 (1.30)
11 pm Number of units 148					
Consultant	0	7	87	26	120 (0.8)
Senior registrar	0	4	10	3	17 (0.11)
Registrar	0	22	16	2	40 (0.27)
Associate specialist Clinical assistant	0	0	5	1	6 (0.04)
GP	0	0	2	0	2 (0.01)
SHO	10	80	26	2	118 (0.8)

Tables 7.1–7.4 give the numbers of the different grades of paediatric staff and their availability for the delivery area at 11 am and 11 pm by the size of unit in August. There were only small differences between the staffing levels and availability on the three weekdays, and the August figures will be used for a more detailed analysis. The units have been put into four groups according to their number of deliveries in 1983 (small — 1–500, medium — 501–2000, large — 2001–4000 and very large — more than 4000).

Figure 7.1 shows the mean number of each grade of doctor available from all sources added together (in the delivery area, in the hospital, within 20 minutes or more than 20 minutes on call) for the four delivery groups at 11 am and 11 pm

TABLE 7.3 Paediatricians by size of unit. Units of 2001–4000 deliveries (August)

	In delivery area	In hospital	<20 minutes	>20 minutes	Total (mean)
11 am Number of units 129					
Consultant	2	89	40	9	140 (1.08)
Senior registrar	2	28	11	0	41 (0.3)
Registrar	8	77	10	2	97 (0.75)
Associate specialist Clinical assistant	2	2	0	0	4 (0.03)
GP	0	1	1	0	2 (0.01)
SHO	23	167	15	0	205 (1.6)
11 pm Number of units 129					
Consultant	1	4	91	20	116 (0.9)
Senior registrar	1	12	19	0	32 (0.25)
Registrar	4	41	16	2	63 (0.5)
Associate specialist Clinical assistant	0	1	2	0	3 (0.02)
GP	0	1	0	0	1 (0.01)
SHO	24	86	11	0	121 (0.94)

on the August study day. The histogram illustrates how the different grades are distributed according to the size of the unit and gives a staffing profile of each group.

Consultant paediatricians are to be found in all four groups of unit but in the small units 11 am, there are only 0.27 consultants per unit, which probably reflects the fact that the majority of these small units are run by GPs, and that only a small number of such units have consultant staff. In the three larger groups of units, the mean number of consultants is just under 1 per unit (0.90–1.08). At 11 pm the numbers are slightly less, 0.24 for the small units and 0.8–0.9 for each of the larger groups of units.

TABLE 7.4   Paediatricians by size of unit. Units of 4000+ deliveries (August)

	In delivery area	In hospital	<20 minutes	>20 minutes	Total (mean)
11 am Number of units 25					
Consultant	0	19	6	0	25 (0.1)
Senior registrar	0	10	1	1	12 (0.48)
Registrar	4	23	0	0	27 (1.08)
Associate specialist Clinical assistant	0	0	0	0	0 —
GP	0	0	0	0	0 —
SHO	8	41	0	0	49 (1.96)
11 pm Number of units 25					
Consultant	0	2	17	3	22 (0.88)
Senior registrar	2	1	7	0	10 (0.4)
Registrar	4	13	1	0	18 (0.72)
Associate specialist Clinical assistant	0	0	0	0	0 —
GP	0	0	0	0	0 —
SHO	7	19	1	0	27 (1.08)

   The mean number of senior registrars per unit increases in proportion to the size of the unit, from 0.06 for groups of small units to 0.48 for very large units. The small mean number, even for the larger units, suggests that many units either do not have a senior registrar doing neonatal work in the labour wards or else these doctors are providing cover for more than one unit.
   The distribution of registrars is very similar to that of the senior registrars though in greater numbers. The mean number per unit for the group of small units is 0.08, rising to 0.38 for medium, 0.75 for large and 1.08 per unit in very large units. The figures suggest that some units do not have any paediatric registrars on duty for the labour wards or that they have duties in more than one

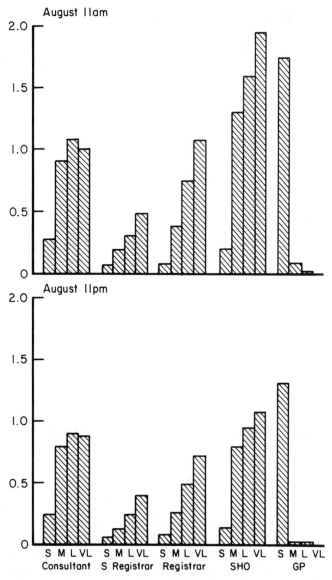

Figure 7.1   Mean number of paediatricians per size of unit at 11 am and 11 pm in August (total units). (S — small, M — medium, L — large and VL — very large)

unit and it is only the very large units that have a registrar on site all day. At 11 pm even the very large units were reduced to a mean of 0.72 registrars/unit.

Analysis of the distribution of registrars with or without the MRCP diploma shows that they are equally distributed in the small, medium and large groups where the proportion of registrars post-MRCP is 58 per cent in small units, 48 per cent in medium units and 51 per cent in large units. In the very large unit, however, the number is 66 per cent suggesting that the larger units have attracted more experienced registrars. It is perhaps surprising that only 56 per cent of all registrars employed at the time of this study had passed the MRCP.

The majority of general practitioners in the survey were in units of up to 500 deliveries per year, where there was a mean of 1.76 per unit. A small number of GPs also work in medium and large units (mean 0.09 and 0.01, respectively).

The number of senior house officers increases with size of unit in a similar fashion to the increase in registrars, the smallest number being in the small unit (0.19 per unit). There is then a large step up in numbers to 1.30 per unit in the medium group, 1.60 in the large and 1.96 in the very large group. At 11 pm there was virtually 1 SHO per unit in large and very large groups, but 0.80 per unit in the medium groups and only 0.14 in the small groups.

The small units are largely run by general practitioners. Figure 7.2 shows that there was always one GP per unit available at all times either in the unit or within 20 minutes' call. There was, however, up to one-third of a GP per unit more than 20 minutes away.

A small number of units in this group have consultant paediatric staff with very small numbers of senior registrars and registrars, and some SHOs; the number of junior staff falls to very low levels on Saturday. A significant proportion of all the paediatric staff in these units was more than 20 minutes away compared with the larger units. For example, the percentage of consultants more than 20 minutes away ranged from 30 per cent at 11 pm on Wednesday to 35 per cent at 11 pm on Saturday. The percentage was higher for senior registrars (50 per cent) and registrars (62 per cent) and lowest for the GP (19 per cent). In these units as many as 32 per cent of SHOs were more than 20 minutes away, which is much higher than for other groups of unit at all times. Indeed, in this group of units, 22 per cent of all grades of staff were more than 20 minutes away.

In the medium units, there was a mean of 0.9 consultant per unit with a small number of registrars (0.38) and a mean of 1.3 SHOs per unit. In many such units the SHO may be responsible directly to the consultant without any registrar support. The number of all staff greater than 20 minutes away at 11 am ranged from 14 per cent on Saturday to 6 per cent on Wednesday 11 am (see also Figure 7.3). Emergency resuscitation in the labour ward will normally be performed by the paediatric SHO most of whom were on the hospital premises, the maximum percentage of SHO more than 20 minutes away on call was 3.3 per cent on Saturday at 11 pm, compared with 17.6 per cent for the same time in small units.

There was a very small number of GPs (0.09), associate specialists and clinical assistants (0.1) working in this group of units.

The highest mean number of consultants per unit in large units

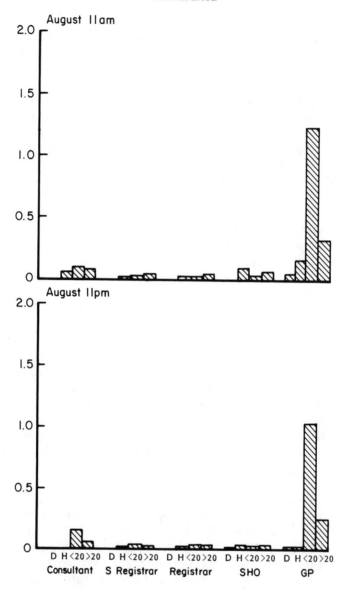

Figure 7.2 Availability of paediatricians in small unit 11 am and 11 pm
D — in delivery unit
H — in hospital
<20 — within 20 minutes' call
>20 — greater than 20 minutes' call

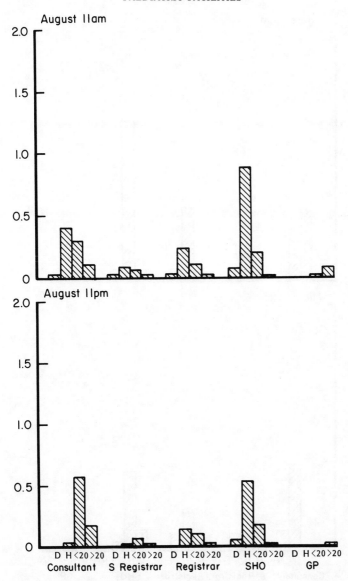

Figure 7.3   Availability of paediatricians in medium unit, 11 am and 11 pm (see Figure 7.2)

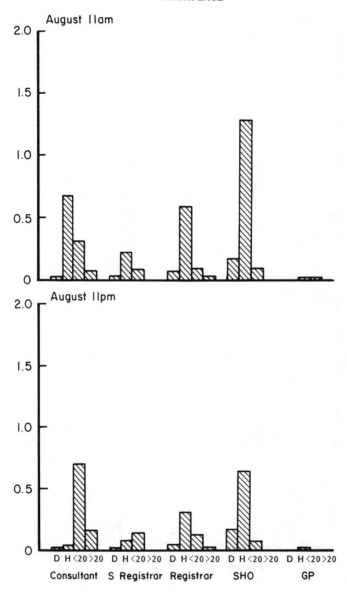

Figure 7.4   Availability of paediatricians in large unit, 11 am and 11 pm (see Figure 7.2)

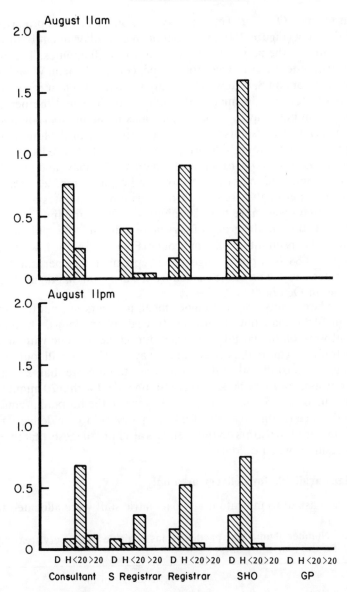

Figure 7.5   Availability of paediatricians in very large unit, 11 am and 11 pm (see Figure 7.2)

was 1.17 at 11 am in October. The majority were on the hospital premises at 11 am on Wednesday (Figure 7.4). At 11 pm on Wednesday and at both sample points on Saturday, the majority were on call within 20 minutes. The number more than 20 minutes away ranged from 6.4 per cent at 11 am on Wednesday to 18 per cent at 11 pm on Saturday. The mean numbers of senior registrars and registrars is greater than in small and medium hospitals and the percentage more than 20 minutes away is less. The maximum number of associate specialists and clinical assistants available at any time during the four months in all these units was only four, similarly, there were only two GPs. The mean number of SHOs was 1.60 per unit at 11 am on Wednesday, and at its lowest was 0.94 at 11 pm. The majority were on the hospital premises at all times though up to 17 per cent were on call from within 20 minutes at 11 pm on Saturday. No SHO was more than 20 minutes away at any time.

There were 26 units in the group of very large units and they had the highest mean number of consultants of all four groups (Figure 7.5). The lowest number at any time was 0.88 at 11 pm in August and September. The percentage more than 20 minutes away at any time ranged from 0 at 11 am on August to 24 per cent at 11 pm in October.

These very large units also had higher mean numbers of senior registrars, registrars and SHOs than units in the other three delivery groups. The majority of these staff were on the hospital premises during the daytime with only one senior registrar being more than 20 minutes away. At 11 pm on all four days the only member of the staff, other than consultant to be more than 20 minutes away, was one associate specialist. Except for one SHO within 20 minutes' call at 11 pm in August and September all SHOs were on the hospital premises all the time and hence readily available for emergency call to the delivery room. The large number of registrars on the premises at 11 pm suggests that they may have been resident when on duty.

Paediatricians available for delivery area only

The units were asked to indicate if any paediatric staff were allocated to the

TABLE 7.5   Number of units with paediatricians available for delivery area only in all units (mean for the four study days)

| | Number of units | |
Number of doctors	11 am	11 pm
None	481	471.5
1	10.75	14.75
2	1.25	0.5
3	0.75	0
Not recorded	27.25	34.75
Total units	521.5	521.25

TABLE 7.6 Number of units with paediatricians available for delivery area only by size of unit (mean for the four study days)

Number of doctors	Small	Medium	Large	Very large
11 am				
None	199.5	170	119.75	21.0
1	0.75	2.25	3.25	4
2	0.5	0.25	0.5	0.5
3	0	0.5	0	0
Not recorded	18.75	11.25	3.75	1
Total units	219.5	184.25	127.25	26.5
11 pm				
None	192.75	140	116.25	21.75
1	3.75	2.75	5.5	3.75
2	0	0	0.5	0
3	0	0	0	0
Not recorded	23	6	5	0.75
Total units	219.5	148.75	127.25	26.25

delivery area with no other duties elsewhere in the hospital. The results are given in Table 7.5. The great majority of units did not have any such member of staff. An average of 10.75 units over the four study days claimed to have an allocated paediatrician at 11 am and 14.75 had such a doctor at 11 pm.

The number of units with one doctor ranged from 0.75 in small units to four in the very large units (Table 7.6). A number of units also claimed to have two or even three paediatricians with no duties other than in the delivery area. Since some of these units were in the small and medium groups it is likely that the question may have been misunderstood.

AVAILABILITY OF PAEDIATRIC STAFF BY WORKLOAD

In order to relate the availability of paediatric staff for the delivery area to the workload, the numbers of staff have been expressed in Tables 7.7–7.10 as number of staff per 100 women in labour at 11 am and 11 pm on each of the study days.

Figure 7.6 shows the total numbers of each grade of staff per 100 women in labour available from all sources (in delivery area, in hospital, less than 20 minutes and more than 20 minutes away) in August. There is a striking difference when compared with Figure 7.1 which shows the mean numbers of staff per unit.

Whereas in Figure 7.1 the mean number of staff (excluding GPs) increases with increasing size of unit, when these numbers are related to workload (Figure 7.6) the reverse is seen. This is most marked for the consultants and SHOs whose numbers per 100 women in labour show a steady fall with

TABLE 7.7   Availability of paediatricians/100 women in labour. Units of 1–500 deliveries (August)

	In delivery area	In hospital	<20 minutes	>20 minutes
11 am Number of women in labour = 42				
Consultant	0	31	64.3	45.2
Senior registrar	0	7.1	7.1	14.3
Registrar	0	11.9	14.3	16.7
Associate specialist				
Clinical assistant	0	14.3	4.8	4.8
GP	21.4	78.6	645.2	166.7
SHO	0	50	21.4	28.6
11 pm Number of women in labour = 28				
Consultant	0	3.5	132.1	61.5
Senior registrar	3.5	7.1	17.8	15.3
Registrar	3.5	10.7	26.0	19.2
Associate specialist				
Clinical assistant	0	0	11.5	0
GP	14.2	10.7	853.8	207.6
SHO	10.7	35.7	26.9	38.4

TABLE 7.8   Availability of paediatricians/100 women in labour. Units of 501–2000 deliveries (August)

	In delivery area	In hospital	<20 minutes	>20 minutes
11 am Number of women in labour = 258				
Consultant	1.1	25.6	18.9	6.5
Senior registrar	0.3	5.0	3.8	0.7
Registrar	1.1	13.9	6.2	0.3
Associate specialist				
Clinical assistant	0	3.1	1.6	1.1
GP	0	0.3	4.2	0.3
SHO	5.0	56.2	12.0	1.1
11 pm Number of women in labour = 170				
Consultant	0	4.1	50.5	15.2
Senior registrar	0	2.3	5.8	1.7
Registrar	0	12.9	9.4	1.1
Associate specialist				
Clinical assistant	0	0	2.9	0.5
GP	0	0	1.1	0
SHO	5.8	47.0	15.2	1.1

TABLE 7.9   Availability of paediatricians/100 women in labour. Units of 2001–4000 deliveries (August)

	In delivery area	In hospital	<20 minutes	>20 minutes
11 am Number of women in labour =375				
Consultant	0.5	23.6	10.6	2.4
Senior registrar	0.5	7.4	2.9	0
Registrar	2.1	20.5	2.7	0.5
Associated specialist Clinical assistant	0.5	0.5	0	0
GP	0	0.3	0.3	0
SHO	6.1	44.4	4.0	1.0
11 pm Number of women in labour = 272				
Consultant	0.4	1.5	33.4	7.4
Senior registrar	0.4	4.4	7.0	0
Registrar	1.5	15.1	5.9	0.7
Associate specialist Clinical assistant	0	0.4	0.7	0
GP	0	0.4	0	0
SHO	8.8	31.6	4.0	0

TABLE 7.10   Availability of paediatricians/100 women in labour. Units of 4000+ deliveries (August)

	In delivery area	In hospital	<20 minutes	>20 minutes
11 am Number of women in labour = 125				
Consultant	0	15.2	4.8	0
Senior registrar	0	6.0	0.8	0.8
Registrar	3.2	18.4	0	0
Associate specialist Clinical asssistant	0	0	0	0
GP	0	0	0	0
SHO	0	32.6	0	0
11 pm Number of women in labour = 63				
Consultant	0	3.1	26.7	4.7
Senior Registrar	3.1	1.5	11.1	0
Registrar	6.3	20.6	1.5	0
Associate specialist Clinical assistant	0	0	0	0
GP	0	0	0	0
SHO	11.1	3.0	1.6	0

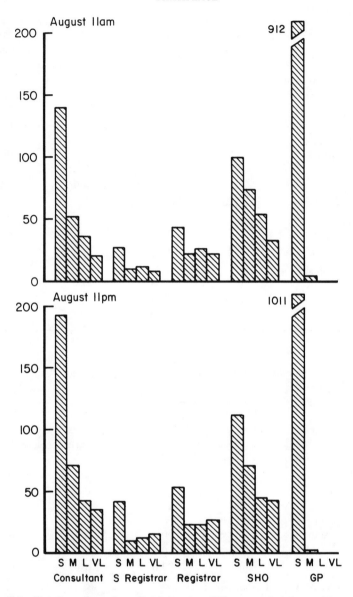

Figure 7.6   Total number of paediatricians per 100 women in labour. (S — small, M — medium, L — large and VL — very large)

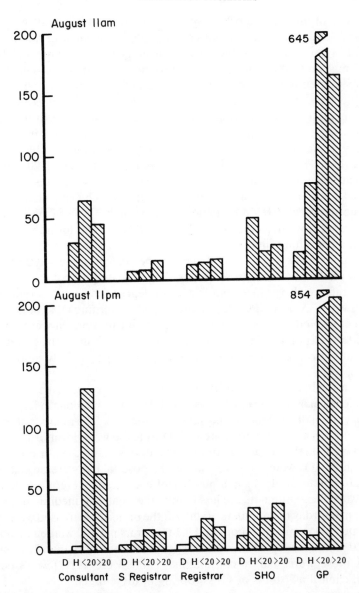

Figure 7.7   Number of paediatricians per 100 women in labour in small unit.
D   — in delivery unit
H   — in hospital
<20 — within 20 minutes' call
>20 – greater than 20 minutes' call

increasing size of unit. The most likely explanation for this is that there is a large number of small units, all staffed but with few women in labour, for example, at 11 am on 1 August there was an average of 0.19 woman in labour per unit in small units; this figure increased progressively with increasing size of unit to 1.75 women in medium, 2.90 in large and 5.0 in very large units.

Small units have the largest number of paediatricians of all grades allocated to women in labour but their availability is scattered compared to the other three unit size groups. Their availability for the delivery area in August (Wednesday) is shown in Figure 7.7. Many of the staff were outside the hospital but were within 20 minutes' call. However, several were more than 20 minutes away even at 11 am on weekdays. The very large numbers of GP/100 women in labour gives a false impression of their availability as each GP will be on call only for the delivery of his own patients, or possibly those of his practice colleagues as well, whereas the hospital staff will be on call for all women in labour in the consultant units.

Medium units have less than half the number of consultants/100 women compared with the small unit group (Figure 7.8). The numbers of other grades of hospital staff are also reduced but to a lesser degree. The greatest reduction in numbers is however in GPs. During the weekday morning most of the staff were on the hospital premises, though a significant proportion were on call from outside at 11 pm. On Saturday the number on call from both less than 20 minutes and more than 20 minutes away increased, particularly among the consultants.

There is a further relative reduction in numbers of consultants, associate specialists, clinical assistants and SHOs per 100 women in labour in large units compared with small and medium hospitals (Figure 7.9). The number of senior registrars and registrars in slightly greater. During the weekday morning most of the staff were on the hospital premises. Some consultants, senior registrars, registrars and SHOs were, however, not in the hospital but were on call from less than 20 minutes; only a small number of each grade were more than 20 minutes away. These numbers are less than in the small and medium units. At night and on Saturday the numbers of staff off the premises increased with up to 7.3 SHOs per 100 women in labour and 9.1 registrars per 100 women in labour less than 20 minutes away. However, very few staff were more than 20 minutes away and these were mainly consultants. There were very few associate specialists, clinical assistants or GPs working in these units.

The very large units have the smallest number of consultants/100 women in labour compared with all other units (Figure 7.10). They also have the lowest number of SHOs/100 women particularly at 11 pm. The numbers of senior registrars and registrars/100 women is similar to the medium and large units by day and slightly higher at night. Except at 11 am in October and 11 pm in November there were no GPs, clinical assistants or associate specialists in these units.

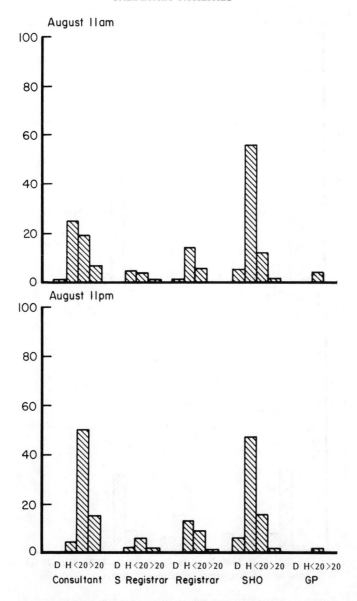

Figure 7.8 Number of paediatricians per 100 women in labour in medium unit (see Figure 7.7)

The availability of the staff is greater than in the small, medium and large units. All SHOs were in hospital at all times except on Saturday at 11 pm and even then there were only 1.2 SHOs/100 women who were less than 20 minutes'

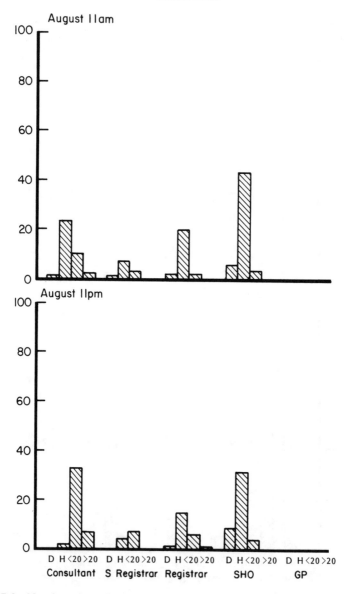

Figure 7.9   Number of paediatricians per 100 women in labour in large unit (see Figure 7.7)

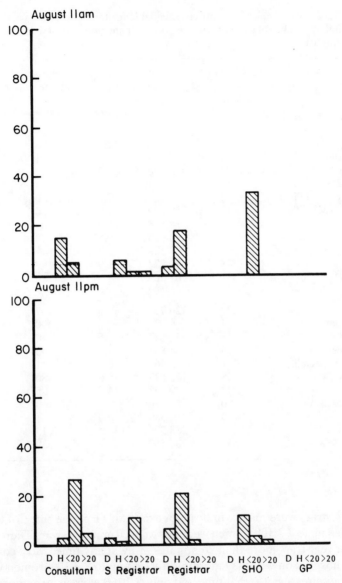

Figure 7.10   Number of paediatricians per 100 women in labour in very large unit (see Figure 7.7)

TABLE 7.11   Most senior paediatrician available for the delivery area and present in the hospital by number of deliveries in previous year and numbers of women currently in labour (August)

	Institutions	Number of deliveries		Number of women in labour who are covered	
		No.	%	No.	%
11 am					
None	228	78 590	11.1	106	13.2
Missing data	4	5 811		1	
Consultant	179	412 490	58.5	477	58.8
Senior registrar	12	27 534	3.9	24	2.9
Associate specialist	2	1 822	0.2	0	0
Registrar (MRCP)	17	49 629	7.0	54	6.6
Registrar	17	38 808	5.5	41	5.0
Clinical assistant	4	3 525	0.5	3	0.3
GP	20	2 129	0.3	5	0.6
SHO	48	84 222	11.9	99	12.2
TOTAL	531	704 560		810	
11 pm					
None	277	126 754	18.0	107	19.8
Missing data	4	6 075		0	
Consultant	15	32 647	4.6	20	3.7
Senior registrar	23	54 832	7.7	42	7.7
Associate specialist	1	2 965	0.4	1	0.1
Registrar (MRCP)	38	111 839	15.8	80	14.8
Registrar	42	100 762	14.3	75	13.9
Clinical assistant	0	0	0	0	0
GP	3	380	0.05	1	0.1
SHO	128	268 306	38.0	213	39.5
TOTAL	531	704 560		539	

call. Registrars were mainly in hospital except at 11 pm on three of the study days when up to 7.3/100 women were less than 20 minutes away. There were no SHOs or registrars more than 20 minutes away at any time. Most consultants were in hospital on weekday mornings though up to 8.3/100 women were less than 20 minutes away at that time and only 0.7/100 women were more than 20 minutes away. At 11 am on Saturday, a greater number (11.9) were less than 20 minutes away, and the number more than 20 minutes away was 3.4/100 women. The number of consultants more than 20 minutes away at any study time was less in these units than in any others, ranging from 0 at 11 am in August to 6.3 at 11 pm in October.

TABLE 7.12 Most senior paediatrician available for the delivery area and present in the hospital by number of deliveries in previous year and number of women currently in labour (September)

	Institutions	Number of deliveries		Number of women in labour who are covered	
		No.	%	No.	%
11 am					
None	246	102 450	14.5	94	12.7
Missing data	2	5 686		0	
Consultant	57	135 114	19.1	169	22.9
Senior registrar	25	61 929	8.7	66	8.9
Associate specialist	3	4 996	0.7	4	0.5
Registrar (MRCP)	25	72 291	10.2	79	10.7
Registrar	35	91 305	12.9	83	11.2
Clinical assistant	4	6 139	0.8	6	0.8
GP	12	1 244	0.1	0	0
SHO	114	223 984	31.7	236	32.0
TOTAL	523	705 138		737	
11 pm					
None	282	157 345	22.3	122	22.2
Missing data	4	8 618		0	
Consultant	8	16 168	2.2	14	2.5
Senior registrar	24	63 177	8.9	66	12.0
Associate specialist	1	2 556	0.3	3	0.5
Registrar (MRCP)	37	115 859	16.4	79	14.3
Registrar	32	73 054	10.3	57	10.3
Clinical assistant	3	5 300	0.7	2	0.3
GP	7	926	0.1	1	0.1
SHO	125	262 135	37.1	205	37.3
TOTAL	523	705 138		549	

PAEDIATRICIANS ON SITE

The availability of the paediatric staff for emergency neonatal resuscitation has been assessed by looking at the grade of the most senior paediatrician present, either in the delivery area or elsewhere on the hospital site, at 11 am and 11 pm on each of the four study days, remembering that for emergency purposes they should be within two minutes' call. Tables 7.11–7.14 show the grades of most senior paediatrician on site in relation to the number of units, number of deliveries in those units in 1983 and the number of women in labour at the survey times. The variations in 1983 deliveries between the months depends on the units which are open in each month. We did not include the 1983 birth

TABLE 7.13   Most senior paediatrician available for the delivery area and present in the hospital by number of deliveries in previous year and numbers of women currently in labour (October)

	Institutions	Number of deliveries		Number of women in labour who are covered	
		No.	%	No.	%
11 am					
None	218	79 224	11.4	87	9.9
Missing data	3	5 810		0	
Consultant	184	412 391	59.3	536	61.2
Senior registrar	11	28 069	4.0	31	3.5
Associate specialist	2	2 853	0.4	1	0.1
Registrar (MRCP)	10	30 568	4.4	41	4.6
Registrar	16	33 098	4.7	43	4.9
Clinical assistant	2	980	0.1	0	0
GP	19	2 596	0.3	4	0.4
SHO	56	99 828	14.3	132	15.0
TOTAL	521	695 417		875	
11 pm					
None	262	119 003	17.1	103	16.3
Missing data	6	11 355		0	
Consultant	19	35 714	5.1	39	6.1
Senior registrar	19	46 803	6.7	46	7.2
Associate specialist	0	0	0	0	0
Registrar (MRCP)	34	95 528	13.7	83	13.1
Registrar	41	94 915	13.6	86	13.6
Clinical assistant	0	0	0	0	0
GP	3	2 824	0.4	1	0.1
SHO	137	289 275	41.6	273	43.2
TOTAL	521	695 417		613	

numbers data in any month, if a unit was missing. In fact, it made very little difference — only 1000 in 700,000 (0.14 per cent).

Figure 7.11 shows the comparison of the grades available at 11 am and 11 pm on Wednesday with Saturday. There were a large number of units which did not have any member of the paediatric staff or a GP on site at the study times. The number of these units ranged from 218 (40 per cent of the total) at 11 am in October, to 282 (54 per cent of units) at 11 pm on Saturday 1 September. The number of deliveries in those units in 1983 ranged from 79, 224 to 157, 345 that is from 11.4 per cent to 22.3 per cent of all births. This method of analysis may be thought to give a misleading impression as many of these units without on-site paediatric cover may have been small GP units, and may have no paediatric doctor or GP present because there were no women delivering at that time.

TABLE 7.14   Most senior paediatrician available for the delivery area and present in the hospital by number of deliveries in previous year and numbers of women currently in labour (November)

	Instututions	Number of deliveries		Number of women in labour who are covered	
		No.	%	No.	%
11 am					
None	224	76 507	11.0	88	10.7
Missing data	2	5 450		1	
Consultant	175	392 038	56.4	467	56.4
Senior registrar	12	28 796	4.1	41	4.9
Associate specialist	2	4 898	0.7	5	0.6
Registrar (MRCP)	12	32 109	4.6	34	4.1
Registrar	11	30 341	4.3	41	4.9
Clinical assistant	1		0.1	0	0
GP	19	4 150	0.6	3	0.3
SHO	64	119 009	17.1	147	17.7
TOTAL	522	694 217		827	
11 pm					
None	266	114 376	16.5	100	17.5
Missing data	4	3 989		2	
Consultant	15	38 733	5.5	31	5.3
Senior registrar	22	44 954	6.4	49	8.4
Associate specialist	2	7 177	1.0	11	1.8
Registrar (MRCP)	26	77 284	11.1	76	13.0
Registrar	41	103 854	14.9	64	10.9
Clinical assistant	0	0	0	0	0
GP	4	2 738	0.3	6	1.0
SHO	142	301 112	43.3	244	41.8
TOTAL	522	694 217		583	

Figure 7.12, however, gives a more valid view by showing the most senior doctor available in relation to the actual number of women in labour at the study times. The same picture emerges, namely that the number of women in labour without cover by a paediatrician or GP on site ranges from 9.9 per cent (October 11 am) to 22.2 per cent (September 11 pm). It would be interesting to know what arrangements exist should the need arise for the emergency resuscitation of any of this large number of babies, some will be consultant units where if there is no paediatrician there should be an obstetrician or anaesthetist. In the GP units, in the absence of a doctor on site, the responsibility must be with the midwife.

On weekdays at 11 am the consultant was the most senior grade of paediatrician in the hospital, covering from 35.3 per cent to 33.5 per cent of all units (Figure 7.11), and 61.2 per cent to 56.4 per cent of women in labour (Figure

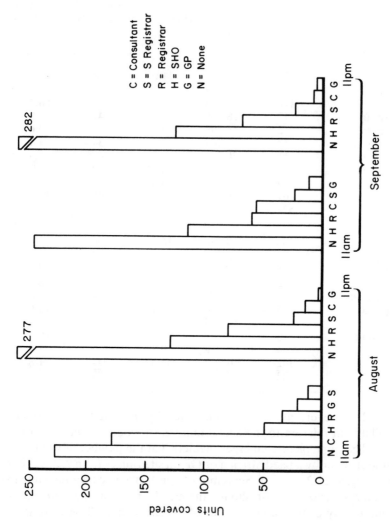

Figure 7.11   Most senior paediatrician on site by number of units

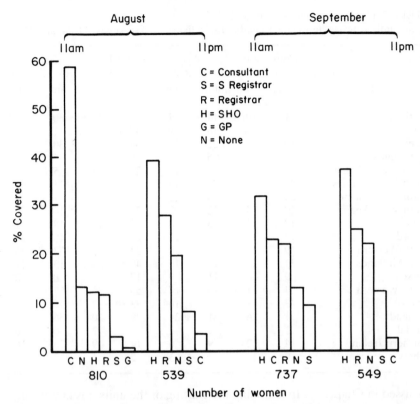

Figure 7.12   Most senior paediatrician on site by percentage of women in labour

7.12). The consultants were followed in order of frequency by SHOs (9 per cent), registrars (6.4 per cent) and GPs (3.8 per cent), senior registrars (2.3 per cent) and associate specialists plus clinical assistants (1.1 per cent). The figures in brackets are the percentage of units covered at 11 am on 1 August. On Saturday morning and evening and on weekday evenings, the SHO was the most senior doctor on site, covering from 27.9 per cent of units at 11 pm in November to 23.9 per cent of units at 11 pm in September. Next in frequency were the registrars, then consultants on Saturday morning but senior registrars in the evenings. Associate specialists were the most senior doctor in three units, and clinical assistants in four units. The largest number of units with a GP as the most senior doctor on site was 20 (11 am August).

REGIONAL AVAILABILITY

The regional distribution of maternity units according to their size and type is

TABLE 7.15   Paediatricians by regions
Total number of paediatricians available for delivery area – August 11 am and 11 pm

	Consultant		All registrars		Senior house officer		General practitioner	
	am	pm	am	pm	am	pm	am	pm
Northern	21	19	14	7	27	18	30	9
Yorkshire	29	25	16	9	40	19	1	10
Trent	19	20	22	14	34	20	30	21
East Anglia	9	8	5	3	15	9	5	2
North-West Thames	20	18	20	18	28	18	5	6
North-East Thames	22	20	27	13	30	21	11	13
South-East Thames	22	20	14	12	33	20	1	0
South-West Thames	20	14	12	7	20	14	10	9
Wessex	18	14	13	8	26	16	18	11
Oxford	14	14	18	17	22	17	40	23
South-Western	19	19	17	10	24	13	73	46
West Midlands	31	27	17	15	40	24	13	11
Mersey	9	8	11	9	17	7	0	0
North-Western	24	21	19	17	55	37	57	43
Wales	27	18	21	16	33	17	16	10
Scotland	31	26	31	24	29	20	56	49
Special	1	3	1	2	3	2	0	0
Northern Ireland	14	12	9	6	14	9	26	16
Others	10	10	3	3	2	1	7	7

discussed in Chapter 2. In analysing the staffing of the units it is important to bear in mind the variations of population and geography of the health regions as well as the numbers and types of their maternity units. Tables 7.15–7.17 give the total numbers of paediatricians available for the delivery area, the numbers on site/100 women in labour and the percentage of the total more than 20 minutes away, at 11 am and 11 pm on the August (Wednesday) study day. Although the special units and others are included in these tables, they will not be discussed further in this section for they are small.

Consultants

The total number of consultants available from all sources (either on site or on call) at 11 am on Wednesday ranged from 9 in Mersey and East Anglia to 31 in the West Midlands and Scotland. At 11 pm the numbers were only slightly less, 8 in Mersey and East Anglia and up to 27 in West Midlands. The numbers on Saturday were very similar to those for weekday evenings.

When availability is related to workload by examining the number of consultants on the premises/100 women in labour (Table 7.16) the range at 11 am on Wednesday is from 12 in Northern Ireland to 33.3 in South-West

TABLE 7.16   Paediatricians by regions
Number of paediatricians on premises/100 women in labour – August 11 am and 11 pm

	Consultant		All registrars		Senior house officer		General practitioner	
	am	pm	am	pm	am	pm	am	pm
Northern	27.5	3.6	27.5	21.4	60	50	2.5	0
Yorkshire	20.4	2.4	24.1	7.3	61.1	31.7	0	0
Trent	15.9	2.3	23.8	15.9	52.4	45.4	9.5	0
East Anglia	29.2	10	12.5	20	58.3	70	4.2	0
North-West Thames	30.3	0	45.4	20	72.7	42.8	0	2.8
North-East Thames	25	2.6	35	23.7	43.3	50	3.3	0
South-East Thames	23.2	4.6	17.8	13.9	53.6	39.5	0	0
South-West Thames	33.3	0	30	19.2	60	50	3.3	0
Wessex	20	0	22.5	33.3	50	86.7	2.5	0
Oxford	18.2	0	22.7	29.2	43.2	54.2	9.1	0
South-Western	24.1	4	37.9	16	75.9	48	27.6	8
West Midlands	29.7	6.1	16.2	18.4	51.3	44.9	2.7	0
Mersey	27.3	9.1	45.4	31.8	63.6	31.8	0	0
North-Western	30.6	3.8	29.0	34.6	69.3	92.3	4.8	0
Wales	31.1	4.5	28.9	31.8	66.6	59.1	4.4	0
Scotland	18.2	0	29.9	19.7	26	22.7	11.7	2.2
Special	9.1	0	9.1	16.6	27.3	33.3	0	0
Northern Ireland	12	0	16	35.7	24	42.8	2	0
Others	28.6	16.6	28.6	16.6	0	0	57	66.7

Thames but at 11 pm there is a large reduction to none in six regions and a maximum of 10 in East Anglia.

On Saturday there were none at 11 am in Mersey and 17.2 in South-West Thames. At 11 pm nine regions had no consultants on site with a maximum of 16.7 in Northern Ireland. This latter figure is very much higher than the next highest figure of 4.5 in Wales.

The percentage of consultants more than 20 minutes away varied from none at 11 am on Wednesday in East Anglia, South-East Thames, West Midlands, Mersey and North-Western to 38.9 per cent in Wessex; at 11 pm only East Anglia had no consultants more than 20 minutes away while Wessex had as many as 57.1 per cent. On Saturday the figures varied from none in Oxford to 43.7 per cent in Wessex at 11 am with East Anglia being none at 11 pm and Wessex again highest at 56.2 per cent.

Registrars

The total numbers of registrars and senior registrars available for the delivery area are given in Table 7.15. Their availability on site/100 women in labour

TABLE 7.17   Paediatricians by regions
Percentage of total number of paediatricians >20 minutes away – August 11 am and 11 pm

	Consultant		All registrars		Senior house officer		General practitioner	
	am	pm	am	pm	am	pm	am	pm
Northern	19	21	0	0	0	0	10	0
Yorkshire	20.7	24.1	0	0	0	0	0	0
Trent	10.5	25	0	0	0	0	23.3	28.6
East Anglia	0	0	0	0	0	0	0	0
North-West Thames	10	27.8	0	0	0	0	0	0
North-East Thames	13.6	35	0	0	0	0	9.1	7.7
South-East Thames	0	18.2	7.1	8.3	0	0	0	0
South-West Thames	25	35.7	8.3	14.3	0	0	0	0
Wessex	38.9	57.1	15.4	37.5	7.8	6.25	0	9.1
Oxford	7.1	7.1	22.2	17.6	5.9	5.9	32.5	26.1
South-Western	10.5	15.8	17.6	30	0	0	24.6	30.4
West Midlands	0	7.4	11.8	6.7	0	0	0	0
Mersey	0	12.5	0	0	0	0	0	0
North-Western	0	19	0	0	15.4	21.6	42.1	48.8
Wales	11.1	5.5	9.5	12.5	0	0	31.2	10
Scotland	16.1	26.9	12.9	8.3	13.8	5	0	4.1
Special	0	0	0	0	0	0	0	0
Northern Ireland	14.3	8.3	0	0	0	11.1	0	0
Others	20	10	0	0	0	0	0	28.6

(Table 7.16) ranged from 16 in Northern Ireland to 45.4 in Mersey and North-West Thames at 11 am on Wednesday. At 11 pm there were 7.3 in Yorkshire and 35.7 in Northern Ireland.

On Saturday the lowest number was 8.8 in South-East Thames and the highest 33.3 in North-West Thames at 11 am. In the evening the range was from 7.7 in Northern region to 42.4 in Scotland.

The percentage of registrars more than 20 minutes away was none in nine regions and up to 22.2 per cent in Oxford at 11 am on Wednesday; and at 11 pm it was still none in the same nine regions but up to 37.5 per cent in Wessex. On Saturday at 11 am only five regions had no registrars more than 20 minutes away at 11 am while Wessex had 28.6 per cent. At 11 pm the range was from none in seven regions to 42.8 per cent in Wessex.

Senior house officers

The total number of senior house officers available for the delivery areas is given in Table 7.15 and their availability on site/100 women in labour is shown in Table 7.16. It ranged from 24 in Northern Ireland to 75.9 in South-Western region. Except for Northern Ireland and Scotland all regions had more than 43 senior house officers/100 women in labour at 11 am on Wednesday. The lowest figure at 11 pm on Wednesday was 22.7 in Scotland and the highest 92.3 in North-Western region.

On Saturday the range was from 30 in East Anglia up to 55.2 in Wales at 11 am and from 12.5 in East Anglia to 116.7 in Northern Ireland at 11 pm. Only four regions had any senior house officers more than 20 minutes away at 11 am on Wednesday, 5.9 per cent in Oxford up to 14.5 per cent in North-Western region. The same four regions plus Northern Ireland had up to 21.6 per cent more than 20 minutes away on Wednesday evening.

On Saturday there were seven regions with senior house officers more than 20 minutes away ranging from 3.7 per cent to 11.8 per cent at 11 am and six regions at 11 pm ranging from 4.5 per cent to 13.3 per cent. It is noteworthy that Wessex had a high percentage of all grades of hospital staff more than 20 minutes away at all study times, frequently more than any other region.

General practitioners

Apart from Mersey, all regions had some general practitioners available for delivery areas at some time. Total numbers are given in Table 7.15. Their presence on site/100 women in labour at 11 am on Wednesday (Table 7.16) varied from none in four regions (including Mersey) to 27.6 in South-Western region. At 11 pm fourteen regions had no general practitioners on site but there were eight in South-Western region. On Saturday ten regions had no general practitioners on site at either 11 am or 11 pm and the remainder varied from 2.9 in North-Western region at 11 am to 14.3 in South-Western region at the same time. South-Western and North-Western regions and Scotland had the largest numbers of general practitioners working in the delivery areas. The percentage of general practitioners, more than 20 minutes away was none at 11 am on Wednesday in ten regions and up to 42.1 per cent in North-Western region. On Saturday the numbers were none in ten regions at 11 am and up to 66.7 per cent in Yorkshire at 11 pm.

PAEDIATRIC FLYING SQUAD

The role of the paediatric flying squad differs from that of the obstetric flying squad for while it is able to provide any emergency treatment at the place of delivery, its main function is the transport of small or sick neonates from the place of birth to a unit where more appropriate or specialized facilities are available. Most such transfers will be from a GP unit, a smaller maternity unit without a special care baby unit, or even one with a special care baby unit of limited facilities to a larger special care baby unit based at a district general hospital. Others will be transfers to a regional centre for babies needing more

TABLE 7.18   Paediatric flying squads

Type of unit	Number with paediatric flying squads	Number without paediatric flying squads	Not recorded
NHS consultant unit	81 ⎱	110 ⎱	2
Combined GP and consultant unit	37 ⎰ 121	72 ⎰ 185	3
Combined unit and private unit	3 ⎰	3 ⎰	0
General practitioner unit	12	179	2
Private unit in NHS hospital	1	1	0
Armed services	0	6	0
Private hospital	1	5	0
Other (1)	1	1	0
Other (2)	0	1	0
TOTAL	136	378	7

prolonged intensive care or specialist services such as paediatric cardiology or surgery.

It has to be remembered that the provision of a paediatric flying squad may place a considerable strain on the resources of the unit, particularly the staffing levels, since most transfers will involve a trained nurse and a doctor of SHO or registrar grade being absent from the hospital often for a whole day, and therefore not available for their normal duties. This will be particularly difficult at night or weekends when staffing levels are lowest. Consequently one would expect the paediatric flying squad service to be provided mainly by the regional centres.

Table 7.18 shows that 136 (26.1 per cent) of the 521 institutions provide a paediatric flying squad service. As expected 121 (88.3 per cent) of these come from consultant units; it is however noteworthy that 12 (8.8 per cent) paediatric flying squads seem to come from general practitioner units (this probably reflects GP units in the same building as a consultant unit). However, 185 consultant units (59.4 per cent) did not have a paediatric flying squad service.

SPECIAL CARE BABY UNIT

A detailed analysis of special and intensive care services for the newborn was not part of this study; however the availability of such services to the place of birth is a relevant aspect of a study into the facilities available, particularly for those institutions caring for high risk pregnancies. Institutions were asked to record if a special care baby unit (SCBU) was available on site and, if so, how many cots there were. They were also asked how many of these cots were available for intensive care, defined in the survey instructions according to the BPA/BAPP guidelines as 'Care given in a special or intensive care nursery which provides continuous skilled supervision by nursing staff and 24-hour resident medical cover. Such care includes long-term mechanical ventilation, CPAP, care of babies less than 1.5 kg birthweight or less than 30 weeks' gestation, and parenteral nutrition.'

The report of the expert group on special care for babies (Sheldon, 1971) recommended that there should be six special care cots per 1000 live births per year[2]. The BPA minimum standards state that there must be five special care cots and one intensive care cot for each 1000 deliveries per year.[4] It has been suggested in the *Lancet* more recently that the number of intensive care cots should be increased beyond this recommendation to cope with modern advances in neonatal intensive care and the improved survival of the very low birthweight baby[5].

Details of SCBU staffing and equipment were outside the scope of this study and recommended levels have been given elsewhere but hospitals were asked how many of their designated intensive care cots were in fact fully staffed and equipped. It is recognized that the replies will have been based on local opinion and not necessarily according to recommended levels. Data on this are marked with an asterisk (*) in the last columns of Tables 7.19, 7.20 and 7.21.

There were several hospitals where there was more than one delivery unit on the same site sharing a single SCBU facility. This has been taken into account when analysing the SCBU data so that the same SCBU is not reported twice. Consequently the number of delivery sites is less in this section than in other parts of the survey report. There were 277 SCBUs identified in the survey with a total of 4794 cots of which 641 were available for intensive care.

The distribution of these cots by number of units is shown in Figure 7.13; 216

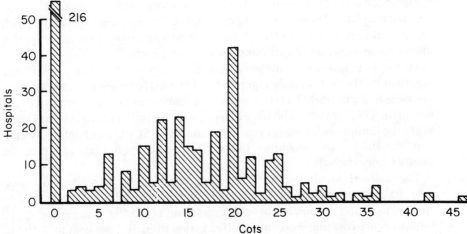

Figure 7.13   Distribution of special care baby unit cots by hospitals

TABLE 7.19   Special care baby units – number of intensive care cots

Number of IC cots	Number of hospitals with designated IC cots	Reported fully staffed cots*
0	316	351
1	26	29
2	52	40
3	30	21
4	26	19
5	11	9
6	20	16
7	1	2
8	1	1
9	2	—
10	4	2
11	—	—
12	2	1
13	—	—
14	—	—
15	3	2
Not known	6	7
TOTAL	500	473

* See text for amplification of this.

hospitals had no SCBU on site, 14 hospitals had a SCBU with 5 or fewer cots and 39 had units of 6 to 10 cots. The majority of SCBUs (154) had 11 to 20 cots. There were 13 units with more than 30 cots, the largest being one of 46 cots.

The number and distribution of intensive care cots is shown in Table 7.19: 184 SCBUs (66.5 per cent) have one or more intensive care cots, the maximum being fifteen cots. There were 52 units with two cots and 134 units had between one and four cots. There were 11 units with five intensive care cots and 20 with six cots but only 13 units with more than this number, though there were three units with as many as fifteen intensive care cots each.

Of the 641 designated intensive care cots only 473 (73.9 per cent) were regarded by the staff as fully equipped and staffed for intensive care and it is arguable that this could be taken as the true number of neonatal intensive care cots in the UK, for those who have to work with the staff and equipment locally know the limitations of the service. The number of SCBUs with intensive care cots was 184 but this would be 149 SCBUs when account was taken of the number fully staffed.

The regional distribution of SCBUs and numbers of cots is given in Figure 7.14. Excluding specials and others, the number of SCBUs per region ranges from 10 to 27 and the number of cots ranges from 142 to 593. The percentage of intensive care cots that were fully staffed varied from 31.7 per cent in Wales to 92.7 per cent in North-East Thames.

TABLE 7.20 Special care baby units – regional distribution of cots

Region	No. of hospitals	No. of SCBUs	Total cots	Intensive care cots	Fully staffed IC cots* No.	Fully staffed IC cots* %
Northern	29	20	278	24	15	62.5
Yorkshire	30	19	325	46	33	71.7
Trent	34	17	342	38	35	92.1
East Anglia	15	8	142	23	17	73.9
North-West Thames	20	18	297	42	28	66.6
North-East Thames	26	19	345	41	38	92.7
South-East Thames	26	19	269	25	20	80
South-West Thames	16	14	191	12	8	61.5
Wessex	30	11	178	27	22	81.5
Oxford	19	10	203	24	14	58.3
South-Western	34	10	203	41	24	58.5
West Midlands	31	21	419	54	39	72.2
Mersey	10	10	188	15	13	86.6
North-Western	25	20	353	46	42	91.3
Wales	38	15	232	44	13	31.7
Scotland	72	27	593	92	74	80.4
Northern Ireland	27	10	157	20	13	65
Specials	2	2	40	11	11	100
Others	16	7	39	16	14	87.5
TOTAL	500	277	4794	641	473	73.8

There were 729 233 live births in the UK in 1984 and according to the BPA guidelines this number of births would require 4375 special and intensive care cots. From Table 7.21, it can be seen that in this survey we found there were 507 more special care cots than recommended but on these theoretical numbers there were 88 (12 per cent) fewer intensive care cots than there should be. Further, there were 256 fewer (a 35 per cent shortfall) in fully staffed and equipped intensive care cots. It would be interesting to know how many of the apparent excess of special care cots were in fact being used to cover the intensive care shortage on the one hand, and how many were providing transitional care rather than special care, particularly in the smaller units.

TABLE 7.21 Nationally available special and intensive care – neonatal cots

	Recommended	Actual	Difference
Total cots	4375	4794	+419
Special care	3646	4153	+507
Intensive care	729	641 (designated)	−88
		473 (fully staffed)	−256*

* See text for amplification of this.

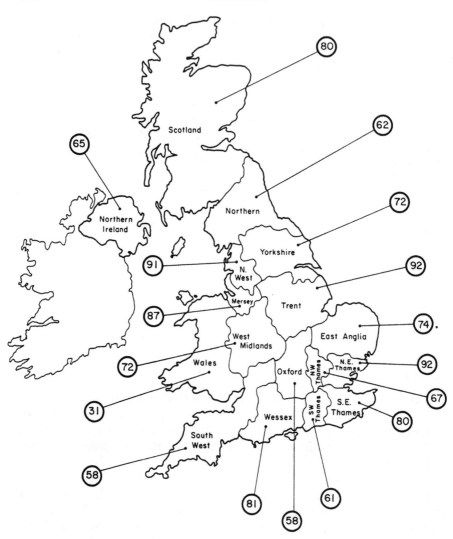

Figure 7.14   Percentage of intensive care cots in SCBU which are fully staffed by regions—see text (August)

CONCLUSIONS

In the majority of small units delivering fewer than 500 women a year, the medical care of the neonate is provided by the GP. Some of these units do have consultant paediatric cover with supporting junior staff mainly at SHO level.

With increasing size of unit there is an increase in mean number per unit of consultants, registrars and SHOs. There are very few GPs, clinical assistants or associate specialists in units over 500 deliveries/year.

When medical staffing is related to workload in terms of number of women in labour rather than as mean number of doctors per unit, the reverse is seen. There are more paediatric staff/100 women in labour in small units than in large ones and the number of staff/100 women in labour falls markedly with increase in size of unit.

Availability of staff is related to size of unit. With increase in size of unit a greater proportion of the staff are on site. In the small units, 22 per cent of all staff may be more than 20 minutes away compared with 6 per cent in the medium units, 2 per cent in large units, and 1 per cent in the very large units.

Very few units have a member of the paediatric staff with duties only in the delivery area.

Between 40 per cent and 54 per cent of units had no paediatrician or GP on site at the survey times. This means that 9–22 per cent of all women in labour had no paediatrician or GP immediately available for emergency neonatal resuscitation.

Where a doctor was on site, in 33–35 per cent of units the most senior grade was consultant, the next most commonly on site was a SHO. At weekends and nights the SHO was the most senior doctor on site covering 28 per cent of units.

One hundred and thirty six units provide a paediatric flying squad: 88 per cent of these are consultant units but there are twelve squads run by GPs.

Regional variation in type of unit is reflected in their staffing, e.g. Mersey has no GP units whereas South-Western and North-Western regions have many. Wessex was notable for the high percentage of its staff more than 20 minutes away.

There were 277 special care baby units: 54 had less than 10 cots. The median size was 20 cots in 43 units. There were 13 units with more than 30 cots.

On the basis of six cots/1000 live births and the 1984 birth rate, nationally there was an average overprovision of total SCBU cots of 9.6 per cent, but there was a 12 per cent underprovision of intensive care cots and only 73.8 per cent were fully staffed and equipped. This in effect meant 35 per cent underprovision for neonatal intensive care.

REFERENCES

1. Recommendations for the improvement of infant care during the perinatal period in the United Kingdom. BPA/RCOG Liaison Committee. 1978.
2. Report of the Expert Group on Special Care for Babies. Chairman Sir Wilfred Sheldon. DHSS. Report on Public Health and Medical Subject. No. 127. London: HMSO, 1971.
3. House of Commons Second Report from the Social Services Committee, 1979–80. *Perinatal and Neonatal Mortality*. London: HMSO, 1980.
4. British Paediatric Association. Minimum standards of neonatal care. *Arch. Dis. Childh.*, 1983, **58,** 943.
5. Falling short. *Lancet*, 1984 (1), 326.

APPENDIX

TABLE 7A.1   Place of birth
Paediatricians by size of unit at 11 am – August

Group (No. of dels 1983)	Con-sultant	Senior registrar	Regi-strars	Associate specialist and clinical assistants	GP	Senior house officer
	No.	No.	No.	No.	No.	No.
In delivery area						
1–500	0	0	0	0	9	0
501–2000	3	1	3	0	0	13
2001–4000	2	2	8	2	0	23
4001+	0	0	4	0	0	8
Not grouped	0	0	0	0	0	0
TOTAL	5	3	15	2	9	44
In hospital						
1–500	13	3	5	6	33	21
501–2000	66	13	36	8	1	145
2001–4000	89	28	77	2	1	167
4001+	19	10	23	0	0	41
Not grouped	2	1	0	0	0	4
TOTAL	189	55	141	16	35	378
Within 20 min						
1–500	27	3	6	2	271	9
501–2000	49	10	16	4	11	31
2001–4000	40	11	10	0	1	15
4001+	6	1	0	0	0	0
Not grouped	0	0	0	0	0	0
TOTAL	122	25	32	6	283	55
Greater than 20 min						
1–500	19	6	7	2	70	12
501–2000	17	2	1	3	1	3
2001–4000	9	0	2	0	0	0
4001+	0	1	0	0	0	0
Not grouped	2	0	0	0	0	0
TOTAL	47	9	10	5	71	15

TABLE 7A.2   Place of birth
Paediatricians by size of unit at 11 pm – August

Group (No. of dels 1983)	Con-sultant	Senior registrar	Regi-strars	Associate specialist and clinical assistants	GP	Senior house officer
	No.	No.	No.	No.	No.	No.
In delivery area						
1–500	0	1	1	0	4	3
501–2000	0	0	0	0	0	10
2001–4000	1	1	4	0	0	24
4001+	0	2	4	0	0	7
Not grouped	0	1	1	0	0	1
TOTAL	1	5	10	0	4	45
In hospital						
1–500	1	2	3	0	3	10
501–2000	7	4	22	0	0	80
2001–4000	4	12	41	1	1	86
4001+	2	1	13	0	0	19
Not grouped	0	0	0	0	0	2
TOTAL	14	19	79	1	4	197
Within 20 min						
1–500	37	5	6	3	222	8
501–2000	87	10	16	5	2	26
2001–4000	91	19	16	2	0	11
4000+	17	7	1	0	0	1
Not grouped	2	1	0	0	0	2
TOTAL	234	42	39	10	224	48
Greater than 20 min						
1–500	16	4	5	0	54	10
501–2000	26	3	2	1	0	2
2001–4000	20	0	2	0	0	0
4001+	3	0	0	0	0	0
Not grouped	3	0	0	0	0	0
TOTAL	68	7	9	1	54	12

TABLE 7A.3 Place of birth
Paediatricians by size of unit at 11 am – September

Group (No. of dels 1983)	Con- sultant	Senior registrar	Regi- strars	Associate specialist and clinical assistants	GP	Senior house officer
	No.	No.	No.	No.	No.	No.
In delivery area						
1–500	1	1	0	0	5	1
501–2000	2	1	2	1	0	10
2001–4000	3	5	6	0	0	25
4001+	0	0	0	0	0	7
Not grouped	0	0	0	0	0	1
TOTAL	6	7	8	1	5	44
In hospital						
1–500	4	3	1	1	20	12
501–2000	18	6	20	4	0	93
2001–4000	24	14	46	2	0	101
4001+	8	8	17	0	0	29
Not grouped	1	2	2	0	0	3
TOTAL	55	33	86	7	20	238
Within 20 min						
1–500	27	4	2	2	234	10
501–2000	71	11	17	4	3	19
2001–4000	81	10	26	0	0	9
4001+	14	1	0	0	0	0
Not grouped	2	0	0	0	2	0
TOTAL	195	26	45	6	239	38
Greater than 20 min						
1–500	16	3	5	2	53	5
501–2000	34	3	4	1	0	4
2001–4000	17	1	2	1	0	0
4001+	4	0	0	0	0	0
Not grouped	0	0	1	0	0	0
TOTAL	71	7	12	4	53	9

TABLE 7A.4 Place of birth
Paediatricians by size of unit at 11 pm – September

Group (No. of dels 1983)	Con- sultant	Senior registrar	Regi- strars	Associate specialist and clinical assistants	GP	Senior house officer
	No.	No.	No.	No.	No.	No.
In delivery area						
1–500	0	0	0	0	5	1
501–2000	0	0	1	0	0	8
2001–4000	1	1	5	0	0	14
4001+	0	0	3	0	0	7
Not grouped	0	0	0	0	0	1
TOTAL	1	1	9	0	5	31
In hospital						
1–500	2	2	1	0	6	3
501–2000	2	4	19	3	0	83
2001–4000	2	12	33	1	0	87
4001+	1	5	13	0	0	20
Not grouped	0	2	1	0	0	3
TOTAL	7	25	67	4	6	196
Within 20 min						
1–500	31	5	6	1	220	10
501–2000	85	11	18	8	2	24
2001–4000	98	15	26	0	0	21
4000+	19	2	4	0	0	1
Not grouped	3	1	0	0	2	0
TOTAL	236	34	54	9	222	56
Greater than 20 min						
1–500	18	3	4	2	37	3
501–2000	31	2	5	1	0	4
2001–4000	23	2	2	0	0	0
4001+	2	0	0	0	0	0
Not grouped	0	1	1	0	1	0
TOTAL	74	8	12	3	38	7

TABLE 7A.5 Place of birth
Paediatricians by size of unit at 11 am – October

Group (No. of dels 1983)	Con-sultant	Senior registrar	Regi-strars	Associate specialist and clinical assistants	GP	Senior house officer
	No.	No.	No.	No.	No.	No.
In delivery area						
1–500	1	0	0	0	6	1
501–2000	4	2	3	0	1	17
2001–4000	2	0	4	0	0	20
4001+	0	0	1	0	0	6
Not grouped	0	0	1	0	0	0
TOTAL	7	2	9	0	7	44
In hospital						
1–500	18	3	5	1	27	18
501–2000	77	18	34	10	1	125
2001–4000	92	27	66	3	0	142
4001+	22	9	20	1	0	38
Not grouped	4	0	4	0	0	8
TOTAL	213	57	129	15	28	331
Within 20 min						
1–500	30	5	7	3	303	8
501–2000	42	9	13	2	9	19
2001–4000	47	9	13	1	0	17
4001+	7	1	1	0	0	0
Not grouped	5	0	0	1	10	0
TOTAL	131	24	34	7	322	44
Greater than 20 min						
1–500	12	5	3	3	60	3
501–2000	13	2	6	0	2	3
2001–4000	7	1	0	0	0	0
4001+	1	1	0	0	0	0
Not grouped	0	0	0	0	0	0
TOTAL	33	9	9	3	62	6

TABLE 7A.6 Place of birth
Paediatricians by size of unit at 11 pm – October

Group (No. of dels 1983)	Consultant	Senior registrar	Registrars	Associate specialist and clinical assistants	GP	Senior house officer
	No.	No.	No.	No.	No.	No.
In delivery area						
1–500	0	0	0	0	4	1
501–2000	3	0	2	0	0	15
2001–4000	1	4	4	0	1	18
4001+	0	0	2	0	0	7
Not grouped	0	0	2	0	0	0
TOTAL	4	4	10	0	5	41
In hospital						
1–500	3	2	4	0	0	9
501–2000	5	6	20	0	0	87
2001–4000	7	8	39	0	0	88
4001+	0	5	9	0	0	20
Not grouped	0	1	2	0	0	8
TOTAL	15	22	74	0	0	212
Within 20 min						
1–500	28	3	4	6	234	8
501–2000	79	15	8	7	5	17
2001–4000	93	22	24	3	0	11
4001+	19	5	5	0	0	0
Not grouped	9	0	1	1	10	0
TOTAL	228	45	42	17	249	36
Greater than 20 min						
1–500	16	5	2	1	46	5
501–2000	26	2	3	1	3	10
2001–4000	17	0	2	0	0	0
4001+	6	0	0	0	0	0
Not grouped	0	0	1	0	0	0
TOTAL	65	7	8	2	49	15

TABLE 7A.7   Place of birth
Paediatricians by size of unit at 11 am – November

Group (No. of dels 1983)	Con-sultant	Senior registrar	Regi-strars	Associate specialist and clinical assistants	GP	Senior house officer
	No.	No.	No.	No.	No.	No.
In delivery area						
1–500	2	0	0	0	7	1
501–2000	0	2	0	0	0	11
2001–4000	4	1	6	0	0	22
4001+	0	1	1	0	0	11
Not grouped	0	0	1	0	0	1
TOTAL	6	4	8	0	7	46
In hospital						
1–500	8	3	3	0	27	10
501–2000	79	18	32	7	0	134
2001–4000	88	29	58	1	3	144
4001+	21	8	22	0	0	31
Not grouped	5	1	4	0	0	5
TOTAL	201	59	119	8	30	324
Within 20 min						
1–500	33	5	5	1	269	13
501–2000	52	7	26	3	13	18
2001–4000	38	6	13	2	0	6
4001+	12	2	2	0	0	0
Not grouped	1	0	0	1	10	0
TOTAL	136	20	46	7	292	37
Greater than 20 min						
1–500	15	3	4	1	79	4
501–2000	15	1	5	1	6	3
2001–4000	12	2	3	0	0	0
4001+	1	0	0	0	0	0
Not grouped	0	0	1	0	4	0
TOTAL	43	6	13	2	89	7

TABLE 7A.8   Place of birth
Paediatricians by size of unit at 11 pm – November

Group (No. of dels 1983)	Con-sultant	Senior registrar	Regi-strars	Associate specialist and clinical assistants	GP	Senior house officer
	No.	No.	No.	No.	No.	No.
In delivery area						
1–500	0	0	0	0	4	0
501–2000	0	1	1	1	1	10
2001–4000	0	0	7	0	0	27
4001+	1	0	3	0	0	4
Not grouped	0	0	0	0	0	1
TOTAL	1	1	11	1	5	42
In hospital						
1–500	0	1	3	0	1	12
501–2000	8	11	18	0	0	80
2001–4000	2	8	36	0	0	91
4001+	4	2	13	1	1	23
Not grouped	0	1	1	0	0	3
TOTAL	14	23	71	1	2	209
Within 20 min						
1–500	36	5	5	1	245	8
501–2000	85	12	16	3	12	23
2001–4000	102	16	18	2	0	10
4001+	18	4	6	0	0	0
Not grouped	4	1	0	1	10	0
TOTAL	245	41	57	7	267	41
Greater than 20 min						
1–500	17	4	5	1	66	3
501–2000	32	1	2	1	0	3
2001–4000	15	0	4	0	0	0
4001+	5	0	0	1	0	0
Not grouped	0	0	1	0	0	0
TOTAL	69	5	12	3	66	6

Birthplace
G.V.P. Chamberlain
© 1987 John Wiley & Sons Ltd.

CHAPTER 8

Home Deliveries

PHILIPPA GUNN

INTRODUCTION

During the last fourteen years, the number of deliveries taking place outside the maternity units has decreased from 12.4 per cent to 1.4 per cent. Although the demand for home deliveries remains small, health authorities are required to make provision for any woman who requests one. The district health authority is also required to provide emergency cover for women in the community regardless of their intended place of birth.

In 1984, the Maternity Services Advisory Committee made recommendations for the midwifery and medical cover of women giving birth at home and the equipment that should be available[1]. It also stated that the community midwife on call for a home delivery should be sufficiently experienced and up to date in current practice to provide a satisfactory service. The Family Practitioner Committee was advised to provide a list of general practitioners willing to care for women having a home delivery; these doctors should be present for at least part of the labour and make themselves accessible easily at other times. The Committee recommended that the necessary equipment for a home birth should include provision for analgesia, resuscitation and some form of two-way emergency call system.

THE QUESTIONNAIRE

The questionnaire for examining the facilities at domiciliary deliveries was prepared and is described in Chapter 1. Each midwife attending a home delivery in one of the four 24-hour periods under review was asked to complete the relevant data on one page. This aimed to provide information about the personnel present and available to the woman at home, the equipment on the premises, emergency services, medical cover and any further arrangements for

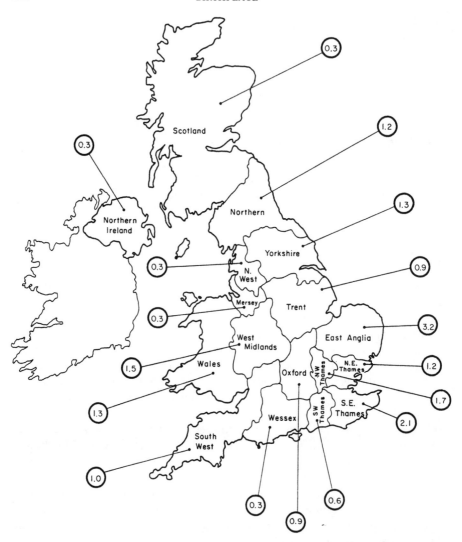

Figure 8.1 Home deliveries as a percentage of total deliveries reported from each region (August)

transfer of mother or baby. A section was provided for comments made by the midwife present. These findings were examined against the background of the mother's booking arrangement for her delivery.

During the four survey days, 86 domiciliary deliveries were reported. These contributed 1.4 per cent of the total deliveries for the United Kingdom during these four days. Examining national data showed that an average of 21 home deliveries occurred each day in the United Kingdom. If extrapolated, it

TABLE 8.1   The number of home deliveries reported by region compared with total
(four study days)

	Home deliveries	Total deliveries	Home deliveries as % of total deliveries
West Midlands	12	809	1.5
South-East Thames	12	565	2.1
East Anglia	9	279	3.2
North-West Thames	8	467	1.7
North-East Thames	7	591	1.2
Yorkshire	7	527	1.3
Northern	5	419	1.2
Trent	5	564	0.9
Wales	5	391	1.3
South-Western	4	420	1.0
Oxford	3	344	0.9
Scotland	2	691	0.3
North-Western	2	614	0.3
South-West Thames	2	350	0.6
Wessex	1	355	0.3
Northern Ireland	1	319	0.3
Mersey	1	356	0.3
TOTAL	86	8061	mean 1.0

might be expected that 84 domiciliary deliveries would be recorded in any four
days.

GEOGRAPHICAL DISTRIBUTION

The distribution of deliveries by geographic region is shown in Table 8.1. Each
region and country reported at least one delivery during the four days although
the numbers ranged from one in Wessex, Northern Ireland and Mersey to
twelve in West Midlands and South-East Thames. When examined against
total deliveries reported for the four days, the three regions with highest
numbers also showed the highest rates in two instances, South-East Thames
(2.1 per cent) and East Anglia (3.2 per cent). The West Midlands rate of 1.5 per
cent emphasizes that with more deliveries reported than from any other region
or kingdom, absolute numbers are less useful. Eight regions had data below the
mean.

DAY OF THE WEEK

In Table 8.2, the distribution of deliveries is shown by day of the week. Fewest
deliveries were reported on the Saturday, mirroring the total trend. This day
difference was not marked.

TABLE 8.6   The number of home deliveries reported by survey day

August (Wednesday)	26
September (Saturday)	16
October (Monday)	25
November (Thursday)	19

BOOKING ARRANGEMENTS

The booking arrangements made by the mother for her delivery had the greatest effect on the facilities available on the premise at birth (Table 8.3). Fifty-seven women (66.2 per cent) were booked for a home delivery. Twenty-five women were booked to deliver elsewhere and of these, one delivered in a doctor's surgery and the remainder in the home. Four women had not made any booking arrangements of which one delivered a stillborn baby of 28 weeks following a concealed pregnancy. No other perinatal deaths were reported. The survey was planned to allow data collection about women delivering outside an institution in transit, but no such cases were reported. It suggests that while there may have been a number of women in this group, the community midwife had not arrived in time or had not been called so the delivery was not reported to us. Had the midwife arrived before the woman's departure, these mothers may have been included in the group of home confinements delivered by the midwife with an ambulance crew outside.

ATTENDANTS PRESENT AT DELIVERY

Deliveries attended by neither midwives nor doctors

Of the 86 women delivering at home, 13 (15.1 per cent) were not attended by either a midwife or a doctor at delivery (Table 8.4). Only one of these women was in the group booked for home delivery; the midwife who subsequently attended this woman commented that this outcome had been predicted. The woman wanted to deliver unattended and the midwife had not anticipated

TABLE 8.3   Booking arrangements for home delivery

	No.	%
Booked for home delivery	57	66.2
Booked elsewhere but a home delivery	24	27.9
Unbooked but delivered at home	4	4.6
Booked elsewhere but delivered in doctor's surgery	1	1.1
TOTAL	86	

TABLE 8.4   Personnel present at the home delivery

	Booked for home delivery		Not booked for home delivery		
	No.	%	No.	%	
None	1	1.8	9	31.0	
Ambulance men only	0	—	3	10.3	
1 Midwife	13	22.8	7	24.1	
2 Midwives or 1 midwife + 1 student midwife	26	45.6	5	17.2	
Midwife + GP	17	29.8	5	17.2	
TOTALS	57		29		86

being called until after the event. Of the twelve women unattended by professional staff and not booked for home delivery, three were attended by ambulance personnel only.

Midwives present at delivery

Eighty-five per cent of all home deliveries were attended by one community midwife regardless of the booking arrangements; sometimes she was accompanied by a student midwife or general practitioner. At eighteen of the deliveries there were two trained midwives present (Table 8.5). In the group booked for home deliveries there were sixteen cases (28 per cent) with a second midwife present for their delivery. One midwife was hospital based and thirteen were community based. There were two nursing officers present at delivery; one attended the delivery with a new midwife under community orientation and at the second a director of nursing services and supervisor of midwives had arranged this day as her annual supervisory visit. In a further case, at which two midwives attended a home delivery, the midwife commented that the mother had requested that her general practitioner should not be present at the delivery.

TABLE 8.5   Trained midwives present at home delivery

	Booked for home delivery		Not booked for home delivery		
	No.	%	No.	%	
None	1	1.8	12	41.4	
1 Midwife	40	70.2	15	51.7	
2 Midwives	16	28.0	2	6.8	
TOTALS	57		29		86

TABLE 8.6   Student midwives present at home delivery

		Booked for home delivery		Not booked for home delivery		
		No.	%	No.	%	
None		35	61.4	25	86.2	
1 Student midwife		19	33.3	4	13.8	
2 Student midwives		3	5.3	0	—	
	TOTALS	57		29		86

The recommendation of *Maternity Care in Action*[1] is that 'The midwife should be assisted by another responsible person'. In districts in which student midwives are gaining experience in the community, their attendance at the delivery will give the community midwife such support during any emergencies. However, in eight of the cases at which there were two trained midwives there was also either a student midwife or a general practitioner. It is the policy of some district health authorities to make available two midwives for home delivery routinely. In two cases the midwife did comment on this policy.

Student midwives present at delivery

Student midwives generally gain community experience in the district in which they train (Table 8.6). In England and Wales there were midwifery training schools in 172 out of 201 districts and in Scotland twelve out of fifteen boards have colleges providing midwifery training. However, student midwives may be allocated to neighbouring districts in which there are no midwifery training schools in order that they can gain sufficient community experience. This would produce attachments to an even greater number of districts.

Of the 86 deliveries, student midwives were present at 26 (30.2 per cent), Table 8.6. Student midwives were obviously more likely to be present at a delivery booked for the home and two student midwives were present at three of these cases.

TABLE 8.7   General practitioners present at home delivery

		Booked for home delivery		Not booked for home delivery		
		No.	%	No.	%	
Not present		40	70.2	24	82.8	
Present		17	29.8	5	17.2	
	TOTALS	57		29		86

TABLE 8.8   General practitioners present during labour in home delivery

| | Booked for home delivery | | Not booked for home delivery | | |
	No.	%	No.	%	
Not present	33	57.9	23	79.4	
Present	24	42.1	6	20.6	
TOTALS	57		29		86

General practitioners present at delivery

General practitioners were present at 22 out of 86 deliveries and present in a higher proportion at those booked for home delivery (Table 8.7) and 24 general practitioners were present at some time during the labour (Table 8.8).

Of those general practitioners who attended at delivery all but two had been booked for that delivery. The woman who delivered in the doctor's surgery was attended by a community midwife and a receptionist but not the general practitioner.

EQUIPMENT ON THE PREMISES OF DELIVERY

Nine items of equipment were surveyed in the domiciliary questionnaire: three related to communication and emergency call systems — telephone, two-way radio and bleep; three were associated with care of the fetus and resuscitation of the newborn — Doppler ultrasound, neonatal laryngoscope, oxygen for the baby; the last three related to emergency resuscitation for the mother — intravenous giving set, intravenous fluids and oxygen for the mother (Table 8.9).

TABLE 8.9   Equipment available on the premises for home delivery

| | Booked for home delivery | | Not booked for home delivery | | |
	No.	%	No.	%	
Telephone	50	87.7	15	51.7	
2-Way radio	5	8.7	5	17.2	
Bleep	31	54.3	10	34.4	
Doppler/ultrasound	20	35.0	5	17.2	
Neonatal laryngoscope	13	22.8	2	6.8	
Oxygen for baby	49	85.9	13	44.8	
IV giving set	16	28.0	5	17.2	
IV fluids	16	28.0	3	10.3	
Oxygen for mother	15	26.3	4	13.7	
TOTALS	57		29		86

Telephones were readily available in the houses of those booked for home delivery; a high proportion (87.5 per cent) had a telephone in the home compared with the national average of 78 per cent (OPCS 1984)[2]. In view of their isolation, women accepted for home delivery might be expected to have a telephone but seven were without. The two-way radio was a less commonly available item of communication than the bleep, a one-way method. Without ready access to a telephone, a bleep is of limited value. One might wonder if the two-way radios had not been available to the midwives, they may not have been called to the delivery and some of these cases may have delivered in transit and not been reported to the survey.

Women booked for home delivery

Oxygen for the baby was present in nearly all cases. Hand held fetal heart Doppler ultrasound was available in one-third of these cases but items such as neonatal laryngoscope, intravenous giving sets and fluid, and oxygen for the mother were only available in about one-quarter of the cases (Table 8.9). Intravenous giving sets and fluids, and oxygen are essential for the emergency resuscitation of the mother and although the establishment of an intravenous line does not fall within the training and practice of midwifery, many experienced midwives have set up drips in an emergency. In the event of an emergency to which medical staff would be summoned, if they were not already there, midwives are expected to carry out emergency treatment. In these cases the items of equipment for dealing with these complications were not available to midwives and may not have been available until the arrival of medical aid, assuming the general practitioner was carrying such equipment.

Women not booked for home delivery

In those cases not booked for delivery, it must be remembered that 40 per cent did not have the presence of either the midwife or general practitioner and by virtue of that, certain items of medical equipment would not be available.

TABLE 8.10   Medical cover for labour at home delivery

	Booked for home delivery		Not booked for home delivery		
	No.	%	No.	%	
GP booked	56	98.2	9	31.0	
GP not booked	1	1.8	20	69.0	
TOTALS	57		29		86

TABLE 8.11   Flying squad availability for home delivery

	Booked for home delivery No.	Not booked for home delivery No.	Total	
			No.	%
Obstetric	53	24	77	89.5
Paediatric	33	15	48	55.8

Oxygen for the baby was nevertheless available to nearly half of these cases but the remaining items of medical equipment were present in less than one-sixth of cases.

EMERGENCY FACILITIES AND MEDICAL COVER

Medical cover for labour

Of the 57 cases booked for home delivery only one was not booked with a general practitioner for labour care (Table 8.10). There were, however, two midwives at this delivery; it was noted that a general practitioner could be on call and that the obstetric flying squad was available in this case.

Among those not booked for home delivery were nine women booked for labour care by the general practitioner for delivery in a general practitioner bed in a local hospital.

Obstetric and paediatric flying squads

An obstetric flying squad was available to a little under 90 per cent of all the home deliveries and a paediatric flying squad was available to just over half (Table 8.11). There was little difference in the availability of the two flying squads between the two groups of those booked for home delivery and those not booked.

TRANSFER OF MOTHERS AND BABIES IN FIRST 24 HOURS

There were no transfers reported in the four days of either mothers or babies in the group that had been booked for home delivery. Among the remaining 29 not booked for home deliveries more than half were transferred to hospital (Table 8.12). Eighteen mothers were transferred to hospital and all admitted to a postnatal ward. One mother remained at home and her baby was transferred to a hospital ward for observation. Nineteen babies were transferred and fourteen of these accompanied their mothers on to the postnatal wards. Four

TABLE 8.12   Numbers of mothers and babies transferred in the first 24 hours after birth at home

| | Booked for home delivery | | Not booked for home delivery | |
	No.	%	No.	%
Mother	0	—	18	62.1
Baby	0	—	19	65.5

babies were transferred to a special care baby unit: one was reported as premature; a second had suffered an apnoeic attack five hours after delivery and was admitted for observation; a third was a macerated stillbirth born following a conealed pregnancy; the remaining baby was admitted with no reason given on the questionnaire.

There were nine ambulance crews present at those deliveries not booked for home confinement — one third of all non-booked cases reported. While numbers are small, if they were extrapolated to a year, it would imply some 800 deliveries a year attended by ambulance personnel, one-tenth of all home confinements.

CONCLUSIONS

This chapter covers the facilities available to the 1 per cent of women delivering in the home. One-third of these had not been planned as home confinements and the most significant findings are the differences in the facilities for these women as compared with those who had planned a home delivery. Although the sample is small, the proportion of women not booked for a home delivery compares closely with the findings in a larger survey of home deliveries carried out by Campbell et al. in 1979[3].

The women with an unplanned home delivery were less likely to have a midwife or general practitioner in attendance or, and even less likely, to have essential items of equipment than those for whom it had been planned.

With few home deliveries occurring there is less opportunity for student midwives and general practitioners to gain experience in the community service. These are two groups who might be asked for advice in the future and yet they are not building up the expertise to consider the advantages and disadvantages. Student midwives and general practitioners were present at less than one-third of deliveries.

If the main drawback of home confinement lies in the management of an emergency of which the two most likely are maternal haemorrhage and neonatal asphyxia, without proper equipment, the best obstetrical midwifery skills cannot be offered. However, in only one-quarter of booked home confinements were items of vital resuscitation available. For the domiciliary service to provide an alternative service, it would be reasonable for inexpensive and easily portable items such as laryngoscopes, Doppler ultrasound, maternal intranvenous fluids and giving sets to be available at all deliveries.

REFERENCES

1. Maternity Services Advisory Committee, *Maternity Care in Action Report:* Part II. London: HMSO 1984.
2. OPCS, *Family Expenditure*, London: HMSO, 1984.
3. Campbell, R., Macdonald Davies, I., MacFarlane, A., and Beral, V., Home birth in England and Wales, 1979: perinatal mortality according to intended place of birth. *Br. Med. J.*, 1984, **289:** 721–724.

CHAPTER 9

Less Than One A Day

GEOFFREY CHAMBERLAIN

The pattern of facilities available at the place of birth in the United Kingdom ranges widely; it depends on the local history of medical and midwifery services, the geographic spread of the population, the management and the patterns of spending before and since the start of the Health Service in 1948. District or regional planning has come late to this scene finding many delivery units difficult to fit into an ideal pattern of obstetrical services. Much of the past activity cannot be assessed in a survey such as the Confidential Enquiry into Facilities Available at the Place of Birth but examination of one extreme end of the range may be helpful. Reports of the 1983 delivery numbers ranged from eight units where there were less than ten births a year to six units with over five thousand deliveries annually.

It is obvious that at the lower end of the size range will be units used only occasionally; where it cannot be expected that facilities would match those of the larger unit where it is more economical to keep a variety and number of staff or equipment. *Small is beautiful*, but when one is trying to give a service, what is too small and therefore less efficient? Are there units in which equipment that obstetricians and midwives expect to have at a delivery will not be found? Even more importantly, does this matter? Some would argue that if we had an ideal screening system so that only women at no risk were allowed to deliver at small units, it would not matter if the special equipment and skills needed to deal with complications was not available. However, everybody in obstetrics and midwifery knows that antenatal screening is not perfect; we must always make provision for the occasional more difficult case. This will happen less often in a screened population at lower risk but still occurs occasionally by the laws of probability.

The vast majority of women in the United Kingdom live near a large town; only a few live in isolated areas of the country where travel to the nearest large maternity unit can be many miles. Parts of outer Scotland, mid-Wales, Yorkshire and the South-West of England might be expected to have problems in providing maternity facilities due to their geography; these are the same difficulties as with other facilities provided by society, such as the emergency ambulance service or the fire brigade.

METHOD

In this section, we have examined all units which reported delivering less than 365 babies in 1983, that is on average one delivery a day. They represent a subset of the under 500 deliveries a year group which is found in many tables throughout this volume; the data are brought together here to emphasize the problems that exist in smaller units.

Of the 531 units in the August reporting day of the survey which reported their 1983 figures, 200 (38 per cent) reported less than 365 deliveries a year, that is less than one a day. Their distribution was skewed towards the lower end of the workload scale as seen in Table 9.1 for two-thirds of these very small units were delivering less than three women a week.

There was little change in distribution when data were examined from each day in the four months of the survey; with figures as small as these any variations were not significant and so all data reported were from the August survey day.

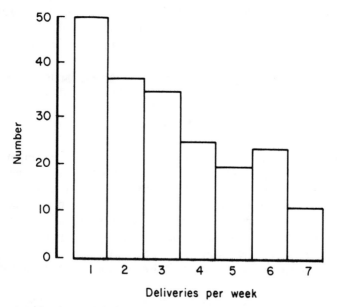

Figure 9.1 Numbers of minute units which reported less than one delivery a day illustrating how few deliveries some units perform

TABLE 9.1   Very small units by average number of deliveries each week. Reported from 1983 data ($n = 200$) (August)

Units reporting:	
Less than one delivery a week	48
Less than two deliveries a week	39
Less than three deliveries a week	37
Less than four deliveries a week	25
Less than five deliveries a week	19
Less than six deliveries a week	22
Less than seven deliveries a week	10
Total units	200

Regional distribution

Table 9.2 shows the distribution by regions of the subset of the units delivering less than 365 babies a year, arranged in ranking order. Reported are the 177 very small isolated maternity units geographically separated from a consultant unit and in this table the 23 very small units in association with consultant cover are not included.

TABLE 9.2   Distribution of very small isolated units as a percentage of all units, in regions in ranking order ($n = 177$) (August data)

	Number	%
Scotland	44	61.1
South-Western	22	59.4
Wales	18	48.6
Wessex	14	45.1
Trent	14	40.0
East Anglia	6	37.4
Northern Ireland	10	37.0
Oxford	8	36.2
Yorkshire	9	30.0
Northern	6	21.4
West Midlands	7	17.0
North-Western	4	13.3
South-East Thames	3	11.1
North-East Thames	3	9.6
North-West Thames	2	9.0
South-West Thames	1	5.8
Mersey	0	0.0
Special hospitals	6	37.5
All United Kingdom	177	37.6

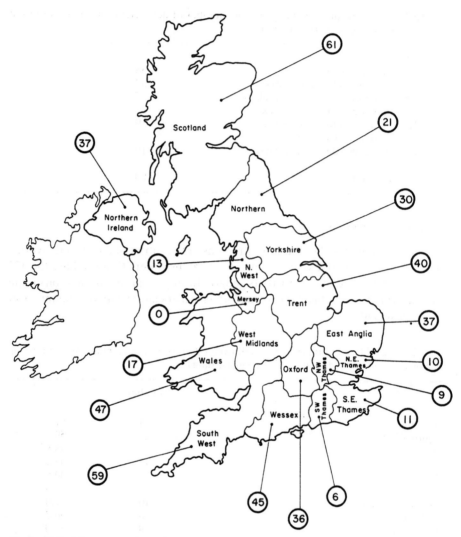

Figure 9.2   The proportion of all units of those doing less than one delivery a day
(365/year) (August)

Throughout the United Kingdom, the mean proportion of these very small
isolated units to the total delivery units was 37.6 per cent.

The highest proportions were in the South-West and Scotland where the
population is most widely spread. Wales and Wessex both reported nearly 50
per cent of these units and again this might be related to the geography of such
rural regions. However, Oxford and East Anglia reported over one-third of
their delivery units in this group. At the bottom end of the table are found the

four Thames regions, all of them with less than 12 per cent of smaller units; the South-West Thames region had only one such unit. From Mersey came no reports of very small isolated units delivering less than 365 babies in 1983.

The information in Table 9.2 reflects to a large extent what might be expected. In the South-East of the United Kingdom, where women are close to reasonable sized and equipped units, the usage made of isolated very small units is low. In the sparsely populated parts of the United Kingdom, as in Scotland and the South-West, the need for very small units is more rational for geography and population concentrations dictate. However, it is less easy to understand in regions like Oxford where the larger towns are well spaced and no one is far by road from a consultant unit with its concentration of equipment and staff.

Analysis of these data by the four survey days did not show any significant changes and so the August and October data are used mostly.

Services

Table 9.3 shows the availability of services. These figures are small and not

TABLE 9.3 Services reported in all very small units ($n = 200$) August data

	Isolated unit $n = 177$	Integrated unit $n = 23$	Missing data
Blood storage			
Available—in hospital	35	8	
—elsewhere	62	9	
Not available	76	4	6
Operating theatre (dedicated)			
Available—in hospital	8	13	
—elsewhere	15	2	
Not available	131	5	26
Operating theatre (shared)			
Available—in hospital	38	5	
—elsewhere	12	0	
Not available	109	7	29
Epidural anaesthesia			
Available—on demand	4	2	
—when possible	6	2	
Not available	162	17	7
Special care baby unit			
Available	3	17	
Not available	172	5	3

capable of statistical evaluation but the trends can be set against tables for the larger units in Chapter 3.

Blood storage facilities were not available in 80 of the 200 units (40 per cent), 76/177 isolated units and 4/23 integrated ones. In about 35 per cent, blood was available elsewhere and in about 17 per cent there was blood in the hospital; in 4 per cent blood was actually stored in the delivery area. Facilities were generally better in the integrated units.

Obviously such a perishable and scarce commodity as stored blood cannot be distributed widely through the country; conversely, if deliveries are to take place in units which are not viable haematologically, arrangements must be made to get blood there swiftly. This is second-best obstetrics, for the replacement of blood is often an urgent matter to be done in minutes rather than hours. In the past the obstetrical flying squad has been used to provide emergency blood supplies but this service has atrophied in the Health Service of the 1980s. In many districts, the flying squad is but a shadow of its previous service due to lack of experience and calls.

The availability of an operating theatre for such very small units might be expected to be sparse. There was no operating theatre available exclusively for obstetric use reported in 136 units (three-quarters of the isolated units compared with one-quarter of the integrated ones). There was not even a shared theatre in 116 (two-thirds of isolated units and one-third of integrated units). Probably the demands for such a theatre would be small and provided the very occasional emergency Caesarean section operation could be performed in a converted labour room, this would match the demand.

Similarly, there was no recovery room in 121 units (109/177 isolated and 12/23 integrated units) but this also should not be a facility that was needed very often if properly selected women only deliver in the smaller units. A recovery room is best close to the operating theatre where an anaesthetist and skilled nursing staff are available. Hence, if there was no theatre there would be no recovery room.

It was disappointing to find that at almost 90 per cent of the very small units, no epidural service was available as a form of analgesia in labour. Indeed, among the 177 isolated units, it was only available on demand in four and when possible in six. More women in 1984 were asking for epidural analgesia yet at the same time a vocative number were wanting to be delivered in very small units. They may not be the same women but if an effective epidural service could be rendered safely by competent anaesthetists, it might make the use of the very small unit more acceptable to more women. That is not to say that epidurals should be done by less skilled doctors but possibly that more senior skilled anaesthetists should be available at such units. However, if an epidural anaesthetic is started, it is desirable that a skilled anaesthetist stays in the unit. This is the limiting factor for there are not enough anaesthetists to satisfy this basic safety factor.

As might be expected, a similar proportion of small units (89 per cent) reported that no special care baby unit (SCBU) was present. If required, obstetricians and midwives would probably utilize the services of the neonatal flying squad (see Chapter 7). Indeed, of the 20 smaller units that reported that they had SCBU services, 17 were small units integrated with consultant units. The other 3 small units may have misinterpreted the question for such a highly labour-intensive service could hardly be justified at a delivery place of a few apparently normal women.

Equipment

The same sampling items of equipment were examined as in all other institutional units. The constraints of this method are considered in Chapter 3. A similar picture to that of services exists with the samples of equipment surveyed. It would be unrealistic to expect all of the items examined on the questionnaire to be present in very small units. However, certain of them should be available anywhere a baby delivers. Several replies to this part of the questionnaire were not filled in well from the very small units. It may be that a midwife completing the questionnaire from a unit delivering one baby a week would consider that to ask about a fetal pH monitor in such a small unit was so much beyond the facilities provided that she did not even fill in the form but she responded well to questions about oxygen for the mother or neonatal resuscitation. In this particular section up to 36 per cent of units did not respond and so no statistical analysis is worth while in many instances.

Of the items that were sampled, delivery beds were present in all but five of the 200 very small units, oxygen for the mother in all but three and in only one unit was there no neonatal laryngoscope; all units that reported had a bag and mask for neonatal resuscitation. These are all pieces of equipment which one might consider as absolute necessities for safe delivery. At a slightly lower level of need might be the presence of a neonatal resuscitation table which was only missing in five and a neonatal overhead heater which was not present in 11 per cent of the very small units from which a reply to this question was received.

More sophisticated equipment for modern labour monitoring includes the fetal heart monitor which was not present in 76 per cent of reporting very small units. There was no pH meter reported in nearly all and no real-time ultrasound machine in 57 per cent of units which answered the question. In places that do few inductions an infusion pump might seem a luxury and this was reported absent in 48 per cent of all very small units.

Perhaps more germane was that an anaesthetic might be required anywhere a woman delivers and yet there was no anaesthetic machine in 25 per cent while 53 per cent of very small units reported no ventilator. Dealing with the problems that might arise, a labouring woman might require an ECG machine (missing in 54 per cent) and possibly a cardiac arrest trolley (missing in 43 per cent).

TABLE 9.4   Very small units reporting equipment ($n = 200$) August

	One	Two or more	None	Missing data
Obstetric equipment				
Real-time ultrasound	20	4	114	62
Fetal heart monitor	25	8	106	61
Fetal pH monitor	2	0	126	72
Delivery beds	91	89	5	15
Birth chair	14	0	120	66
Infusion pump	28	18	96	58
Oxygen for mother	102	86	3	9
Paediatric equipment				
Neonatal laryngoscope	116	79	1	4
Resuscitation table	167	19	5	9
Overhead heater	126	35	23	16
Bag and mask	140	51	0	9
Anaesthetic equipment				
Anaesthetic machine	107	4	51	38
ECG machine	32	1	108	59
Ventilator	26	0	107	67
Cardiac arrest trolley	61	4	86	49

Note: The data presented in this table were collected with the same constraints as in larger assets and need the same care in interpretation as is outlined in Chapter 8.

In some cases it might be argued, such equipment could be brought by the visiting obstetrician or anaesthetist but in others, if it was required at all, it would be wanted so swiftly that it should be on the spot.

It is encouraging to find that the absolute essentials of delivery seem to be well provided. Perhaps a little less reassuring is that some of the equipment required for monitoring the fetus and for dealing promptly with certain complications in the mother is not so freely available in these very small units.

Load

The deliveries reported during the days of the survey were small. While there

TABLE 9.5   Reported numbers of women in labour at sample times on the four survey dates in all the very small units ($n = 200$)

Reported in labour at	August	September	October	November
11 am	41	30	29	30
11 pm	20	19	22	20

TABLE 9.6   Numbers of women in labour at 11 am and 11 pm (by region) in the very small units (October data)

	Number of very small units reported	Women in labour (11 am)	Women in labour (11 pm)
Northern	6	0	1
Yorkshire	11	6	5
Trent	14	3	2
East Anglia	7	0	0
North-West Thames	2	4	1
North-East Thames	5	0	0
South-East Thames	4	0	0
South-West Thames	2	0	0
Wessex	15	1	0
Oxford	10	1	2
South-Western	23	1	3
West Midlands	11	2	3
North-Western	9	2	0
Wales	18	1	0
Scotland	44	3	2
Northern Ireland	11	4	2
Others	6	1	1
TOTAL	196	29	22

Note: (1) There were no small units reported from Mersey RHA or the special hospitals.
(2) Four units of this size did not report numbers of women in labour at this survey point.

were fewer at night time, there were no significant differences between the four survey days. As an example, Table 9.5 shows that about 2 per cent of all women in the country deliver in these very small units which however make up 38 per cent of the total units which cover the obstetrics in the United Kingdom.

Table 9.6 indicates the regional distribution of deliveries and the very small units. There is no relation between the numbers of the very small units open and the women who were in labour.

Midwives

The provision of midwives to look after the women in labour at the small units was analysed. With such small numbers of deliveries, this was expressed as midwives per 100 women in labour and only those institutions which had a central delivery area were assessed. The midwife is the pivot of management in these very small units.

As shown in Table 9.5, there were few women in labour at the sample times in these units and so it is reasonable that staff would be moved to other parts of

TABLE 9.7   Midwives per 100 women in labour in less than one a day units with a central delivery area (n = 189)

		Number of institutes with women in labour	Mean ratio of midwives per 100 women in labour
August	11 am	15	207
	3 pm	15	247
	7 pm	9	115
	11 pm	12	136
September	11 am	11	186
	3 pm	14	257
	7 pm	15	123
	11 pm	16	144
October	11 am	13	258
	3 pm	13	393
	7 pm	5	130
	11 pm	11	100
November	11 am	13	227
	3 pm	11	200
	7 pm	7	161
	11 pm	13	134

the unit or if community midwives be on call from home. The ratio of both sister and staff midwife (taken together) to 100 women in labour was over 100 in samples at all times, being highest at the 3 pm sample point. These ratios were maintained through all four survey days.

Medical staff

The medical staffing was analysed from the October sample point for all the 189 very small units with central delivery areas performing less than 365 deliveries a year in 1983, by grade, speciality and at two sample times (11 am and 11 pm). The majority of doctors in the hospital and on call within 20 minutes were general practitioners covering obstetrics, paediatrics and anaesthesia. Obviously many general practitioners were on rotas to be available; while at the delivery rooms there were about 33 GPs per 100 women in labour at 11 am (Table 9.8), there were 35 GPs in other parts of the hospital (106/100 women in labour) or 880 on call within 20 minutes 2904/100 women). Similar data were obtained about family doctors covering paediatrics and anaesthesia (Tables 9.9 and 9.10).

However, if the consultant staff and their hierarchy are examined, much lower ratios were seen. For example, at 11 am on the sample day there were ratios per 100 women in labour of 58, 42 and 52 of a consultant obstetrician, paediatrician or anaesthetist respectively in the building with ratios of 79, 82

TABLE 9.8   Obstetricians on duty to provide care for women in delivery areas of very small units on 1 October 1984 by seniority of doctor and availability. Units with central delivery areas only ($n = 189$ at 11 am and 188 at 11 pm)

Grade and sample time	In delivery area	In hospital	On call	
			<20 minutes	>20 minutes
11 am 33 women in labour				
Consultant	1	19	26	13
Senior registrar	0	5	1	7
Registrar	0	9	9	6
Senior house officer	1	17	2	3
General practitioner	10	35	880	203
Other	0	5	4	3
11 pm 22 women on labour				
Consultant	0	2	30	18
Senior registrar	0	1	3	6
Registrar	0	7	8	4
Senior house officer	1	10	3	5
General practitioner	9	6	744	124
Other	0	0	4	1

TABLE 9.9   Paediatricians on duty to provide care for women in delivery areas of very small units on 1 October 1984 by seniority of doctor and availability. Units with central delivery areas only ($n = 189$ at 11 am and 188 at 11 pm)

Grade and sample time	In delivery area	In hospital	On call	
			<20 minutes	>20 minutes
11 am 33 women in labour				
Consultant	0	14	27	12
Senior registrar	0	2	5	5
Registrar	0	4	5	3
Senior house officer	1	14	6	3
General practitioner	6	27	302	60
Other	0	1	3	3
11 pm 22 women in labour				
Consultant	0	3	25	16
Senior registrar	0	2	2	5
Registrar	0	3	3	2
Senior house officer	1	7	6	5
General practitioner	4	0	230	46
Other	0	0	6	1

TABLE 9.10   Anaesthetists on duty to provide care for women in delivery areas of very small units on 1 October 1984 by seniority of doctor and availability. Units with central delivery areas only (n = 189 at 11 am and 188 at 11 pm)

Grade and sample time	In delivery area	In hospital	On call	
			<20 minutes	>20 minutes
11 am 33 women in labour				
Consultant	2	15	26	8
Senior registrar	0	3	4	5
Registrar	0	6	6	2
Senior house officer	0	9	1	3
General practitioner	5	14	112	16
Other	0	0	3	2
11 pm 22 women in labour				
Consultant	0	2	33	13
Senior registrar	0	3	3	7
Registrar	0	4	6	2
Senior house officer	0	4	5	5
General practitioner	6	0	90	6
Other	0	0	4	1

and 78 of the same consultants being on call within 20 minutes. The number of women, therefore, whose labours were closely covered by consultant staff is much less than in larger units. With good screening of a woman in the antenatal period, this may well be an acceptable risk ratio, but it must be realized that many women in such very small units have no consultant cover within 20 minutes. Numbers were too small to relate this to any geographic distribution of units.

The much reduced number of obstetricians in training at these very small units is shown in ratios per 100 women in labour. At 11 am on the sample day in October, senior registrar, registrar and SHO obstetricians provided ratios of 15, 27 and 52 staff members per 100 women in labour respectively in the hospital (columns 1 and 2 in Table 9.8) with 70, 3 and 27 on call within 20 minutes (column 3 in Table 9.8). In paediatrics, the ratios were 4, 12 and 42 and 15, 15 and 18 while in anaesthesia there were 9, 18 and 27 and 12, 18 and 3 per 100 women in labour respectively.

Such low ratios reflect the concentration of training staff away from very small units. This is probably not a deliberate policy but could emphasize that the most efficient teaching takes place where there is a high concentration of women on whom to teach. However, it must also be understood that much of the service load of an acute labour ward care is really in the hands of this grade of doctors and so the skills of the senior registrar and registrar are not so readily available in the very small units. These are considered training grades in theory but in the present confusion of manpower in the NHS much of the abnormal obstetrics is actually managed by them under consultant cover.

CONCLUSIONS

Over one-third of obstetric delivery units in the United Kingdom are minute and only 2 per cent of women deliver in them. Midwifery staffing is similar to larger units but medical staffing shows that most of the work and immediate cover is by general practitioners.

Where the population is widely spaced, obviously smaller units are required but their economy and efficacy need constant examination. Where populations are denser and communications good women and their relatives can travel easily to central units. The provision of very small units may be too costly; concentration of staff and equipment may be a wiser solution in the future.

Glossary

AGENCY MIDWIFE: Trained midwife employed through a commercial nursing agency.

ANAESTHETIC: A substance that abolishes the sensation of pain. This may work by the loss of consciousness, blocking the transmission of painful impulses along nerves or numbing nerve end points.

ANAESTHETIST: A doctor who specializes in the administration of anaesthetics.

ANAESTHETIC MACHINE: A moveable trolley carrying equipment used to administer an anaesthetic to a patient. It is usually self-contained with cylinders of anaesthetic cases and equipment for giving them to the patient, monitoring equipment and all the drugs needed by the anaesthetist.

ANAESTHETIC VENTILATOR: Mechanical equipment which continues the chest movements of respiration artificially.

ANTENATAL BEDS: Hospital beds allocated for use by mothers during pregnancy and prior to going into labour.

ASSOCIATE SPECIALIST: This is a senior doctor with a similar training background to that of a consultant. However, they do not have full clinical responsibility. They usually work as senior members in a team of doctors.

BAG AND MASK RESUSCITATION: Manual revival of a patient using an air-refillable bag and close fitting face mask to force air into the lungs.

BANK MIDWIFE: Trained midwife employed on an occasional basis through a hospital bank of pool of midwives and nurses.

BIRTH CHAIR: Chair designed for use by the mother during childbirth so that she can deliver sitting upright.

BLEEP: Radio signal equipment providing communication over several miles.

BLOOD STORAGE AREA: A site with refrigerated equipment to enable storage of donor blood prepared for transfusion.

BREECH DELIVERY: Delivery in which the baby's buttocks or feet present first and the head follows.

CAESAREAN SECTION: An operation by which the baby is delivered through an incision in the abdominal and uterine wall.

CARDIAC ARREST TROLLEY: A collection of items of equipment for resuscitation of the mother kept on one trolley for easy mobilization. It is used specifically in cardiac or respiratory arrest.

CENTRAL DELIVERY AREA: Single geographical site within a maternity unit designed for deliveries.

CLINICAL ASSISTANT: A part-time post held by less experienced doctors who work under the supervision of senior hospital staff. Many such posts are held by GPs who wish to keep up some special aspects of their hospital learnt skills.

CONSULTANT: A specialist doctor with a full- or part-time appointment in a National Health Service hospital. A consultant is ultimately in charge of the management of women admitted to hospital under his care; he directs the policies of the medical teams.

COMMUNITY MIDWIFE: Trained midwife providing service mainly outside the hospital for women in the community.

CONTINUOUS FETAL HEART RATE MONITOR: An electronic computer used to check the fetal state in labour by recording continuously the fetal heart rate and its variations.

CONTINUOUS POSITIVE AIRWAY PRESSURE (CPAP): A mechanical method for the administration of artificial respiration to infants in the specific treatment of hyaline membrane disease.

DELIVERY AREA: The part of a hospital where delivery rooms are gathered together with the staff and equipment needed for the care of labouring women.

DELIVERY ROOM: A room in which vaginal deliveries take place; emergency facilities for all other deliveries are often available but it would be unusual to perform Caesarean sections in such a room unless there was some temporary block of the proper facilities.

DOPPLER ULTRASOUND: A portable machine using high frequency sound waves to detect the fetal heart rate and its variation.

ELECTIVE LOWER SEGMENT CAESAREAN SECTION: A Caesarean section which has been planned prior to the onset of labour for maternal or fetal complications.

ELECTROCARDIOGRAPHIC MONITOR: Electronic equipment providing a recording of the electrical activity of the heart.

EMERGENCY LOWER SEGMENT CAESAREAN SECTION: A Caesarean section which is performed as a result of complications arising in the mother or fetus during labour or because of some unforeseen event such as bleeding.

EPIDURAL ANAESTHESIA: A local anaesthetic injected around the spinal sac causing temporary numbness and loss of sensation in the lower part of the body. When given in labour the pain of uterine contractions is virtually abolished, as is that of the stretching of the vagina and the floor of the pelvis.

FETAL HEART RATE MONITOR: A machine which records and displays continuously the rate of the fetal heart. It may be used in late pregnancy or in labour.

FETAL pH MONITOR: Biochemical equipment used for the analysis of blood samples taken from the fetus during labour to assess shortage of oxygen in the baby.

FORCEPS DELIVERY: An operative method of controlling delivery of the baby through the birth canal by applying suitably curved metal blades to the sides of the baby's head. This can only be done once the cervix is fully dilated in the second stage of labour.

GENERAL ANAESTHETIC: Anaesthetic agents given to a patient which brings about complete loss of consciousness and consequent unawareness of any painful stimuli.

GENERAL PRACTITIONER: A general practitioner is a family doctor who has total overall care of patients. The general practitioner is the primary health practitioner but in addition some doctors may have extra experience and qualifications in different specialities, e.g. obstetrics, general medicine, anaesthesia, and may undertake to use them in the care of labouring women.

HOSPITAL PORTER: Porter employed by health authority in larger units where he helps in the transport of patients and equipment between parts of the hospital.

HYPOXIA: A lack of oxygen which may occur in either mother or fetus. This needs prompt treatment to prevent perinatal damage.

INFUSION PUMP: Electronic equipment which regulates the flow of an intravenous infusion.

INTENSIVE CARE BABY UNIT: A special ward or intensive care nursery which provides continuous skilled supervision of sick newborn infants by nursing staff and a specially trained medical staff. Care includes long-term mechanical ventilation, care of babies of less than 1.5 kg or less than 30 weeks' gestation and parenteral nutrition.

INTUBATION: The passing of a tube into the trachea to establish an unobstructed airway.

LARYNGOSCOPE: An illuminated splint used to provide an airway into the larynx at the time of intubation.

LOCUM DOCTOR: The employment of a doctor on a non-permanent basis to cover the absence of medical staff during holidays or sickness. In this study we asked only about locum posts of more than two weeks' duration since we were examining the effects of the long-term locum only.

LOW BIRTHWEIGHT BABIES: Babies delivered with a birthweight of less than 2.5 kg (approximately 5½ pounds).

MATERNITY UNIT: That part of hospital or nursing home which provides services for the mother in pregnancy and childbirth and for both mother and baby afterwards.

MEDICAL STUDENTS: All those training to be doctors must do some practical obstetrical work. This is usually in their fourth year of a five-year programme.

MIDWIFE: One who specializes in the care of women during pregnancy, childbirth, puerperium and in the care of the newborn infant. The midwife undergoes a training of three years (or 18 months if she is already a state registered nurse) and passes an examination to become a registered midwife. To continue practising the midwife must attend a statutory refresher course every five years and notify her intention to practise to the health authority every year in which she works.

MIDWIFERY SISTER: A trained midwife with some additional experience who has generally been promoted after practising as a staff midwife.

MORBIDITY: A deterioration in the quality of life in the mother or infant; more generally expressed as illness or having some disease.

NEONATAL DEATH: A death occurring in the first 28 days of life. If such a death is in the first seven days, it is further categorized as an early neonatal death; such early neonatal deaths are grouped with stillbirths to derive a perinatal mortality rate.

NORMAL DELIVERY: A spontaneous vaginal delivery which occurs with the baby born head first.

NURSING OFFICER (SENIOR MIDWIFE GRADE): Trained midwife with considerable experience in midwifery who now fills a greater administrative role.

OBSTETRIC DELIVERY BED: A special bed that will allow operative procedures and has a capacity for rapid tilting — head up or head down. It is usually provided with a thick sorbo rubber mattress.

OBSTETRICAL EMERGENCY TEAM (FLYING SQUAD): A team of obstetrical and midwifery personnel available to provide emergency services outside the hospital to the mother in pregnancy or immediately following childbirth.

OBSTETRICIAN: A doctor who specializes in the care of pregnant women, their deliveries and the immediate time afterwards.

OPERATING THEATRE: This is a part of the delivery unit of the hospital set on one side for surgical operations and the administration of anaesthesia.

OVERHEAD HEATER: An electrical apparatus which provides heat over a cot where the newborn baby is lying.

OXYGEN: The essential ingredient of air which is used to revive unconscious people. When it is needed for resuscitation of mothers and babies it is available from a central piped supply or from portable cylinders.

PAEDIATRICIAN: A doctor specializing in the care of infants and children; some paediatricians specialize in looking after newborn babies — neonatologists.

PAEDIATRIC FLYING SQUAD: A team of paediatricians and neonatal nurses available for the emergency treatment of neonates outside the hospital. They frequently provide a service transferring babies born in general hospitals to specialist hospitals.

PARAMEDICAL PERSONNEL: Those involved in the care of women who are not qualified in medicine or midwifery. Important paramedical workers include ambulance staff, physiotherapists, dieticians and radiographers.

PARENTERAL NUTRITION: Nutrients are given by intravenous infusion so that they bypass the stomach and intestinal tract.

PERINATAL MORTALITY RATE: The number of stillbirths and early neonatal deaths (deaths occurring during the first week of life) per 1000 total births.

POSTNATAL BEDS: Hospital beds allocated for the care of women following childbirth.

REAL-TIME ULTRASOUND: Electronic equipment using the reflection of high frequency sound waves to produce the image of intrauterine events on a screen. From this, the position of the fetus and its size may be assessed; so can the volume of amniotic fluid and the site of the placenta.

RECOVERY ROOM: An area for the care and observation of patients following an anaesthetic.

REGISTRAR (PRE- AND POST-HIGHER DEGREE): In the United Kingdom, most doctors wishing to train in obstetrics, paediatrics or anaesthesia, serve in this grade after having been a senior house officer. Some are promoted to a senior registrar after three or four years in the grade. While registrars, most will obtain a higher diploma of the appropriate supervising body thus showing that they have learned a certain amount and are capable of further training. Potential obstetricians will become Members of the Royal College of Obstetricians and Gynaecologists (MRCOG), paediatricians Members of the Royal College of Physicians (MRCP) and anaesthetists Fellows of the Faculty of Anaesthetists of the Royal College of Surgeons (FFARCS). All these diplomas are obtained at the same level of training, usually four to six years after qualifying.

RESUSCITATION TABLE (NEONATAL): A table with equipment prepared for the emergency treatment of the newborn baby. Often the resuscitator is portable and taken to the labour ward as required.

SENIOR HOUSE OFFICER: Doctors wishing to train in obstetrics start after a pre-registration year of general medical and surgical training performed after qualifying. Some senior house officers are gaining enough experience to enter the speciality permanently. From the latter group, registrars are appointed after about two years in the grade.

SENIOR REGISTRAR: After six to eight years of more junior posts, the potential specialists are promoted to the most senior of the training grades. From here, most become consultants after three to four years of senior registrar work. They are the future consultants.

SPECIAL CARE BABY UNIT: This unit provides care of the newborn in a special nursery or transitional ward providing observation treatment falling short of intensive care but exceeding normal care, which includes monitoring the baby, the use of supplemental oxygen, tube feeding and the care of babies requiring constant nursing supervision and medical advice.

STAFF MIDWIFE: A trained midwife with a clinical role.

STILLBIRTH: A baby who is born dead after the 28th week of pregnancy; those born dead before this are classified with abortions. The stillbirths are grouped with early neonatal deaths to derive a perinatal mortality rate.

STUDENT MIDWIFE: All those training to be midwives.

STUDENT NURSE: Students undertaking training to become a state registered nurse. During the training the student nurse will spend a short period of time in the maternity unit on a supernumerary basis. She is not permitted to carry out deliveries.

THEATRE TRAINED NURSING STAFF: Staff with a minimum of one year's experience in operating theatre work and employed specifically for the theatre area. In this survey, they are not included in any of the midwifery grades on the list.

TWIN DELIVERY: A delivery of two babies from one mother in the same pregnancy.

TWO-WAY RADIO: Communication equipment allowing midwives or doctors away from their bases to receive and transmit information.

VACUUM EXTRACTION: A method of delivering the baby by applying suction to a metal cap applied to the head of the baby. The baby's scalp is then drawn into the cup by the use of vacuum and guided by the doctor through the birth canal to assist delivery.

VAGINAL CEPHALIC OPERATIVE DELIVERY: A vaginal delivery with the head delivering first with the use of assisting instruments, either forceps or vacuum extraction.

WARD CLERK: Secretarial personnel employed to carry out administrative duties, such as organizing admissions and hospital records or enquiries.

APPENDIX

Maternity Unit Profiles

MIRANDA MUGFORD

The chapters in this report have explored in some detail each of the different categories of staff and equipment typically available to maternity units. It is also possible to use the data to form an overall picture of resources available to units surveyed, and then to place an individual unit in that context. One way of doing this is to create unit profiles which graphically portray how an individual unit relates to the overall distribution for chosen items of staff and equipment. In this way, any unit which contributed can compare its own, say, midwifery staffing, with the range for units of a similar size of type.

Looking at different categories of staff and equipment simultaneously emphasizes their interdependence, and may help to explain apparently unlikely values for specific items. The profile will show the overall pattern of provision against which the single unit's profile will show for what items it has normal provision and for what items it is markedly different from the majority of similar units. A further advantage of this approach is that it provides a simplified view of the mass of data that have been collected. However, the use of profiles should be seen as an aid to formal statistical analysis or interpretation, rather than a substitute.

We have constructed an example of such a profile to illustrate what can be done. The method has been derived from that used by Selbman and colleagues to create profiles of units contributing to the Bavarian Perinatal Survey[1], and uses the graphical methods developed by Yates and colleagues[2] for inter-district comparison of hospital statistics.

The first problem is to select the key items. The smaller the number of items included, the fewer the specific questions that can be addressed. The larger the

283

MATERNITY UNIT PROFILE   HOSPITAL: XXXX   CATEGORY: All units in survey

Based on data from the NBTF Confidential Enquiry of facilities at the place of birth.

	Range of values within category	Value for this unit	Position relative to other units in this category expressed as a percentile (0 — 100)
1983 RATES			
Low birthweight	0–38.5	6.63	
Caesarean section	0–39.1	13.2	
Perinatal mortality	0–29	9.8	
ACTIVITY RATES ON SURVEY DAY			
Normal delivery	0–100	62.5	
Forceps and vacuum	0–100	0	
Caesarean section	0–40	31.3	
STAFF IN HOSPITAL AT 11.00AM SURVEY DAY			
Midwives	0.5–28	1.8	
Senior obstetricians	0–800	33.3	
Junior obstetricians	0–850	66.6	
GP obstetricians	0–1000	0	
Senior paediatricians	38–3600	288.9	
Junior paediatricians	0–900	88.9	
Senior anaesthetists	0–900	33.3	
Junior anaesthetists	0–700	44.4	
STAFF IN HOSPITAL AT 11.00PM ON SURVEY DAY			
Midwives	0.5–16	4.5	
Senior obstetricians	0–500	0	
Junior obstetricians	0–700	300	
GP obstetricians	0–600	0	
Senior paediatricians	0–300	0	
Junior paediatricians	0–1000	200	
Senior anaesthetists	0–500	50	
Junior anaesthetists	0–700	200	
EQUIPMENT IN UNIT AT TIME OF SURVEY			
Delivery rooms	0–963	203.5	
Delivery beds	0–1538	271.3	
Oxygen for mother	0–2085	162.8	
Anaesthetic machines	0–5391	1628	
Fetal heart monitors	0–1696	814	
Laryngoscope	0–1339	407	
Bag and mask	0–2718	814	

Figure A1   Definitions of variables used in maternity unit profiles

LOW BIRTHWEIGHT   Number of births weighing less than 2500 g in 1983 as per cent of 1983 deliveries.

CAESAREAN SECTION   Number of 1983 deliveries by Caesarean section as a per cent of 1983 deliveries.

PERINATAL MORTALITY   Stillbirths and first week deaths per 1000 total births in 1983.

ACTIVITY RATES ON SURVEY DAY
Normal delivery   Deliveries excluding breech and operative deliveries as per cent of all deliveries in 24-hour period.
Forceps and vacuum extractions   Expressed as a per cent of all deliveries in 24-hour period.
Caesarean sections   Elective and emergency Caesarean section operations as a per cent of all deliveries in 24-hour period.

STAFF IN HOSPITAL ON SURVEY DAY
Midwives   Qualified midwives in delivery area and available for delivery area per 100 women in labour at the time.
Medical staff   Staff members per thousand 1983 deliveries. Senior staff includes consultants and post college membership registrars.

EQUIPMENT IN UNIT AT TIME OF SURVEY
Items of equipment in the delivery area per thousand 1983 deliveries.

number of items, the more difficult it is to take in the unit profile at a glance. The solution adopted by Selbman was to create a simple *general profile* and a series of *special profiles* designed to answer specific questions. The wider issue of what information would be needed for a review of facilities for perinatal care in a region has been discussed elsewhere[3].

Figure A.1 shows an example of a unit profile for all hospitals in the survey. The profile describes the workload, the staff present at the time of the survey, and the equipment available. All the variables are expressed as rates. Midwifery staff figures and survey day activity rates are per 1000 women in labour at the time, and other rates are expressed in terms of 1983 births. A percentile bar is displayed for each variable showing the minimum, maximum and median values for all units of that size. The profile for the unit in question is drawn by marking the position for that unit on each percentile bar, thus showing whether the unit lies close to the central value or has unusually high or low rates for any particular item in the profile. The shaded area marks values falling outside the interdecile range: 80 per cent of all units will have values within these limits, and thus a value falling within the shaded area could be called unusual.

REFERENCES

1. Selbman, H.K., Warnke, W., and Eissner, H.J. (1982). Comparison of hospitals supporting quality assurance. *Meth. Inform. Med.*, **21:** 75–80.
2. *DHSS Performance Indicators Handbook*. Appendix 4. DHSS, 1986.
3. Mugford, M., Mutch, L., and Elbourne, D. (1985). Standard perinatal data: suggestions for regular review of facilities for perinatal care within a regional health authority. *Community Med.*, **7:** 157–168.

Index

Index compiled by Peva Keane